THE SEA
AND HISTORY

THE SEA
AND HISTORY

EDITED BY E.E. RICE

SUTTON PUBLISHING

First published in 1996 by
Sutton Publishing Limited · Phoenix Mill
Thrupp · Stroud · Gloucestershire · GL5 2BU

British Library Cataloguing in Publication Data
A catalogue record for this book is available from the British Library

ISBN 0 7509 1096 8

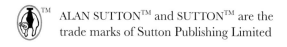

ALAN SUTTON™ and SUTTON™ are the trade marks of Sutton Publishing Limited

Typeset in 10/12 Baskerville.
Typesetting and origination by
Sutton Publishing Limited.
Printed in Great Britain by
WBC Limited, Bridgend.

CONTENTS

LIST OF FIGURES

Chapter Six

Chapter Seven

LIST OF CONTRIBUTORS

E.E. Rice is Fellow and Domestic Bursar of Wolfson College, Oxford, where she teaches ancient history and archaeology. She is the author of *The Grand Procession of Ptolemy Philadelphus* (1983), editor of *Revolution and Counter-Revolution* (The Wolfson College Lectures, 1989; 1991) and a contributor to *Who Was Who in the Greek World* (1982) and *A Dictionary of Ancient History* (1994).

Geoffrey Rickman is Professor of Roman History at the University of St Andrews. He is the author of *Roman Granaries and Storebuildings* (1971) and *The Corn Supply of Ancient Rome* (1980), and is currently working on a study of Roman ports in the Mediterranean. He was elected a Fellow of the British Academy in 1989.

Elisha Linder is founder of the Centre for Maritime Studies at the University of Haifa, where he researches and lectures in ancient maritime history and marine archaeology. He is also co-founder of the Man and Sea Society.

N.C. Flemming is Director of the European Global Ocean Observing System in Southampton. He has published about fifty papers on the submarine archaeological remains of ancient ports in the Mediterranean, and has edited books and conference proceedings on scientific diving.

Anthony Laughton made his career in research oceanography at the National Institute of Oceanography (later the Institute of Oceanographic Sciences), where he was Director from 1978 to 1988. He was knighted in 1987 for services to oceanography.

Seán McGrail, formerly Professor of Maritime Archaeology at the University of Oxford, is now Visiting Professor of Maritime Archaeology at the University of Southampton. His publications include *Logboats of England and Wales* (1978), *Rafts, Boats and Ships* (1981), *Ancient Boats in North-West Europe* (1987) and *Medieval Boat and Ship Timbers from Dublin* (1993).

A.J. Parker is Senior Lecturer in Archaeology at the University of Bristol. He has made a special study of ancient shipwrecks and their importance as documents of Graeco-Roman trade and technology. His *Ancient Shipwrecks of the Mediterranean and the Roman Provinces* was published in 1992. A Vice-President of the Nautical Archaeology Society, he has been active in survey and excavation underwater for twenty-five years, especially around Sicily.

Sarah Arenson is Director and co-founder of the Man and Sea Society. Previously she was a lecturer at the University of Haifa, specializing in Middle Eastern history and the history of maritime civilizations. She is the author of *The Encircled Sea: the Mediterranean Maritime Civilization*.

Admiral Sir James Eberle retired from the Royal Navy in 1983, having held the appointments of a member of the Board of Admiralty, the Commander in Chief UK Fleet, the Allied Commander in Chief of the NATO Channel Command, the NATO Commander in Chief Eastern Atlantic and Commander in Chief of the Royal Naval Home Command. He is also a former Director of the Royal Institute for International Affairs.

John Keegan is a military historian. He taught for many years at the Royal Military Academy Sandhurst and is now the Defence Editor of the *Daily Telegraph*. His publications include *The Face of Battle, The Mask of Command, Battle at Sea* and *A History of Warfare*, which was awarded the Duff Cooper Prize in 1994.

PREFACE

The 1995 Wolfson College Lectures on 'The Sea and History' took their inspiration from an idea put forward by Dr Elisha Linder of the Center for Maritime Studies, University of Haifa, when he was in residence at Wolfson as a Visiting Scholar in 1992. Knowing my interest in naval history and maritime archaeology, he approached me with a plan for eight lectures examining various aspects of the study of the sea, and we were delighted when the college approved the scheme for 1995. The general aim of the series was to investigate various aspects of the relationship between man and the sea, past and present. Such a wide-ranging theme allowed for the integration of several academic disciplines: archaeology, history, literature and art in the humanities; economics and marine law in the social sciences; coastal geology and physical oceanography, among others, in the sciences; and technological studies, including ship-building, harbour construction, and seafaring and navigational techniques. From this point of view the papers complement each other and create a multidisciplinary approach to the age-old relationship between man and the sea.

The organization of this series was well under way when the fourth annual Ronald Syme Lecture (established in memory of the Roman historian Sir Ronald Syme, a Fellow of the college for many years) was given at Wolfson in November 1994. The speaker, Professor Geoffrey Rickman of the University of St Andrews, had, quite coincidentally, chosen as his topic *Mare Nostrum*, translated as 'Our Sea', the significant phrase by which the Romans knew the Mediterranean. This lecture gave a comprehensive overview of the physical characteristics of the Mediterranean and its importance in Graeco-Roman times, and proved to be a perfect, if unintended, introduction to 'The Sea and History' series. The college is grateful to Professor Rickman for agreeing to its publication in this volume.

Elisha Linder returned as a Visiting Scholar to Wolfson in the spring of 1995 to be present for the series and to deliver the opening lecture: 'Human Apprehension of the Sea'. He demonstrated the importance of the sea in ancient times by examining various myths and legends about the sea in ancient societies, showing how humans passed from feelings of mystery and fear to an ability to master the oceans on long-distance voyages. The question of cultural diffusion by contact from the sea remains one of the most intriguing areas of investigation for historians and archaeologists today.

Dr Nic Flemming gave a thought-provoking lecture on 'Sea Level, Neotectonics and Changes in Coastal Settlements: Threat and Response'. Post-glacial sea level rise has submerged much of the early evidence of mankind's relationship with the littoral zone. He showed how physical changes in sea levels have had wide-ranging effects on settlement patterns along the shoreline, on the location of harbours and on the development of commercial ports. These processes are illustrated by a discussion of individual sites that Flemming has studied.

The vexed issue of extant marine resources, which we hear frequently debated today, made Anthony Laughton's examination of 'Marine Resources from Antiquity to the Present Day' particularly topical. Throughout the ages the sea has been a source of food, minerals and energy to man, affecting our lifestyle and economic base. For how long can we continue to consume marine resources before the increasing demands of the modern day irrevocably destroy the balance of life systems in the sea? Definite answers cannot always be given, but careful reflection on our continuing exploitation of the sea is required.

Seán McGrail is one of the leading authorities on the ship, the means by which the sea is used as an avenue of transport. 'The Ship: Carrier of Goods, People and Ideas' discussed various types of ancient and medieval ships and the different methods of ship construction used by peoples on many seas. Visual evidence is gathered alike from humble graffito drawings and elaborate artistic representations, and from archaeological investigations of chance remains of shipwrecks and buried ships that happen to have survived.

With the development of the ship and mastery of the sea came commercial and economic possibilities on a grand scale. Toby Parker gave a fascinating account of maritime trade, primarily Roman, in 'Sea Transport and Trade in the Ancient Mediterranean'. Trade routes and their interconnections are indicated by underwater finds of ships' cargoes, leading to hypotheses about the distribution of goods throughout the Mediterranean. In particular, clay amphorae used for transport of wine and other goods, many with identifiable stamps, provide a durable and closely datable deposit on the seafloor.

Bringing the subject of man and the sea forward from antiquity, Sarah Arenson considered 'Navigation and Exploration in the Medieval World', which emphasized the fact that seafaring expertise did not decline after the days of the great naval and maritime fleets of antiquity. Technological developments in seafaring and navigation combined with growing geographical knowledge led to the exploration of further and unknown shores by western, Muslim, Jewish and eastern traders. A new world, for better or worse, was created.

Admiral Sir James Eberle brought us into the modern day with 'The Development of the Command of Sea Power in the Nineteenth and Twentieth Centuries'. The navies of the present world powers and the naval arms race are a world apart from antiquity, and are more familiar to us from our acquaintance with current events. Incredible advances in ship design, navigational techniques and weaponry have changed our relationship with the sea as well as the face of warfare. Man's growing mastery of the sea has allowed for our increasing mastery over our fellow man.

Finally, the eminent military historian John Keegan brought the sea and history back to British shores with his examination of 'The Sea and the English', showing how the sea has always exercised a particular importance and fascination for this island nation. In the light of this we can perhaps see from a different perspective how *Mare Nostrum* was also the British view of the world ocean, and how it came to play as pivotal a role in the lives of the inhabitants of these islands as their *Mare Nostrum* did for the peoples of the ancient Mediterranean.

E.E. Rice
E. Linder

ACKNOWLEDGEMENTS

As convener of the 1995 Wolfson College Lectures in conjunction with Dr Elisha Linder, I should like to thank the President of Wolfson College and Lady Smith, Dr W.J. Kennedy, Dr Michal Artzy, Dr N.C. Flemming, Professor Seán McGrail, Mrs Janet Walker and Ms Jan Scriven for their help and advice before and during the lecture series. Other friends and colleagues who offered support are too numerous to single out. The publication process was eased by Jane Crompton and Clare Bishop of Sutton Publishing Ltd.

E.E. Rice
Wolfson College, Oxford

1

MARE NOSTRUM

Geoffrey Rickman

I start with a quotation:

> I have loved the Mediterranean with passion, no doubt because I am a northerner
> like so many others in whose footsteps I have followed. I have joyfully dedicated long
> years of study to it – much more than all my youth. In return, I hope that a little of
> this joy and a great deal of Mediterranean sunlight will shine from the pages of this
> book.

So wrote the French historian Fernand Braudel in the preface to the first edition of his
great work *The Mediterranean and the Mediterranean World in the Age of Philip II* (Braudel,
1972, p. 17). I share that passion for the Mediterranean, and I have often wondered why
it is that classicists generally seem less aware than they should be of the vital significance
of that very special sea. We somehow take the geographical setting for granted, and in
particular the sea at the heart of it all. Of course, we are promised a new book on the
Mediterranean by Nicholas Purcell and Peregrine Hordern, which will help to put
matters right. Here I want to anticipate that, in a very small way indeed, and to focus on
some of the work that has been done on the Mediterranean, at least on the Roman
period, and on the kinds of question that have been asked about that work.

The subject's importance has been put in a rather startling way recently by Keith
Hopkins, Professor of Ancient History at Cambridge. Again I quote:

> The Mediterranean Sea was the Roman Empire's internal lake. In spite of the
> Romans' reputation as landlubbers, it was not land routes but the Mediterranean
> Sea which afforded Rome the main avenues for its imperial expansion. And when
> the whole of the Mediterranean basin was unified under Roman rule, the
> Mediterranean was called 'our sea' (*mare nostrum*). It was effectively cleared of pirates
> from 36 BC until the third century AD. Prolonged peace brought a decrease of risk
> and an increase of sea borne trade. Ships carried cargoes of wheat, wine, olive oil,
> wood, metals, and luxuries, especially to the city of Rome with its large population
> and unparalleled concentration of wealthy consumers. They also carried soldiers,
> merchants, migrants and slaves, to say nothing of government officials, itinerant
> preachers, and craftsmen, across the sea between Rome and the provinces. Political,
> cultural, and economic integration proceeded hand in hand. Ease of transport and
> communication by sea in some degree compensated for low technology and low
> productivity. In that sense, the Roman Empire was built on water. (Hopkins, 1988,
> pp. 755–77).

That may be obvious to a modern observer – a very intelligent modern observer – but how far were the Romans themselves aware that theirs was – what Peter Garnsey and Richard Saller call it in the first chapter of their new book – 'A Mediterranean Empire'? (Garnsey and Saller, 1987). After all, in their more enthusiastic moments, as in Virgil's *Aeneid* (I. 278–9; *cf.* VI. 794–5), the Romans saw their lot as extending their empire forever – *imperium sine fine*.

It was not a Mediterranean Empire, but an empire without bounds. In more sober moments, of course, the Romans admitted that the habitable world was both finite and surrounded, so far as they could tell, by an uncrossable ocean. The attitude of an author like Strabo, writing at the time of Augustus, to the possibility of other inhabited worlds beyond his own was, as the Israeli scholar Zeev Rubin pointed out, like ours towards that of life in outer space (Rubin, 1986, pp. 13–62). What mattered to Strabo was what he called '*our* inhabited world' (*he kath hemas oikoumene*, Strabo 2.5.4). This *oikoumene* (in Latin this *orbis terrarum*) became conveniently confused in Roman minds with *orbis noster* or *orbis Romanus*, even though by the time of Ptolemy in the early second century AD the world geographically was known to stretch from Iceland (Thule) to Ceylon (Taprobane) and beyond. The fiction nevertheless had been created that the world was, or potentially could be, all under Roman domination. It was an infinity of attitude rather than of actual practice.

In fact the centre of their world was the Mediterranean Sea, and domination depended on Roman control of it. Writers in Latin, as Rubin said, are rarely explicit on the matter. Polybius, a Greek, was more so. Writing in the mid-second century BC, and trying to explain Rome's rise to power, he stressed how, even at the moment when Rome's very existence seemed threatened by Hannibal's invasion of Italy, a change had come about in world affairs (1.3.1):

> Previously, the doings of the world (the *oikoumene*) had been, so to say, dispersed – as they were held together by no unity of initiative, results, or locality; but ever since this date (i.e. 140th Olympiad, 220–216 BC), history has been an organic whole, and the affairs of Italy and Africa have been interlinked with those of Greece and Asia – all leading up to one end.

Polybius' story after this is about the way the Romans became lords both of the land and of 'our sea' (*he thalassa he kath hemas*). Rubin suggested that, even so, the Roman upper classes felt no need to stress for Polybius their control of the sea, but emphasized instead the domination of the land. If that is true, and was typical of their attitude, they were to pay a heavy price for it in the dangerous rise of piracy in the first century BC. Cicero, in his famous speech on behalf of the law of Manilius in 66 BC, bore witness to the chaos that had been caused by Roman loss of sea control.

To be fair to the Romans of the Republic, we should acknowledge that in trying to control the Mediterranean Sea, as indeed in trying to understand it, land and sea have to be taken together as a unit. Domination of Cilicia, the pirates' homeland in southern Asia Minor, was no less important than victories over them at sea. Similarly, in trying to understand the '*longue durée*' of the history of the Mediterranean, we must, as Braudel has shown, study the coasts, the peninsulas and the mountain ranges no less than the sea itself.

Strabo understood something of all this, as Garnsey and Saller emphasized. He was interested in 'the diversified details, with which our geographical map is filled'. Among these he included the favourable positions of cities, peninsulas, the broken texture of coastlines and so on (Strabo 2.5.15ff.). He pointed, for example, to the length of Italy's peninsula, how the Apennines extended down much of its length, how climate varied in relation to these, and how important that was in guaranteeing a varied and comprehensive range of foodstuffs.

This is in its way sharp, 'Braudelian' stuff, since regional variety in landscape and climate is crucially important in the Mediterranean, with many more deviations from any norm than we tend to think. Why the Mediterranean world mattered to Strabo more than elsewhere is also interesting. It was above all because it was the haven of civilization. He wrote (Strabo 2.5.18):

> Again we wish to know about those parts of the world where tradition places more deeds of action, political constitutions, arts, and everything else that contributes to practical wisdom; and our needs draw us to those places with which commercial and social intercourse is attainable; and these are the places that are under government, or rather under good government. Now, as I have said, our sea (*he par hemin thalassa*) has a great advantage in all these respects, and so with it I must begin my description.

In short, he saw a link between historical action and geography.

Although not all had the fullness of understanding of Strabo, it was Greek writers, from Plutarch and Appian, through Aelius Aristides to Cassius Dio, who most overtly expressed the sense of the importance of the Mediterranean Sea. Aelius Aristides, the Greek sophist and rhetorician was particularly important. What was exceptional about him was his emphasis on the economic role played by the Mediterranean. He delivered a panegyric of Rome on his visit to the capital in AD 143/144. After the traditional flattery about the unlimited nature of Rome's empire, he said, revealingly:

> But the sea is like a belt that extends in the middle of the *oikoumene* as well as in the middle of your empire (*To Rome*, 80). Around this sea, the great continents extend far and wide, incessantly augmenting your wealth with something of their own. From every land and sea the products of every season, and the crops of all rivers and lakes, as well as the craftsmanship of the Greeks and the Barbarians is imported to you – so much so that if anybody wanted to survey all these things, he would either have to watch them in his travels all over the world, or be in this city. Of all that is grown or manufactured by each and every people, there is nothing that would not be here in abundance. So many freight ships arrive here from everywhere, carrying every merchandise, throughout all seasons, until the very end of every autumn. . . . Arrivals and departures of ships never cease, so much so that one may wonder how sufficient room can be found for the freight ships not merely in the harbour but in the entire area.

There is, of course, much rhetoric here, but also – we are coming to believe, and I shall return to this shortly – much truth as well.

First, what are the physical properties of the Mediterranean Sea? (Bascom, 1976) What is its size? It has a surface area of 2.96 million square kilometres and a volume of 4.24 million cubic kilometres. It is the biggest inland sea. Its main basins are as deep as oceans, the western one having a flat floor at about 2,700 metres, while the eastern basin, though of the same average depth, is not so flat. The shallow areas are the Aegean, the Adriatic and a large area south-west of Sicily, where there is very little water deeper than 500 metres. The bottom is composed mainly of two kinds of material. In the deeper areas and for 90 per cent of the Mediterranean there are calcareous muds and clays, while in the Aegean, and in those shore areas with steep hills and with high erosion rates, rocks and sand predominate.

The sea level relative to the adjacent land has changed in a number of places. This seems, however, not to be the result of some general change in the sea level. Nicholas Flemming's authoritative study showed that since the early Bronze Age, the sea level has altered by no more than plus or minus half a metre (Flemming, 1969, pp. 1ff.; see also *infra*). Explanations for the drowning, or uplifting, of particular coastal areas have to be looked for in local changes. The most obvious example of this in the western Mediterranean is the local tectonic shifts that have affected the area near Naples. Here, volcanic activity has resulted in the drowning of various harbour installations at Portus Iulius, while leaving others in the same area near Puteoli at a higher level. The coasts of the Mediterranean, of course, differ markedly from one another anyway in their suitability for ports and harbours, and those differences have increased since the Bronze Age (that is from about 3000 BC) (Rickman, 1985). Erosion by the sea, sedimental deposits from rivers, together with winds, have tended to straighten coastlines and to eliminate natural harbours, but the process has been faster on shallow, shelving coasts than on deeply indented ones. The northern shore of the Mediterranean is a steep, indented coast, and has therefore changed little over the past 5,000 years. With its bays, headlands and numerous islands, it affords many small natural harbours and landing places. What has changed there in a significant manner is the extent and shape of the lagoonal areas just behind the coasts, which were once used for, and were of great importance to, navigation and trade. The southern shore of the Mediterranean by contrast was less well endowed by nature and has changed much more. It has few islands offshore and virtually no natural harbours for hundreds of miles. The eastern coast of Tunisia in particular has very shallow and treacherous water the further south you go.

Tides in the Mediterranean are very small generally, rarely exceeding a few centimetres, but, considering this, currents are surprisingly large. These are caused mainly by evaporation. Winds dried by surrounding deserts evaporate extraordinary quantities of water, taking about 1,000 cubic miles of water a year, or an average of about 80,000 tons a second. This amount of water cannot be made up by the rivers, which compensate for only some 25 per cent of the loss, or from the Black Sea, which provides another 4 per cent. The remaining 71 per cent, therefore, is constantly replaced by an inflow through the Straits of Gibraltar from the Atlantic. There is a double current here. Heavier, more saline Mediterranean water falls and flows out into the Atlantic in a deep subsurface current, while lighter, less saline Atlantic water flows into the Mediterranean in a fast surface current, which averages a speed of about 6 knots. This interchange has two effects. First, it helps to control the salinity of the Mediterranean, admittedly at a higher level than the Atlantic, but so as to prevent evaporation turning the Mediterranean into a huge dead sea. Second, it sets up a general current flowing in a counterclockwise direction. In the western Mediterranean the current flows eastwards along the north coast of Africa, branches along the north coast of Sicily, then north-westwards up the coast of Italy, and so round in a circle back towards Gibraltar. Within this general flow there are a couple of secondary currents moving in the same counterclockwise direction: one north from Algiers; the other westwards from the Tiber. There was a similar system in the eastern Mediterranean, partly fed from the inflow through the Dardanelles from the Black Sea. In general, these currents, although they could be helpful allies, did not really impede navigation in antiquity, and only became dangerous in narrows like the straits of Messina, where the waters of the Tyrrhenian and Ionian seas try to change places every twelve hours, creating whirlpools and tidal rips – the notorious Scylla and Charybdis.

Winds were far more important than currents for navigation in antiquity, not least because the ships were predominantly square-rigged (Pryor, 1988, pp. 12–24). In winter, a series of rapid depressions from the Atlantic creates unstable and often foul weather in the western basin of the Mediterranean; while the eastern Mediterranean, subject to the conflicting influences of an anticyclone over Siberia and depressions from the desert, has good and bad days, but there was no way in antiquity of predicting their duration. In summer, on the other hand, good weather prevails throughout with no atmospheric turmoil. In the western basin, high pressure from the Azores brings a mixture of prevailing winds from the north-west and north-east, while in the eastern basin a low over India and Persia also sets up prevailing winds from the north and north-west. These were the famous Etesian winds of antiquity.

All this dictated a certain pattern to navigation, up until the medieval period. Winter was essentially a period of *mare clausum*, with sailing officially discouraged from October to April, or even from September to May. Of course, not all navigation stopped. Small-scale tramping from port to port was still possible, even if risky, but the great ships of commerce, and those on state business, stayed in harbour waiting for better and more reliable weather. That came with the summer. This in itself is an oversimplification in that there were, and are, not two seasons in the Mediterranean but four, with spring and autumn important in their own right. These provided a greater variety of winds than normal, and that could be helpful for navigation in these intermediate periods.

More help for navigation could be gained also from local climatic conditions, of which there are many in the Mediterranean. The conjunction of the body of water and its surrounding land masses, together with the particular configuration of certain coasts, produce both on- and offshore breezes, plus significant local winds.

The breezes arise at the edge of the sea, because the different temperatures of sea and land create differences in pressure. At night the land is colder than the sea, a condition that produces a breeze blowing seawards; during the day the land is warmer than the sea and the breeze blows towards the land. The breezes are mainly a phenomenon of the summer in the Mediterranean and do not blow all day, but they are of great importance to navigation. Their effect can be felt up to 12 miles away from the coast, and they can therefore counteract to some extent the effect of the prevailing winds. They allow a ship to sail in the opposite direction. In a region where the prevailing wind was onshore, as for example at Carthage, an offshore breeze in the late evening would help a ship to leave port, as we know from one of the journeys of St Augustine (*Confessions*, 5.8.15).

The local winds, on the other hand, are often much more dramatic and dangerous, particularly where the mountains fall straight into the sea. The most famous is still the *mistral* of Provence or *tramontana* of Liguria, an icy blast of cold air from the Massif Central, or from the Alps, drawn into the local depressions over the Gulf of Genoa through the Rhone gap, usually in spring or autumn. The wind accelerates as it leaves the coast, rushing towards Corsica and Sardinia. In the Adriatic, the *bora* is a similar phenomenon of the Dalmatian coast, and, channelled by the coastal relief, can be even more violent than the *mistral*. The scale of the danger can be calculated. When the wind exceeds 40 knots, full storm waves in the Mediterranean reach 5 to 7 metres in height. They not only endanger shipping, but can do great damage to port works that are not properly positioned or constructed. With the *bora*, gusts can reach more than 100 knots and waves can regularly rise to between 7 and 10 metres high. There are other, less dangerous, local winds such as the *gregale*, which blows across the Ionian sea from Albania and Greece, as well as individual winds around peninsulas, but virtually the only exception to the prevailing northerly winds are the various forms of the *scirocco* from the south. The south coast of the Mediterranean is less rugged and the winds tend to be more restrained, but there can be a sudden rush of air from the Sahara northwards. These hot winds can be violent, bringing dust storms to the whole southern coast of the Mediterranean, and are of little help to navigation.

For both ancient and medieval ships, dependent on wind and human muscle, all these physical factors combined to make the southern coast of the Mediterranean less attractive, or positively dangerous. Prevailing winds from the north, varied by storms from the same direction, made the south coast a dangerous lee shore, against which ships might be dashed. Shallow waters, rocky shoals and sandbanks, low-lying coasts with no landmarks, and a lack of natural harbours for hundreds of miles compounded the problem. The northern coasts by contrast were relatively kind to mariners. High coastal profiles with good landmarks, many bays and protected beaches where ships could shelter in the lee of land in inclement weather, good depths of water close to land, and a wind from the shore – all conspired to help, or reassure, sailors.

So far we have talked of the Mediterranean as a unity, or perhaps as two or three basins: western, central and eastern. However, there is evidence to suggest that the ancients originally viewed the Mediterranean as a series of smaller seas. The French scholar Jean Rougé has shown that some twenty-one named sea areas can be distinguished in the sources (Rougé, 1966, pp. 41–5). What is interesting is that the names are of Greek origin and most often drawn from islands or coasts, such as *mare Tyrrhenum* and *mare Balearicum*. These date back, according to Rougé, to a period when coastal trade was the norm. The more an area of sea was broken down into such named areas, the more, so he argued, we can deduce early vigour of sailing activity. What emerges is what we have come to expect. The coast of Africa seems to have been less important than other coasts for navigation. However, the big distinction is between the eastern and western Mediterranean. The east is broken up into many more named areas, which suggests that the western Mediterranean was an area where navigation developed later. By then, particularly in the Roman period, high-seas trading had become more important than coastal trade. The Romans, using the high seas with confidence, never felt the need to create a whole new nomenclature for the coastal sea areas: they took the names from the Greek past. When they wanted to talk about the whole sea, they referred to it as *mare nostrum, mare magnum*, or – and this is the most interesting – *mare internum*. The sea after all provided the internal routes of communication and empire. The term *mare mediterraneum* does not appear until Solinus used it in the second half of the third century AD.

It is perhaps doubtful whether we shall ever be able to map the main ancient shipping routes as we can those of the modern Mediterranean. It has been argued by Hopkins that we should not even try to do so, since such a map would give a false impression of regularity and systematization, which is too 'modern'. However, Rougé has made a noble attempt to collect the evidence in the written sources regarding the routes taken by shipping in the eastern and western Mediterranean. The only map he has published is, however, highly schematic and related to Diocletian (1966, pp. 88–9). For the period of the Roman Empire, certain generalizations do seem possible from Rougé's work, although they are not well illustrated by this map. At least until the founding of Constantinople, Rome was the capital of the oikoumene, and it was on Rome's ports that the great maritime routes converged. At the start, that was Puteoli in the bay of Naples, then Portus at the Tiber mouth, then finally Rome itself.

The most famous of these routes was that bringing the wheat of Egypt from Alexandria. Working against the prevailing Etesian winds from the north and north-west, the ships could go either north or south. The main northerly route was by way of Cyprus, Myra in southern Asia Minor, either Rhodes or Cnidos, south of the island of Crete, on to Malta and then Messina, and up the west coast of Italy. The southerly was along the African coast, trying to take advantage of the alternating land and sea breezes as far as Cyrene. Either journey could take at least a month, and sometimes two. The journey back to Egypt before the wind was both easier and quicker. The routes from the east and from Asia Minor or the Aegean grafted themselves on to these routes. By the end of the first century AD, more grain was coming to Rome from Africa than from Egypt. The main route for ships from Carthage, certainly after the development of Portus by Trajan, seems to have been up to the east coast of Sardinia, as far as the Straits of Bonifacio between Sardinia and Corsica, and then with the wind behind them they made for the Tiber mouth.

This route in fact linked up with other traditional routes from the West. The routes from Spain – from Cadiz in the south, or from Tarraco (Tarragona) in the north – either linked up with the African route south of Sardinia or headed directly through the straits of Bonifacio. Granted that the route from Narbonne in Gaul also led between Corsica and Sardinia, it is hardly surprising that the Straits of Bonifacio can be shown to have been a veritable ships' graveyard. So long as Rome flourished, as a great centre of wealth, a great consumer and a great entrepot, so did these routes. There were also, of course, many others, as we can still see from the Diocletian Edict on Maximum Prices, where the rates of transportation of goods to a number of different areas are given.

The precise extent and vigour of trade in general in the Roman Empire and the role of the sea in that trade has been a subject of controversy. Rostovtzeff in his masterpiece The Social and Economic History of the Roman Empire wrote in 1926 as if trade in antiquity was no different in kind from modern trade, but only rather less in quantity. After that, a steady process of minimalizing the role of trade in antiquity set in. A.H.M. Jones in the middle of this century stressed the difficulty, slowness and expense of transport by land, and the effort and risk of transport by sea, although that was, he admitted, both easier and cheaper (Jones, 1974). The picture that emerged from Jones' work was of long-distance movement only of those goods that were of direct interest to the state, or of luxury items for which the rich could afford to pay. What that meant was, on the one hand, grain for the capital and for the soldiers, and marbles and long timbers for state building contracts; and on the other, silks, perfumes and unusual manufactured items for the pampered few. Most inhabitants of the empire, for Jones, were peasants living at subsistence level and not involved in such goings-on. Moses Finley, in his book The Ancient Economy published in 1973, built on Jones' work to a point that went beyond merely minimalizing the role of trade (Finley, 1985). The economy of the ancient world, according to Finley, was different not just in extent but in kind from that of the modern world. It was a 'primitive' economy, with no sense of the real potential of 'capital', or of the creative use of 'profits'. It was not a market economy at all, as we would understand it. Ancient society, for Finley, was dominated by a desire for status. That might involve displays of wealth, whether in private consumption or expenditure on public benefactions, but it did not involve productive investment or involvement in mercantile trade by land or by sea. Finley's position was developed with searing intelligence, and many polemics against those who differed from him, and he was a formidable opponent. However, from the beginning the Finley 'model' of the ancient economy failed to convince some scholars, particularly those with archaeological knowledge, such as the late Martin Frederiksen (Frederiksen, 1975). It failed to account for, or even to match, what they knew could be found in excavations all over the empire: a great, and sometimes dense, scatter of material objects – as Kevin Greene has shown in his book (Greene, 1986) – which had come to these places from elsewhere, and often from far away.

That early reaction of disbelief of the Finley thesis, founded largely on what had been discovered by land archaeology, has since been reinforced by the ever-increasing discoveries of underwater archaeology in the Mediterranean. The development of aqualung diving has led to the discovery of more than 800 sites of shipwrecks to date, and an increasing sophistication in studying them. Of course, some of the earliest underwater excavations in the 1950s were crude and inaccurate. Some parts of the Mediterranean have been more systematically explored than others, and more wrecks have been found (29 per cent) in shallow water than in deep sea. However, some of the excavations have been exemplary, as at Madrague de Giens near Hyéres in southern France by the French archaeologists Patrice Pomey and André Tchernia (Tchernia, 1978). Toby Parker of Bristol University has shown, with appropriate caution, what legitimate general conclusions can already be drawn from this evidence (Parker, 1984, pp. 99–113; 1992; see also infra). There can now be little doubt that the period from 200 BC to AD 200 saw a more intense traffic by sea than was to occur again for more than a thousand years; that quite large ships carrying some 340 to 400 tons of cargo were common; and that most often these cargoes were made up of mixed goods from quite different sources. In the same ship you might find amphoras, pottery, lead ingots and bronze vessels, all from different places. Parker has emphasized, correctly, how much transshipment and harbourside dealing is implied by the make-up of such cargoes, how much speculative buying and selling is implied and how often small quantities of goods rode 'piggy-back' on other larger cargoes. Sea trade clearly flourished.

Keith Hopkins, stimulated by this new kind of evidence, therefore redefined the Jones–Finley model of the ancient economy and ancient trade (Hopkins, 1983; 1988, pp. 755–77). What he has tried to do is to keep faith with the essence of that model – that is, to acknowledge the limitations of transport to which Jones drew attention, and to avoid those anachronistic modern economic terms and concepts, which were Finley's bête noire. He has argued that we should not talk of ancient trade with a capital 'T' as if it were one thing, of single character. We should instead distinguish short-haul, middle-range and long-distance trade, but see that they meshed with one another. We should admit that the great bulk of the trade in the empire was short haul and had to go overland, whatever the difficulty, mainly from local countryside to neighbouring town. It was largely that agricultural surplus, beyond their subsistence requirements, that the population of the empire sold or exchanged so as to pay their taxes, and buy such goods as they could afford, from wherever they might come. This process was lubricated in many areas by the use of coinage. Whatever its original state purpose was meant to be, it had come to be used by quite ordinary people in their everyday transactions, as Fergus Millar showed in his study of Lucian's *The Golden Ass* (Millar, 1981).

In so far as there were great motors and stimuli to this and to other trade over longer – sometimes much longer – distances, they were not so much individual entrepreneurial motives, as we might understand them in John Major's Britain, as the state's needs. First, a circulation of money and goods was created by the state's collection of its taxes and payment of its dues, above all to its soldiers, often stationed in remote provinces. Second, the state's need to feed the privileged population of the city of Rome with massive imports of wheat drawn over the sea from the southern Mediterranean, and to feed its troops, created a whole structure of harbours, quayside arrangements, credit facilities and ship sailings that, once they existed, could be used for a whole range of other trade as well.

Of course, this model of the ancient economy may need to be refined in its turn, and Duncan-Jones in his book *Structure and Scale in the Roman Economy* has set about that task, arguing that the circulation of goods was more regionally defined, and resulted from a more complex set of factors. However, the Hopkins model does, I think, have the virtue of trying to explain how, at one and the same time, trade in general, at least in the republic and early empire, was of no conscious interest to the state, and yet trade was somehow governed by the state's imperatives, rather than by totally independent, economic imperatives of its own. Naturally, once these state rhythms were established, and with them the whole infrastructure of roads and ports, individual merchants or groups of merchants could pursue profitable motives of their own. However, these men could not by themselves, and from their profits alone – even if they had thought of it – have created that infrastructure, from which they, and the world in which they lived, derived such benefit.

The whole seems to hinge upon a human act of will, but at the level of the state. It was an act of political will, to make sure that what the emperors saw as their interests were properly served. Perhaps the most obvious and famous expression of this will in the Mediterranean was the creation of an artificial double harbour near the mouth of the Tiber by the emperors Claudius and Trajan (Rickman, 1991, pp. 103–18). The effort was prodigious and took decades to complete in each case – from AD 42 to, possibly, AD 64, and from AD 100 to AD 112.

However, this spectacular achievement should not monopolize our attention completely. Rome had long made use of the great natural harbour further south at Puteoli in Campania. This was an integral part of Rome's port complex in the late republic and seems to have had its role enhanced in the early Empire. It was probably Augustus who built the famous arcaded mole there, which was a functional utility, a wonder of hydraulic engineering and a tourist attraction. From that a whole series of docks and warehouses stretched northwards along the shoreline, the *ripa hortensiana*, and it was these that made Puteoli the great port it was. They may have reached and included the facilities now drowned by the sea but still visible underwater near Portus Iulius and the Lucrine Lake. The recently discovered wax tablets from Murecine near Pompeii have confirmed the role played by grain from Alexandria in the speculations of the merchants at these Puteolan docks under the Emperor Gaius in the first century AD. The interest of all the early emperors in this area is quite clear. Claudius himself sent an urban cohort to Puteoli, as well as to Ostia, to act as a fire service.

The emperors' concern was also for the dangers of the route through the Mediterranean to Puteoli, and from there up to the Tiber mouth. Josephus praises the Emperor Gaius for beginning the enlargement of the harbour at Rhegium, on the toe of Italy, specifically for the benefit of the Alexandrian grain fleet. That was a notoriously dangerous point, as we have seen, on the journey through the Straits of Messina. Similarly, the great *horrea*, built by Hadrian in southern Asia Minor at Patara and Myra, were precisely at the point where Alexandrian grain ships could call, as we know from the story of St Paul. Also, Hadrian, according to Dio, was generous in providing and improving harbours generally.

The sea route north from Puteoli up the west coast of Italy to Ostia, open to storms from the north-west and poorly provided with natural harbours, was equally in need of attention. Julius Caesar, who contemplated the building of a harbour at Ostia, had intended also to construct an inland canal from at least Terracina to Rome. Nero revived the idea and made a determined effort to link the area of Puteoli with the Tiber, by means of canals and inland waterways all the way from Lake Avernus (south of Cumae) to Ostia, and from Ostia to Rome. Traces of that effort (18 metres wide, 4 metres deep, with quays and roads) still exist near the Lago di Paolo at Circeii. The project was started, significantly, in AD 64, which the commemorative coinage suggests was the date of the completion of work on the Claudian harbour. It was therefore all part of a coherent strategy, involving both Campania and the Tiber, for dealing with the problem of Rome's ports, although that is not how it was represented by Tacitus and Suetonius, who saw it as pure folly. On the coast itself, harbours were also built at Antium, and probably Astura, both so big that they could have served as harbours of refuge for grain ships coming up from Puteoli by sea. By the end of the first century AD a direct land route between the Campanian harbours and the capital had also been created, when Domitian built a magnificent new road, much praised by Statius. This left the *Via Appia* near Sinuessa and (avoiding Capua) headed straight for Puteoli and Naples.

Claudius' harbour at Portus should therefore be seen as no more than a complement to the arrangements in Campania that were expected to continue. It had the limited purpose of making an area near the Tiber mouth safer for a greater amount of shipping. As we know from Tacitus, it was not completely successful even in that.

Trajan's project, although it appears simply to be creating an inner basin, or *cothon*, for the Claudian harbour, was in fact quite different, as Nicholas Purcell has emphasized. It marked a serious attempt to centralize the commerce of the capital, particularly its grain supply, on Ostia and the harbours at Portus. The new basin guaranteed security for a variety of shipping, and massively increased the granaries and storehouses available near the Tiber mouth. The whole ensemble of basins and canals covered some 1,300,000 square metres, providing anchorage for 600 or more ships without counting those doubled up, or in the centre of the basins. It is by far the single biggest port complex known to us from antiquity. At the same time, under Trajan and Hadrian in Rome, the embankments, mooring facilities, and warehouses in the Emporium district and in the old Forum Boarium were all systematically improved. It seems that, with the attempt at an inland canal now definitely abandoned, Rome was not to be permitted to be so dependent on the distant Campanian harbours. That was reinforced by Trajan's construction of two further harbours nearby, one to the north of the Tiber at Centumcellae, the other to the south, redeveloped at Terracina (each of 100,000 square metres). In a unique grouping, these were to act as satellites for the great new double harbour at Portus. Significantly, they also were connected to Rome by good roads. All these facilities, once they existed, could be, and were, used for the transport and trade of a whole host of goods other than grain.

The safe passage of both goods and people all over the Mediterranean was guaranteed by a system of imperial military fleets. Out of the chaos of the late republic, the suppression of Sextus Pompeius and the naval victory at Actium, Augustus emerged with a group of warships, which he originally based at Forum Iulii in Gaul. That base was supplanted by two military harbours in Italy itself: Misenum, just north of Naples, near the ports of the west coast was one; Ravenna, on a lagoon south of the River Po and the port of Aquileia in the Adriatic, was the other. Italy, of course, was traditionally free of military garrisons, but by these means, as Chester Starr has reminded us, the emperor could ensure some control both of Italy and of the avenues of approach to it (1989). The sailors may have numbered no more than 15,000, or with the other provincial flotillas and detachments perhaps 30,000, compared with the great mass of legionaries and auxiliaries numbering nearly 300,000. However, the sailors of the imperial fleets were nonetheless organized on military as well as naval lines, depicted themselves on tombstones in military dress and called themselves *milites*, not *nautae*. As Tacitus said in Ann. I.9, 'Armies, provinces, fleets, the whole system was interrelated.' The safety of the seas was secured by the military occupation of former pirate areas, whether in Cilicia or Dalmatia, as well as the positioning of naval detachments at places such as Caesarea in Mauretania, to patrol an area where the mountains so dominate the coast that there is no Roman road for 200 miles. The result, one way or another, was an unchallenged Roman domination, and imperial control, of the Mediterranean Sea.

Men knew that and were grateful. During Augustus' final illness his ship passed an Alexandrian freighter arriving at Puteoli. The passengers and crew, recognizing him, put on white robes and garlands, burned incense, and showered him with blessings and thanks for the safety of the seas (*Augustus Suetonius*, ch. 98). A great age had begun.

When it all came to an end, and why, has been no less a subject of controversy, on which I should like to make a few brief comments, although I know that I should not do so, given the many and subtle warnings by Averil Cameron in her book *The Mediterranean World in Late Antiquity* (1993; see also Randsborg, 1991). A famous debate was triggered off by the thesis of the Belgian scholar Henri Pirenne early this century about Mohammed and Charlemagne. He claimed that the unity of the Mediterranean was destroyed not by the Gothic and Germanic invasions of the fifth and sixth centuries AD but by the rapid and unexpected advance of Islam in the seventh and eighth centuries AD. Pirenne's thesis was much more complicated and subtle than that, but even in this simplified form it sent out shock waves at the time, which have reverberated ever since. Norman Baynes, the British Byzantinist, disagreed immediately (Baynes, 1955, pp. 309–16). He wrote in 1929: 'My own belief is that the unity of the Mediterranean world was broken by the pirate fleet of Vandal Carthage, and that the shattered unity was never restored.' In 1983, Richard Hodges and David Whitehouse, in a book entitled *Mohammed, Charlemagne, and the Origins of Europe*, tried to bring new archaeological evidence and methods to bear on the Pirenne thesis, which had largely been based on written evidence. One particular question they asked, relevant to this discussion, was whether it could be proved, as Pirenne had supposed, that trade in the Mediterranean was still as extensive and vigorous in AD 600 as it had been in AD 400.

Their answer, although still provisional, and subject to emendation by further evidence and the work of other scholars, was interesting, and it chimes with some of the points I made earlier. The archaeological evidence, in their opinion, supports Pirenne's view that we should not exaggerate the effect of the barbarian invasions from the north on the Mediterranean and its trade. Even Alaric's brief capture of Rome in AD 410 and the deposition of Romulus Augustulus in 476 were simply incidents within what was a long, and much more complex, process. Excavations in Carthage, Rome and elsewhere demonstrate, they believe, the persistence of commercial life, although on a diminishing scale, within the Mediterranean until the sixth century AD. However, it is in that century – the 500s AD – that the growing evidence from both urban and rural excavations places, so they think, the critical degradation of Rome. They see the Arab advance after AD 630, therefore, as a consequence and not, as Pirenne thought, as the cause of the catastrophe. If this is correct, then neither Germanic barbarians nor Islam were the culprits in any simple way for the increasing disunity of the Mediterranean.

Rather, what seems to have happened was a progressive inward collapse of imperial will, certainly in the western Mediterranean. It was that imperial will after all that had created and sustained Rome as the greatest and most populous city the world had known – or was to know, until London in 1800. Hodges and Whitehouse estimated that the population of the city fell rapidly to 500,000 by AD 450 then to 100,000 by AD 500. What that meant, as the medievalist Chris Wickham has said, is that even if Vandal Africa was only too happy to go on sending, or selling, *annona* shipments of grain to the city, a diminished and enfeebled Rome no longer needed, or could afford, so much. When that happened, the infrastructure on which so much other trade from Africa was based disappeared, with dire consequences for long-distance trade in general (Wickham, 1988, pp. 189–93).

Even the reconquest of the west by Justinian in the mid-sixth century AD, as Zeev Rubin has argued, could not restore it (1986). The Vandal kingdom might be destroyed, and Byzantine mastery of the sea might be proclaimed, and might be true, in the sense that there was no power to challenge it, but, in practice, Justinian was overstretched financially in trying to fit out naval expeditions to the west. A new situation was emerging there, not because the Mediterranean was actually divided off at any point, but rather for two interlinked reasons. First, Byzantium was no longer capable of taking full advantage of the opportunities the western Mediterranean offered. Second, the western Barbarian kingdoms were in such a rudimentary state of political and economic development that they could not themselves embark on any grand-scale commercial activity without the Byzantine stimulus. Trade continued, of course, in the west, but it was more in the nature of *cabotage* – coasting trade. The high seas were left increasingly empty once more.

In the east the story was rather different, with Egypt still serving the new capital, Constantinople, with supplies of wheat for a while, and mercantile prosperity outlasting that in the west by nearly a century. Nevertheless, Byzantium was being eroded just as the western empire had been, and trade, although it continued, was no longer on a massive scale.

It was a changed world, with the sea not necessarily divided between west and east, or between barbarians and Islam, but, as it so happened, no longer a cohesive unit.

The Mediterranean was no more the monopoly of any single power, ready and able to make that effort of political and administrative will – to impose that interconnection, on which Polybius had remarked – which was the essential foundation for pervasive trade.

That was a fact of immense importance in the history of Europe. It is not surprising that the *Oxford History of the Classical World* should end with it. The last sentence of the last chapter, written by Henry Chadwick and entitled 'On taking leave of antiquity', says simply: 'The Mediterranean was no longer a Roman lake.' (1986).

What that meant was that the empire 'built on water' was gone, and with it a vital element of the classical world.

Author's note

This lecture was given in memory of Sir Ronald Syme at Wolfson College, Oxford, in November 1994. It draws heavily, and overtly, on some of my previous work and that of many other scholars. It was not intended for publication, but I have been persuaded by Ellen Rice that it might form a suitable introduction to the Wolfson Lecture Series on 'The Sea and History'. I offer my thanks to her, and hope that her judgement is correct.

REFERENCES

Bascom, W. *Deep Water, Ancient Ships*, New York, 1976

Baynes, N. 'H. Pirenne and the unity of the Mediterranean world' in *Byzantine Studies and Other Essays*, London, 1955, pp. 309–16 (review in *JRS* 19, 1929, pp. 224–35)

Braudel, F. *The Mediterranean and the Mediterranean World in the Age of Philip II*, London, 1972

Cameron, A. *The Mediterranean World in Late Antiquity, AD 395–600*, London, 1993

Chadwick, H. 'Envoi: on taking leave of antiquity' in *Oxford History of the Classical World*, Oxford, 1986

Duncan-Jones, R. *Structure and Scale in the Roman Economy*, Cambridge, 1990

Finley, M.I. *The Ancient Economy*, London, 1985

Flemming, N.C. 'Archaeological evidence for eustatic change of sea level and earth movements in the western Mediterranean in the last 2000 years', *Spec. Pap. Geol. Soc. Amer.* 109, 1969, pp. 1ff.

Frederiksen, M.W. 'Theory, evidence and the ancient economy', *JRS* 65, 1975, pp. 164–71

Garnsey, P. and Saller, R. *The Roman Empire, Economy, Society and Culture*, London, 1987

Greene, K. *The Archaeology of the Roman Empire*, London, 1986

Hodges, R. and Whitehouse, D. *Mohammed, Charlemagne, and the Origins of Europe*, London, 1983

Hopkins, K. 'Models, Ships, and Staples' in P. Garnsey and C.R. Whittaker (eds), *Trade and Famine in Classical Antiquity*, Cambridge, 1983

——. 'Roman trade, industry and labor' in M. Grant and R. Kitzinger (eds), *Civilization of the Ancient Mediterranean*, New York, 1988, Vol. II, pp. 755–77

Jones, A.H.M. *The Roman Economy* (Studies in ancient economic and administrative history), P.A. Brunt (ed.), Oxford, 1974

Millar, F.G.B. 'The world of the Golden Ass', *JRS* 71, 1981, pp. 63–75

Parker, A.J. 'Shipwrecks and ancient trade in the Mediterranean', *Archaeol. Rev. Cambridge* 3, 1984, pp. 84–113

——. *Ancient shipwrecks of the Mediterranean and Roman provinces*, BAR 580, 1992

Pryor, J.H. *Geography, Technology and War (Studies in maritime history of the Mediterranean, 649–1571)*, Cambridge, 1988

Randsborg, K. *The First Millennium AD in Europe and the Mediterranean: an Archaeological Essay*, Cambridge, 1991

Rickman, G.E. 'Towards a study of Roman ports' in A. Raban (ed.), *Harbour Archaeology*, BAR 257, 1985, pp. 105–14 (for references)

——. 'Problems of transport and development of ports' in A. Giovannini (ed.), *Nourrir la plèbe, Schweizerische Beiträge zur Altertumswissenschaft*, Heft 22, 1991, pp. 103–18

Rougé, J. *Recherches sur l'organisation du commerce maritime en Méditerranée sous l'empire romain*, Paris, 1966, pp. 41–5

Rubin, Z. 'The Mediterranean and the dilemma of the Roman empire in late antiquity', *Mediterranean Historical Review* 1, 1986, pp. 13–62

Starr, C. *The Influence of Sea Power on Ancient History*, New York, 1989

Tchernia, A., Pomey, P. and Hesnard, A. *L'Épave romaine de la Madrague de Giens (Var)*, *Gallia* (Suppl.) 34, 1978

Wickham, C. 'Marx, Sherlock Holmes and late Roman commerce' (review discussion), *JRS* 78, 1988, pp. 189–93

2
HUMAN APPREHENSION OF THE SEA
Elisha Linder

H ere I discuss the ambiguity in attitudes towards, relationships with and reactions to the sea. On the one hand there is awe, the fear of the unknown and the unpredictable, and the impossibility of harnessing its destructive powers. On the other hand there is the challenge, adventure, creativity, imagination and romance; the sea as a vital element of life, a source of food and energy, a bridge between distant people and cultures. Who among us has not at some stage of our lives experienced such a dichotomy while sailing the high seas? The Athenian comic poet, Archippus, who lived in the fifth century BC declared:

> How pleasant is it to watch the sea from land.
> Oh Mother! avoid sailing on ships!

An attempt to trace the earliest records revealing the relationship between man and the sea leads us to myth and legend. We shall follow a constant rule of mythology, 'that whatever happens among the gods above, reflects events on earth' (Graves, 1973).

In mythopoeic thinking of the ancient Near East, the water element was conceived as a primordial ocean – a major component in the creation of the universe linked with the underworld. These waters of chaos from which life emerged appeared everywhere. The sea, one of its manifestations, was considered a constant threat to the earth and its inhabitants, but carried some positive attributes to be reckoned with. Likewise the fresh water descending from heaven, while in bond with threatening clouds, stormy winds and lightning, brings the blessing to growth and vegetation, and to the sustenance of the essentials of life. In Egypt, Mesopotamia and Israel the existing world has emerged from water of chaos. In Egypt the primeval ocean was Nun, also presenting the subsoil waters and the Nile; while in Mesopotamia the fertilizing power in water was personified as the god Enki or Ea. In Israel it was Tehom, the face of the water over which God was moving (Genesis 1:2).

Excerpts from the literature relating to this theme will aid in familiarizing the reader with the sources that have been drawn upon. My examples are taken from the Near Eastern cultures of Egypt, Mesopotamia, Cana'an and Israel. I refrained from including Greece because of the wide scope the sea embraces and the vast literature that signifies it. It becomes a category in itself: one that I hope will be dealt with separately in the future. Among the four cultures, the first two are defined as riverine – whereby the rivers Nile in Egypt and the Tigris and Euphrates in Mesopotamia serve as their 'lifeline'. The third, Cana'an (later Phoenicia), represents a maritime culture *par excellence*. The fourth example, which relates to ancient Israel, is almost an antithesis of maritime and riverine cultures, having originated on the fringe of the desert with its history entrenched in a terrestrial mountainous environment, remote from the sea.

The ancient records of Egypt are scarce in mythological literature pertaining explicitly to the sea. This seems not at all surprising. Although Upper Egypt, where the religious foundations were laid, was in its early history not entirely isolated from the outer world, its populated areas extending along the Nile were flanked by desert, and the sea as a physical entity was out of sight. From the New Kingdom (in the middle of the second millennium BC) we find the 'Astarta Papyrus,' which reached us in a most fragmented state, in Gardiner's words: 'the lamentable wreckage of a most magnificent manuscript' (Gardiner, 1932). This relates to the coming of the Canaanite goddess, Astarta, to Egypt and her role as an intermediary between the Ennead of the gods and the sea. By reconstructing the text it appears that the sea, after meeting Astarta on the shore, desires the goddess and is willing to accept her as a replacement for the tribute he had previously demanded. If refused, the sea threatens 'to cover the earth and the mountains', an act of aggression against the assembly of the gods. Based on conjecture, the tale reflects the animosity and conflict between the sea and the Egyptian gods.

An Egyptian document of a different category – a tale with mythopoeic elements – is 'the story of the shipwrecked sailor', which at a first glance appears to be a remote ancestor of Robinson Crusoe. It is an account of a sailing expedition in the Red Sea led by the king's envoy that failed to reach its destination due to a terrible storm that wrecked the ship off an island, with only one survivor remaining. The adventures of his miraculous escape are retold. The following excerpts will introduce us to the essentials (Erman 1927):

> I had set out for the mines of the sovereign and gone down to the sea in a ship of a hundred and twenty cubits in length and forty cubits in breadth; and therein were a hundred and twenty sailors of the pick of Egypt. They scanned the sky, they scanned the earth, and their hearts were more . . . than those of the lions. They foretold a storm before ever it came, and a tempest when as yet it was not. A storm burst while we were yet at sea, before we had reached land. We flew before the wind and it made a . . . and a wave eight cubits high was within it.
>
> Then the ship perished, and of them that were in it not one survived. And I was cast on to an island by . . . a wave of the sea. Then I heard the sound of thunder and thought it was a wave of the sea. The trees broke and the earth quaked. I uncovered my face and found that it was a serpent that drew nigh. He was thirty cubits long, and his head – it was longer than two cubits; his body was overlaid with gold, his eyebrows were of real lapis lazuli and he coiled himself forward – He said unto me: 'Who brought thee hither, little one'
>
> Then I extended myself on my belly and touched the ground in [his] presence and said unto him: I will discourse on thy nature to the Sovereign and acquaint him with thy greatness. – Thereupon he laughed at me – 'I am the prince of Punt and myrrh, – But it shall happen, when thou are parted from this place, that never shall thou behold this island more, for it will become water' – And he said unto me: 'Safely home, little one, and see thy children, and give me a good home in thy city.'
>
> And he gave me a freight of myrrh, hekenu, iudeneb, incense, elephant-tusks, greyhounds, monkeys, apes and all goodly treasures.

In the story of the shipwrecked sailor, mythical motifs are interwoven with practical realities. When confronting the dangerous powers of the sea, human feebleness is exposed. However, along with the mythical, one finds references to the experienced sailors who had learned to use the winds and currents, and other practices like celestial navigation. They advanced the technology of ship-building and applied it to the service of maritime commercial enterprises.

When turning to Mesopotamia, the Babylonian epic *Enuma Elish* tells, among others, of the battle between Marduk and Tiamat. The sea is represented in the personified form of Tiamat. Marduk is known as the god of the thunderstorm, 'the rider of the clouds'. The following text introduced us to this battle between the elements of nature, wherein the sea threatens to undermine the universal order and Marduk, in the name of the assembly of the gods:

> Tiamat and the expert of the gods, Marduk, engaged, were tangled in single combat, joined in battle. The lord spread his net encompassing her, the tempest, following after, he loosed in her face, Tiamat opened her mouth to devour – he drove in the tempest lest she close her lips, the fierce winds filled her belly, her insides congested and she opened wide her mouth, he let fly an arrow, it split her belly, cut through her inward parts and gashed the heart, he held her fast, extinguished her life (Jacobsen, 1968).

In the Ugaritic literature (Gordon, 1949) we find a similar mythological motif: the battle between the god of rain and thunderstorm against the sea. Ba'al is the god of the rains, while Yam, like in the Biblical texts, represents the sea. At the assembly of the Canaanite pantheon, led by El, Yam sends his messenger to request Ba'al's surrender:

> The message of Yam your Lord,
> of your master, Judge River* . . .
> 'Give up Ba'al [and his partisans]
> Dagan's son that I may inherit his province.'
> As soon as the gods saw them
> Saw the messengers of Yam
> The Emissaries of Judge River
> The gods lowered their heads upon their knees
> Yea upon the throne of their lordships.
> Ba'al rebukes them:
> 'Why O gods, have ye lowered,
> your heads from on top of your knees
> O gods lift up your heads
> I shall answer the messengers of Yam. The emissaries of Judge River.'
> But Ba'al yields for the time being while El surrenders him –
> 'Ba'al is thy slave O Yam,
> Ba'al is thy slave forever
> Dagan's son is thy captive
> He will bring thy tribute like the gods.'

---

* It is suggested that Judge River, in Ugaritic Thapiṭ Nahar, is reminiscent of the trial ordeal referred to in the code of Hammurabi as *anna nari illak*: to the river he shall go, in the river, he shall plunge (Albright, 1936).

. . . but only temporarily – Kothar V'Hasis, the divine craftsman, gave Ba'al two clubs for conquering Yam and proclaimed his victory in the battle:

> Lo thine enemies o Ba'al
> Lo thine enemies wilt thou smite
> Lo thou wilt vanquish thy foes
> Thou wilt take thine eternal kingdom
> Thine everlasting sovereignty
> thou should swoop in the hand of Ba'al
> Like an eagle in his fingers!
> Strike the shoulders of Prince Sea
> Between the hands of Judge River!

Ba'al overcomes Yam.

> Have I not crushed El's darling, Yam
> Nor destroyed the great god River?
> Have I not muzzled Tannin
> Nor crushed the writhing serpent Lotan*
> . . . one of seven heads?

In the Hebrew cosmogony, as it appears in Genesis, the order of the universe is established by God with the place of every element, the waters, sky, sea and land specified:

And it was so, God called the dry land, Earth, and the waters that were gathered together, he called, Seas. And God said 'Let the waters under the heavens be gathered together in one place and let the dry land appear (Genesis 1:9–10).

The deluge narrative again indicates absolute control of the waters by God, who both causes the floods and dries the waters, thus returning the order to the universe. All was under the jurisdiction of Yahweh. Indeed, no strife exists among the deities representing these elements as nature appears under the rule of one God, as is manifested in Psalms 104: 24–27:

O Lord, how manifold are thy works! In wisdom hast thou made them all; the earth is full of thy creatures. Yonder is the sea, great and wide, which teems with things innumerable, living things both small and great. There go the ships, and Leviathan that you formed to sport in it. These all look to thee to give them their food in due season.

Cassuto (1940), Loewenstamm (1969) Fenton (1978) and others have already, some time ago, called our attention to elements of Hebrew epic poetry wherein a struggle between

---

* The monster Lotan is synonymous with the Hebrew Leviathan, as is the crooked serpent with the Biblical Nahas Bariach and Aqualaton. It has been common knowledge that in the Hebrew cosmogony there is only one creator and no recollection of myths in which any pantheon of gods oppose His creation. Is this indeed so, or can one challenge this assumption that there are no mythological traces in the early Hebrew literature?

Yahweh and Yam – the sea – is evident, even if Genesis does not portray any 'theomachia' – a war between the deities – and the so-called 'monsters': 'In that day the Lord with his hard and great and strong sword, will punish Leviathan, the fleeing serpent, Leviathan the twisting serpent and he will slay the dragon that is in the Sea' (Isaiah 27:1). Further: 'Awake, as in the days of old, the generations of long ago. Was it not you who cut Rahav, that did pierce the dragon? Was it not you that didst dry up the sea, the waters of the great deep?' (Isaiah 51:9). Then in the Psalms (74: 13–14): 'Thou didst divide the Sea by thy might, thou didst break heads of the dragons in the waters, thou didst crush the heads of Leviathan,' and when Job (7:12) was complaining in bitterness, and was calling forth: 'Am I the sea or the dragon, that you settest a guard over me?'

It appears as if, initially, the sea had the upper hand. However, in the struggle for power the sea was finally overcome and with him Leviathan, Nachash Bariach, Nachash Aqalaton – the sea 'monsters' as they are named in the Old Testament Hebrew and, as mentioned above, with identical names in the Ugaritic mythological literature. Gordon called our attention to the wide spread of the Leviathan myth. Starting with the third millennium BC, when seven-headed dragons representing Leviathan were depicted on seals dating to the Akkad dynasty, to a corpus of magic incantation bowls with Aramaic inscription that were found in Nippur, Babylon, around 500 BCE, which read: 'I am enchanting you with the spell of the Sea and the spell of Leviathan the Dragon.' No wonder that in the Biblical narratives, and in the later commentaries and literature, the sea and the rivers, as well as the primeval waters, symbolized the force of evil (Gordon, 1966).

It was pointed out (Fenton, 1978) that in the later prophets there is a transformation. The struggles of Yahweh against the sea and the monsters turns into the struggle of Israel against its enemies – cosmogony changes into history. In the following passage (Ezekiel 29:3), Pharaoh the King of Egypt is synonymous with the dragon, which in the 'theomachia' represents the historical enemy:

> Thus says the Lord God,
> Behold I am against you
> Pharaoh King of Egypt
> The great dragon that lies
> in the midst of his streams.

The final victory was also achieved in a historical content (Psalms 114:1, 3)

> When Israel went forth from Egypt . . .
> The sea looked and fled
> Jordan turned back.

Four cultures so very different in their geographical setting, religious background, social organization and political history share in common a negative apprehension of the sea. In the cosmogonic narratives the sea appears as the enemy of universal order, threatening to cover the earth and the mountains while revoking the authority of the other gods. With a certain reservation due to the absence of mythopoeic thought in Israel, even Yahweh, the omnipotent God of Israel, is threatened by Yam and the other 'sea monsters'. We also find similarities in the nomenclature for the sea named Yam in Egypt, Cana'an and Israel, with a possible close etymology in the

Babylonian 'Tiamat', derived from 'Tamtum', the normal form in Akkadian for sea (Jacobsen, 1968).

When similarities among two or more cultural entities appear, we are touching on a problem that occupies anthropologists when comparing cultures with identical features: do we face diffusion or independent development? In the former case the first reaction would be to look for a principal source that could serve as a model for imitation, borrowing or even copying. In our case, when concerned with the making of a myth, we need to know what were the background conditions of religious beliefs, cultic practices and social patterns of behaviours that were supportive to the process of acceptance by the receiving parties. Also, we must discover whether there is a maximum spatial distance between the transmitter and the receiver that allows such a transfer? What is the temporal span in which a process of diffusion occurs? Furthermore, would it require a common 'Sitz in Leben' as a precondition. Indeed, a logical assumption would be to search for a geographical proximity to a coast or the sea for such a setting and an intimate daily acquaintance with the sea. This, however, when judging from an overall historical perspective, was not the case with three of our examples, the only exception being the Canaanite–Ugaritic entity.

How, then, can we explain the adoption by the Egyptians of a myth, a legend or a tale, the core of which is the sea? In its early history the centre of political power, cultural and religious creativity was located in upper Egypt. A vast body of water created by the inundation of the Nile could arouse the collective imagination to perceive the sea in this river. It was only then that the water element became so dominant that it created an allusion of the Nile resembling an open sea. Herodotus compared this flooded landscape to the Aegean Sea with its islands resembling the Egyptian cities surrounded by waters (Book II, ch. 97). The sea, per se, arrives with the advent of sailing and increased activity in the Red Sea. Though navigation in the Red Sea had rather early beginnings, it reached its climax during the middle of the second millennium BC, when regular expeditions set forth to Punt. The descriptions and tales of these sailing expeditions to remote locations remained a mystery. They explain the evolution of the shipwrecked sailor tale, which combines fact and fantasy, and how it caused a sensation of fright along with the desire to explore the Red Sea and develop trade routes in its waters.

The expansion of Egypt's rule along the eastern coast of the Mediterranean in the late Bronze Age, subduing the local population of coastal dwelling seamen as vassals, brought not only the skills of the Canaanite–Phoenician boatbuilders to the delta shipyards of Pru Nefer, but along with them their beliefs; thus Canaanite cult practice flourished there. It seems only logical and natural for Astarta to have been adopted at such a time into the Egyptian pantheon and for myths telling of struggles of the gods of the sea to evolve. Here the principle of diffusion has been implemented.

The importance of the sea was early recognized by the Mesopotamian rulers. The development of international trade, which spread to distant borders, included maritime commercial enterprises that reached out from the Persian Gulf into the Indian Ocean. Sargon I, King of Akkad, defined the borders of his kingdom in the twenty-fourth century BC – 'from the upper sea to the lower sea' – that is, from the Mediterranean to the Persian Gulf. Commercial sailing ventures to Dilmun, Magan and Meluha are well documented in the archives of the third Dynasty of Ur (Oppenheim, 1954). The myth of the wars between Marduk and Taimat demonstrates the unique place that the sea occupied in the imagination of the people.

To which historical epoch can we assign the narratives describing the struggle between Yahweh and Yam? The appropriate time would have been during the reign of Solomon, who established a close relationship with Hiram, King of Tyre, which resulted in developing commercial maritime ventures in the Mediterranean and the Red Sea. At that time the Israelites also achieved a foothold on the Mediterranean coast at the harbour city of Dor. The Israeli awareness of the sea coincided with the penetration of Phoenician religion and cult practices. Yahweh, the god of Israel, fought and overcame the Phoenician Yam and what he represented.

Hence one would expect a prominent role and positive attitude towards the sea in the Canaanite–Ugaritic mythology. Yam and his cohorts the 'sea monsters' were to defeat Ba'al, who represented the terrestrial world. What occurred, however, was just the opposite: it was Ba'al who had the upper hand and, together with his sister goddess, Anat, he claimed victory over Yam.

We have now examined certain features in the historical setting of the various cultures that could have triggered the creation of these myths. The human experience, which was conceived in terms of cosmic events, varied, but still the common denominator was a negative apprehension about the sea.

Can we assume that the sea, being such an overriding, overwhelming factor in the perception and experience of ancient man, could have produced independently primordial fears, such that man cannot control or understand? The spontaneous reaction to this natural phenomenon formed the first phase, a substratum from which mythopoeic thinking was nurtured.

The process of diffusion among the neighbouring cultures came later and formed the second phase. In its background we seek international political contacts, exchanges of ideas and goals with the movement of people.

The third phase answers to the practical experience of part of the population living near and off the sea. They live with all of the advantages that the sea offers: abundant nutrition, raw materials for coastal industries, economic gains from maritime commerce, relative safety from hostile invaders and others. All elements call for a positive apprehension of the sea. Still, there remains the *pericula maris*, dangers of the sea, which grow in proportion to the intensity of the activities at sea of the sailors, fishermen and maritime traders, notwithstanding naval crews.

Indeed, when an attempt is made to historicalize the myth, one could simplify the analysis by applying the following rule: the greater the direct, concrete involvement of a population with the sea and its various related activities, the greater its negative apprehension of that power.

Having dealt with facets of man's negative apprehension of the sea, with all the fear and mistrust, and the concern of the unknown and destructive powers, let me recall briefly the positive apprehension of the sea: ships of eastern and western building technology, the great commercial maritime enterprises, the resources of food and minerals derived from the depth of the ocean, the technological innovations triggered by the sea, the skills of navigation developed throughout the ages and, above all, the human spirit expressed in withstanding all of the *pericula maris*.

Along with the understandings of maritime history derived from the Ugaritic maritime texts and several other epigraphic sources (Linder, 1970), marine archaeology has revolutionized our knowledge of ancient seafaring and triggered interest not only in the Mediterranean where it had its origin. At present, many parts of the world, including the Far East, are engaged in uncovering their maritime heritage.

One of the issues challenging research that in light of recent developments has become very critical is the notion of ancient man's ability to sail great distances and reach new horizons. Historical records tell us of daring sailing ventures into unknown open seas. These are manifestations of the human spirit – adventurous and of inquisitive nature – in which some of the noblest qualities are revealed.

Heyerdahl's experiments in ocean crossing serve as an example, as do the trial sailings with the Kyrenia fourth-century BC merchantman replica and the 'trireme' test initiated by British scientists, reliving chapters of ancient naval warfare.

Elizabeth Mann Borgese is a principle exponent of the law of the sea. In her introduction to *Pacem in Maribus* she said that the oceans have come to pose a problem too serious and too diverse to be left to oceanographers, a problem that is interdisciplinary as it is transnational, postulating the existence of a common heritage of mankind.

REFERENCES

Albright, W.F. 'Zabúl Yam and Thapiṭ Nahar in the combat between Baal and the Sea', *JPOS* 16, 1936, pp. 17–20

Cassuto, M.D. 'Shirat Ha'alila Beyisrael', *Tarbitz* 13, 1940 (in Hebrew)

Erman, A. (trs.). *The Literature of the Ancient Egyptians*, London, 1927

Fenton, T.L. 'Different approaches to the theomachy myth in Old Testament writers' in Y. Avishur and J. Blau (eds), *Studies in Bible and the Ancient Near East*, Jerusalem, (1978)

Frankfurt, H. and H.A. *The Intellectual Adventure of Ancient Man*, Chicago, 1946

Gardiner, A.H. 'The Astarta Papyrus' in *Studies Presented to F.L.L. Griffith*, London, Egyptian Exploration Society, 1932

Gordon, C.H. *Ugaritic Literature*, Rome, 1949

——. 'Leviathan: symbol of evil' in A. Altman (ed.), *Biblical Motifs*, Cambridge, 1966

Graves, R. *New Larousse Encyclopedia of Mythology*, 1973

Jacobsen, T.H. 'The battle between Marduk and Tiamat', *JAOS* 88, 1968, pp. 104–8

Linder, E. '*The maritime texts of Ugarit*', Brandeis University, unpublished PhD thesis, 1970

Loewenstamm, S.E. 'Mithos Hayam Bekitvei Ugarit', *Eretz Israel* 9, 1969 (in Hebrew)

Oppenheim, A.L. 'The Sea Merchant of Ur', *JAOS* 74, 1954

All biblical quotations are taken from *The Revised Standard Version of the Old Testament*, 1952.

3

SEA LEVEL, NEOTECTONICS AND CHANGES IN COASTAL SETTLEMENTS: THREAT AND RESPONSE

N.C. Flemming

OBJECTIVES

The purpose of this chapter is to try to understand how different human communities have, over the last 100,000 years or more, responded to the stresses, disasters and benefits created by changing sea levels, whether rising or falling, during the last Ice Age. I am referring only to actual changes of relative sea level on the coast, not to alluvial silting, deltaic growth or erosion. The field evidence presented shows that archaeological sites of different ages from 2,000 to 50,000 years Before Present (BP) exist underwater on the continental shelf, and hence that they must have experienced inundation and abandonment. One find of submerged artefacts *in situ* indicates that material up to 1 million years old can survive multiple inundations by the sea. The problem is to understand the process of abandonment when the sea rises, and, even more obscure at the moment, the process of occupation of the continental shelf when the sea level falls. Most of the data are available to begin this exercise, which I think will be very rewarding and will contribute much to the interpretation of the origins of human wealth and civilization. I will also present evidence that the rate of acquisition of new data underwater is such as to suggest that the exercise will, over the next decade or so, be successful.

INTRODUCTION

The level of the land and the level of the sea have been changing slowly or rapidly in geological terms throughout geological time relative to the centre of mass of the earth (see, for example, Fairbridge, 1961; Flemming, 1969; Devoy, 1987; Pirazzoli, 1976, 1987; Flemming and Woodworth, 1988; Pirazzoli *et al.*, 1992; Tushingham and Peltier, 1991; Dvorak and Mastrolorenzo, 1990; Richards *et al.*, 1994; Warwick *et al.*, 1996). The two topographic surfaces, that is the mean upper surface of the ocean and the upper surface of the crust of the earth, are controlled by differing and largely independent forces, apart from gravity, and at any given point on the coast they may, at a given time, be moving vertically in the same direction, or in opposite directions. The typical rates of change in both cases under present climatic conditions are of the order of 1 millimetre per year, or 1 metre per millennium. Often the rates of change are much less, and occasionally more, up to a maximum of about 5 to 10 millimetres per year, or 5 to 10 metres per millennium. It is difficult to separate the causes of relative vertical movement of a coastal archaeological site because the statistical variability of sea level change and that of earth movements are rather similar, and the characteristic distributions of rates overlap. The typical rate of rise during the melting of the last glaciation was of the order of 10 metres per millennium, or 0.5 metres in fifty years, which is very noticeable in a human lifetime. The peak rate of rise during the so-called Heinrich events of maximum iceberg release would be about 0.75 metres per fifty years.

For at least 400,000 years the human race has found it convenient to exploit marine resources for food, including shellfish, crustacea, and algae. For at least 50,000 years, people have been able to make open sea crossings of the order of 80 kilometres in sufficient numbers to colonize previously uninhabited land masses. That means that several hundred people, including men and women, must have made a crossing within a few years, not just one chance raft drifting onto an island with one or two men and women (Allen *et al.*, 1977; Jones, 1977). For at least 10,000 years, coastal dwellers have had the skill to go to sea and catch swordfish, tuna, seals and small whales. For at least 10,000 years, people have built villages on the coast and lived in close proximity to places where they sheltered their boats (for example, Galili, 1987). For at least 2,500 years, coastal city dwellers have constructed massive and specialized waterside buildings, and have lived with the risk that the sea level could change and render useless the harbour works and dockside structures representing the accumulated wealth of generations. My enquiry consists of trying to understand how each community in these differing circumstances responded to the threat of changing sea level.

To understand how people responded to a change in sea level and the consequent horizontal movement of the coast, we need to understand why people wished to be near the coast in the first place. If the coast were an irrelevance, just coincidentally adjacent to a living space, then people would tend to avoid it, and would certainly not follow a retreating sea when the sea level dropped. When the sea level rose, people would have no choice but to retreat. The question arises, did they retreat cautiously in advance, or did they try to hold on to their coastal lands and familiar resources until the last minute? What was the perceived value of being on the coast during each age?

ESTIMATING THE VALUE OF LIVING BY THE COAST

In 1981, Pat Masters and I organized a conference at Scripps Institution of Oceanography on Quaternary Shorelines and Archaeology (Masters and Flemming, 1983) at which Dr Geoffrey Bailey of the University of Cambridge suggested that the exploitation of marine food resources, and possibly other benefits of living close to the shore, might have been so important during the late Palaeolithic that one could not explain the final stages of the Palaeolithic and the rise of agriculture and urbanization in the Neolithic without estimating the economic importance of the sea. From recent correspondence and meetings (1995) with Bailey, I know that he holds this view even more strongly now. Since the global sea level was many tens of metres below present sea level throughout the Palaeolithic from about 100,000 years ago to 10,000 years ago, the economic importance of the sea in the Palaeolithic can only be studied by obtaining evidence from under the sea on the modern continental shelf. In publications on his excavations in northern Greece, Bailey (1994) has suggested that the extreme paucity of Palaeolithic finds in the Balkans may be due to the fact that in glacial periods people followed the descending sea onto the present continental shelf, abandoning the colder mountains. As the sea level rose again, people retreated from the continental shelf and once again exploited the shelter and fauna of the hills and mountains. This is consistent with the temporal and spatial discontinuity of known Middle Palaeolithic sites in Greece. This is an unproven hypothesis that both Geoffrey Bailey and I, from our different perspectives, are interested to work on.

The value that people place on the coastal zone, wetlands, shore and shallow waters is largely based on the following:

- intertidal seafood, shellfish, crustacea, algae;
- evaporated salt;
- fish and crustacea in lagoons, creeks and estuaries;
- freshwater and springs on the coastal plain;
- reeds for boats, fences, fish-traps, roofing and shelter;
- fauna on coastal plains – good hunting;
- security on headlands and high promontories;
- equable climate with minimum seasonal temperature range, but windy;
- sea transport: rafts, logs, inflated skins, constructed craft – ability to carry heavy loads;
- sea fisheries, fishing by nets and lines, fixed nets and fish traps;
- food from sea mammals – seals, dolphins and whales;
- offshore islands and nearby land masses, for example the Greek islands;
- ability to cross straits, for example Gibraltar, Sicily Channel, Sunda and Sahul;
- investment in harbours, docks, warehouses, slipways and other maritime structures;
- artificial cultivation of fish and crustacea and algae;
- tourism, high-value and desirable living space (for example Herod, Petronius, Tiberius);
- industrial constructions, dye-works, metal work and modern power stations;
- estuaries and land-locked bays as a focus for industry, habitation and transport.

Throughout the Palaeolithic and Neolithic, the sea level was changing continuously up or down at a rate that was noticeable in a single generation. Why did people choose to stay near the coast, or did they avoid it? A rising sea level would have forced them out of their hunting grounds and familiar fishing shore; a falling sea level might leave them with a barren expanse of saline land and poor vegetation. Is there an analogy with those farmers who insist on returning to the still smoking flanks of erupting volcanoes because of the quality of the soil? In an era before the actual physical investment of capital in stone and brick structures on the coastline, what was the commitment, if any, that made the coast seem so valuable?

It is difficult to understand the value that people placed on sea travel in the prehistoric period. We accept now that a city on the coast has the advantage of access to cheap and efficient bulk transport by cargo ships, and the entrepot value of transshipment between sea, river, road and rail. Did living by the sea carry the same advantage, in whatever primitive form, in prehistoric times? It is evident that people crossed the sea at Gibraltar in the Palaeolithic; from Indonesia to Australia, and to the chains of islands north of Papua New Guinea, including the Admiralty Islands (Birdsell, 1957; Allen *et al.*, 1977); and probably crossed the Red Sea at Bab el

Mandab; and probably from Korea to Kyushu in southern Japan. Was there any advantage of such crossings to the tribes who lived close to the shore on either side? In some primitive form, did they hold the secret skills of navigation, and the knowledge of the weather and currents, so that nobody could cross casually without the skill and support of the local tribes? It seems almost certain that such local knowledge would have been acquired, and exploited, so that some tribes or individuals would have become revered as pilots. Such knowledge would have had value and would have been given up or abandoned with reluctance.

Paul Johnstone has analysed the potential for Palaeolithic and Neolithic tribes to have exploited available materials and technology to make boats and rafts as much as 50,000 years ago. Using ethnological evidence from modern boats of primitive design, log rafts, reed boats, bark boats and skin boats (Johnstone, 1988, pp. 7–43), he suggested how these might have been used in prehistory, before tools were developed for cutting or carving wood with any subtlety (see also McGrail *infra*).

What made early people take the risk of sea crossings on logs and inflated skins? Bamboo, balsa, and reeds provide obvious sources of buoyancy without the need to construct a waterproof, shaped hull, but to cross more than a few kilometres of sea, and particularly to cross more than one could swim, created manifest danger. Early craft and rafts had very low freeboard, and an unexpected wind, current, storm or heavy surf at the point of arrival meant certain capsizing. Since purposeful migration required the transport of women, and probably children, the motives and persistence must have been strong.

The fact that the human race spread to all the continents of the world is a self-evident demonstration that Palaeolithic people were not content to sit in one place and live off the same food caught in the same way for thousands of years. Something compelled people to explore and to expand their range. An average extended horizon of 1 kilometre per year would be sufficient to account for the rate of migration of the human race into new areas. This being so, we do not need to find any peculiar urge that compelled some clans or tribes to explore across sea straits to find new land on offshore islands, or land masses just visible from mountain tops, or because of forest fires visible on the far shore. If tribes tended to increase their range of hunting on land when there was always the risk of impinging on a competitor's territory, then there was an added attraction in crossing the sea to a land where there might have been no human competitors at all.

Palaeolithic and Neolithic methods of subsistence placed considerable stress on the land and its fauna and flora. It takes a large land area to support a family living by hunting and gathering. Aborigine forest burning, slash-and-burn cultivation, the extinction of herds of mammoths and bison, Neolithic and Bronze Age villages razed to the ground with accompanying mass graves: all attest to the competition for resources. Spindler (1994, pp. 251–2) described a Neolithic alpine village that had been burned, and on the edge of which there was a mass grave of slaughtered individuals of all ages. Whether this was a culturally motivated conflict or a struggle for resources and land, it indicates a level of competition and conflict that is all too familiar.

We now have several factors that suggest that, for at least 100,000 years, people have had good reasons for dwelling or hunting close to the sea, and using all of the resources provided by the sea and the shore. To move inland, or to lose contact with the sea, could be to lose an advantage in the competition for survival. The skills and knowledge acquired on the shore were obtained over many years, and often at risk of life or injury. The people with these maritime skills would have had motives to stay close to the sea if possible, and to migrate seawards or inland with falling and rising sea levels.

As the Neolithic period progressed and people built larger and larger cities and, later, harbours, we have to introduce the concept of accumulated capital in the form of houses, streets, docks, breakwaters, lighthouses and slipways, which they would have been very reluctant to abandon. Did it matter more to a Palaeolithic hunter seeing a beloved hunting ground sinking infinitesimally beneath the waves than to us seeing Venice sink into the mud of the Adriatic? When Kangaroo island off the south coast of Australia was cut off by the rising sea, the Aborigine tribes continued to live there for many years, but they gradually died out in spite of the fact that the island was 150 by 50 kilometres in size (Jones, 1977). They tried to hang on, but were defeated by the reduced area for hunting and a limited human breeding population.

As the evidence in this chapter will demonstrate, it is almost certain that the entire continental shelf of the earth surrounding all of the major continents and continental islands was occupied 50,000 years ago, with the possible exception of the Americas and the American continent. A recent discovery off the coast of South Africa (Werz and Flemming, in preparation) suggests not only that some parts of the continental shelf were occupied 1 million years ago, but that the evidence for this occupation can, in suitable circumstances, survive successive transgressions of sea level and be discovered by divers. It appears that for a large proportion of the prehistory of the human race, humans had the freedom to migrate onto and exploit the continental shelf and shorelines that are at present submerged, and that they chose to do so. If it is correct to suggest that the maritime economics of the time were an important factor, there is a great deal of radically new information to be discovered under the sea. The submerged continental shelf of the earth has a total area about the size of Africa, and we know practically nothing about how this submerged continent was occupied during most of the last 100,000, let alone the last 1 million years.

SEA LEVEL CHANGES DOCUMENTED THROUGH THE LAST 100,000 TO 1 MILLION YEARS

There have been about twenty major ice-age climatic cycles in the last 2 million years, each lasting about 100,000 years. The last interglacial, 128,000 years ago, is known as the Eemian, when the sea level was a few metres above its present level. In the intervening period there were four successive cycles of falling and rising sea level, each to a greater depth, culminating in a maximum low sea level well below -100 metres about 20,000 years ago. The most generally accepted curves and regional variations of estimated global mean sea level for the past 1 million years are provided by Shackleton and Opdyke (1973), Emiliani (1978), Chappell (1981), Devoy (1987), Chappell and Polach (1991), and Tushingham and Peltier (1991). These events are being elucidated in increasing detail as a result of research on ocean bed sediment cores, studies of iceberg rafting (Heinrich events), radionuclide dating of submerged stalactites and other speleothems in submerged caves in the Bahamas (Richards et al., 1994), and deep drilling through the ice caps in Greenland and Antarctica. The estimated most probable sea level curve is shown in fig. 1 for the last 1 million years, and fig. 2 for the last 150,000 years. Since the redistribution of mass between ice sheets and ocean water

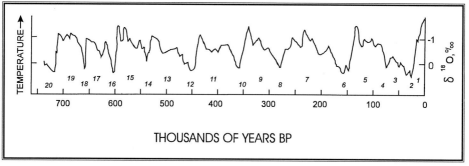

Fig. 1. Generalized palaeotemperature curve for the last 750,000 years, showing nine warm periods when the temperature and sea level rose to the same as or above present conditions, and intervening cold temperature low sea level periods. Note that the last 100,000 years is broken into several subsidiary interstadials, with temperature reversals and intermediate sea level stillstands. This figure is based on Inman (1983), who derived the data from Emiliani and Rona (1969), Broecker and Ku (1969), Emiliani and Shackleton (1974), Emiliani (1978, 1981), Chappell (1981), Shackleton and Opdyke (1973), and Arrhenius (1952). Each cycle of approximately 100,000 years corresponds to a glacial period during which ice caps formed on the continents and the sea level dropped by about 100 m, followed by melting of the ice caps and a rise of sea level. (Source: Inman, 1983)

causes a compensatory redistribution of mass within the mantle of the earth (Walcott, 1972; Clark and Lingle, 1978; Tushingham and Peltier 1991), the crust of the earth changes shape between maxima and minima of sea level changes, and the observed relative change at any point is never exactly as shown in figs 1 and 2. Nevertheless, to a first approximation they give an indication as to how the volume of ocean water increased and decreased during the last 100,000 years.

Because there were stillstands of intermediate high and low sea level during some periods (fig. 2), the maximum rate of change of sea level when the ice sheets are melting or freezing is greater than would be expected from the average rate of change, and has a maximum of the order of 1 metre per century. This is more rapid than the minor fluctuations that have occurred during the last 5,000 years, and would easily be observed during someone's lifetime.

From these curves it is possible to calculate, again to a rough approximation, the areas that were land and sea at each sea level and date in the past. This was carried out by Blanc (1937) for parts of the Mediterranean Sea, and more recently by Birdsell (1957) for Australia, Emery and Edwards (1966) for the east coast of the United States, Van Andel and Llanos (1983) and Shackleton et al. (1984) for the Mediterranean (fig. 3), and Dunbar et al. (1992) for the Gulf of Mexico. Each of these authors theorized about the importance of the continental shelf as a prehistoric living space. Several studies have also been made of the occupation of the floor of the North Sea (for example by Louwe Kooijmans, 1970/1). Only Blanc (1940) conducted fieldwork that revealed vestiges of terrestrial species and human occupation, and that was in sea caves at Palinuro in southern Italy. There is no controversy concerning the probability of occupation of the continental shelf. As Hillaire Belloc said of the microbe covered with

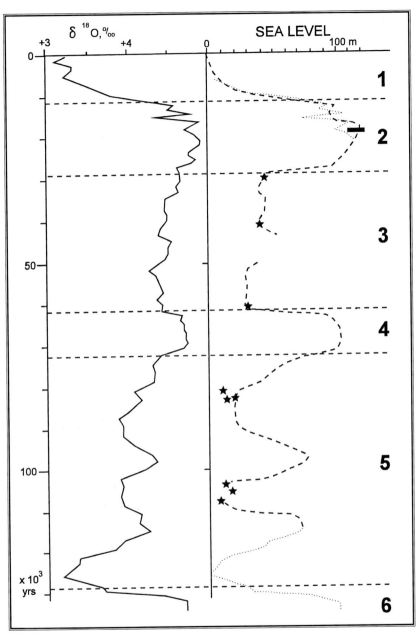

Fig. 2. Sea level changes for the past 130,000 years. Left curve is an oxygen isotope curve based on abyssal benthic Foraminifera indicating removal of water from the ocean (ice age) when the ^{18}O increased, and addition of water to the ocean (interglacial melting), when the ^{18}O decreased. Right curve shows the approximate sea level on the same timescale. Data from raised beaches in areas of uplift are shown by stars. Dashed line indicates sea level in metres below present sea level. Oxygen isotope stages are dated and numbered in the right-hand margin. (Source: Shackleton, van Andel and Runnels, 1984)

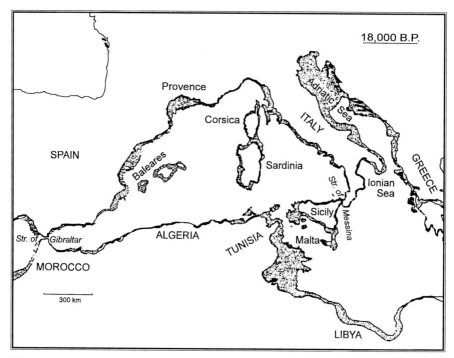

Fig. 3. At the maximum of the last glaciation, 18,000 years ago, the sea level was slightly over 100 m below the present sea level. The continental shelf was exposed, creating a new geographic outline for the continents and islands. This map shows the appearance of the western Mediterranean at this period. (Source: Shackleton, van Andel and Runnels, 1984)

lots and lots of coloured spots: 'Scientists who ought to know assure us that it must be so; let us never never doubt what nobody is sure about.' However, very few people in the academic community have conducted fieldwork to prove occupation of the continental shelf, or to find further details of the human activity on this submerged land mass the size of Africa. A sparse scattering of submerged lithic artefact sites has now been found by divers off the coast of every continent, and these will be described later.

EARTH MOVEMENTS, PLATE TECTONICS AND EARTHQUAKES

In broad terms the distribution of earthquakes is well known from the worldwide map of plate tectonic boundaries, and the many thousands of earthquake epicentres detected from seismic recording stations. Whenever a plate boundary is close to, coincides with or intersects the coast, there is a high probability of vertical earth movements, and hence settlements in the region will be either uplifted or submerged. My research in the Mediterranean has shown that during the last 5,000 years, while the sea level has been constant to within +/- 1 metre, the displacements of the land can be closely correlated with the plate tectonic boundaries and proximity to volcanoes (Flemming, 1969, 1978; Flemming and Webb, 1986; Flemming, 1993).

A further cause of subsidence is the accumulation of sediments around deltas and river mouths, which can result both in later compaction of the sediment and a net subsidence of the earth's crust due to the added weight of the sediment. These processes can only be analysed and related to particular archaeological sites after acquisition of detailed local information on the geology, faulting and composition of unconsolidated sediments.

For classical archaeological sites, the existence of masonry structures, quarries, harbour breakwaters, fish tanks and other cuttings and constructions makes it relatively easy to detect a relative change of sea level (Flemming, 1969; Blackman, 1973; Flemming and Webb, 1986). The earliest known harbour constructions and cuttings of islands to make ship-shelters are approximately 3,000 years old. Earlier Bronze Age coastal towns and settlements of the Mediterranean exhibit no signs of special structures near the water line (see, for example, Harding et al., 1969; Flemming et al., 1978). Neolithic and Mesolithic sites also show no indication of jetties, quays, docks or other special coastal technology at the waterline (Galili, 1987; Andersen, 1980; Flemming, 1983). It is possible that during the period 10,000 to 3,000 BP, when shipping, trade and fishing were active in many parts of the world, the inhabitants of some coastal settlements built small wooden jetties to ease the task of loading and unloading vessels. Such ephemeral structures exist today in many small villages in countries such as Turkey or India. Wooden structures do not survive in seawater unless buried in sediments, and so far no evidence has been found of marine technological waterfront installations from the early Bronze Age or Neolithic, in spite of several thorough excavations of coastal and submerged sites.

Palaeolithic sites found underwater are, by definition, devoid of habitable constructions. Submerged Palaeolithic sites identified so far (Sordinas, 1983; Riccardi et al., 1987; Scuvée and Verague, 1988; Flemming, 1985; Werz and Flemming, in preparation) consist of stone tools in situ under sediments, embedded in peat, or in submerged caves or washed out of submerged sediments and lying in unconsolidated gravels.

Since it is more difficult to obtain data about the older lithic sites than about the classical or Bronze Age sites, I will start the analysis of field examples with the most recent material and work backwards in time. This has the advantage that there are a greater number of known sites in the more recent periods, and the analysis of more recent artefacts provides a credibility that can then be extended cautiously backwards in time to the older sites, which provide less clear evidence.

CLASSICAL COASTAL SITES OF THE MEDITERRANEAN, 1900–2600 BP

To demonstrate the possibility of analysing human response to changing sea level, I will consider four classical sites: Phalasarna, uplifted 6.3 metres on the west coast of Crete; Apollonia, sunk 2.5 metres on the Cyrenaica coast of Libya; Caesarea, partly submerged to a depth of 8 metres on the coast of Israel; and the Phlegrean shoreline of the Bay of Naples, vertically displaced up and down by the volcanic activity in the region of Monte Nuovo.

Phalasarna, Crete, Greece

The ruins of Phalasarna lie on the extreme west coast of Crete. The visible buildings projecting from fields, and on the acropolis hill by the sea, were mapped by Spratt (1865), who proposed that the west end of Crete had been uplifted by more than 5 metres. Over the next century there was no confirmation of Spratt's hypothesis, and it was not certain whether, on archaeological evidence, the remains in the fields were those

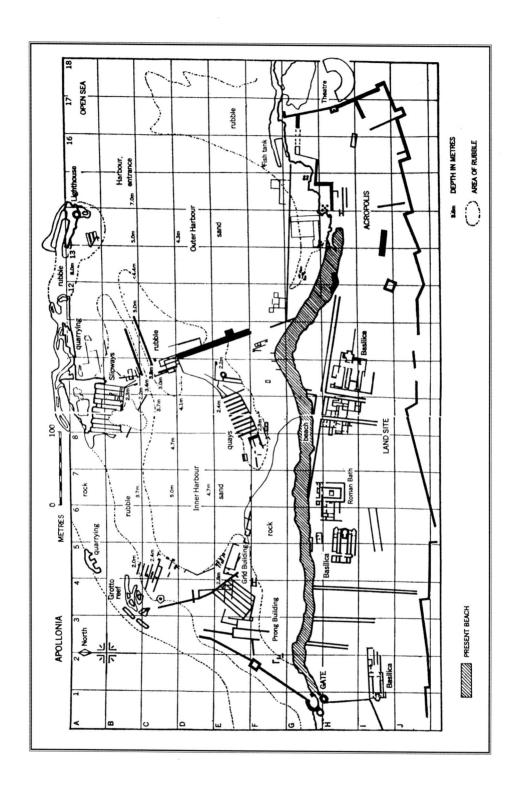

APOLLONIA

North

OPEN SEA

Lighthouse

Harbour, entrance

rubble

7.0m

8.0m

rubble

Fish tank

rubble

ACROPOLIS

Theatre

Outer Harbour

sand

5.0m

4.3m

4.4m

3.0m

quarrying

Slipways

rubble

3.8m

3.4m

3.0m

2.3m 2.2m

3.7m 4.1m

2.2m

Basilica

METRES

0   100

rock

rubble

3.7m

5.0m

Inner Harbour

sand

4.7m

quays

2.4m

2.3m

2.3m

4.7m

rock

LAND SITE

Roman Bath

quarrying

Grotto
reef

2.0m

2.4m

2.2m

Grid Building

rock

Basilica

Prong Building

GATE

Basilica

beach

8.6m   DEPTH IN METRES

AREA OF RUBBLE

PRESENT BEACH

of a harbour or of dwellings and civic structures. Hafemann (1965) studied the marine solution notches and fossil beaches of Crete, and showed conclusively that the western end of the island was uplifted, and this was analysed in more detail by Flemming *et al.* (1973) and Flemming (1978). Phalasarna has been uplifted by 6.3 metres since the time of occupation of the site 2,000 years ago. Flemming *et al.* (1973) deduced that the enclosed harbour area of Phalasarna was indeed in the fields at the foot of the acropolis, as proposed by Spratt (1865), but it was not until the excavations led by Hadjidaki (1988) that this was proven beyond doubt. The excavation showed defensive towers, sea walls, a harbour entrance and water cisterns. Flemming *et al.* (1973) had already drawn attention to the ancient fish tanks at Phalasarna, which aligned with the marine solution notches on the cliffs nearby, confirming the correlation of many structures to the ancient shoreline, 6.3 metres above the present sea level.

The coast on either side of Phalasarna is steep, with cliffs and headlands interspersed with narrow valleys coming down to the shore and small beaches. The city area is partly grassland, grazed by sheep, partly scrub bushes, and partly rock outcrops and quarries. At the level of approximately 6–7 metres above present sea level, all vegetation ceases, and bare rock slopes down to the sea. No buildings, cuttings, foundations or any other human artefact or construction occurs below the level of the old marine solution notches that run across the rock. The date of uplift, and the speed of the geological process that caused the uplift, are uncertain, and different propositions exist (for example Pirazzoli *et al.*, 1992). From the point of view of the current enquiry, the city was uplifted, some time early in the last 2,000 years, abandoned, and the exposed land along the shore was not reoccupied. The zone of tilted uplift extends from Khania, around the western end of Crete, to Elaphonisi at the south-west corner, and then along the south coast to Matala (Flemming, 1978). Small modern fishing villages in sandy bays extend down to the shore, but other classical sites in western Crete (for example Kissamos and Agneion) do not seem to have been reoccupied or rebuilt down to the shoreline after the geological uplift.

It is difficult to separate the devastating effects of the massive uplift of the coast, whether rapid or spread over several centuries, from the economic problems of the decline of the Roman Empire, the slow fragmentation of the Byzantine Empire and local problems of piracy that may have made it dangerous to live on the coast. By the time the uplift was complete, the Cretan economy and the prosperity of individual cities were insufficient to support the rebuilding of the extensive port structures, breakwaters, docks and fortifications at the lower level.

Apollonia, Libya

Apollonia was a Greek foundation on the coast of Cyrenaica, now Libya, in North Africa. The ruins on the shore and underwater were first mapped by Beechey (1827). The nineteenth-century chart of the coast shows submerged buildings spread over the

Opposite: Fig. 4. The Greek colony of Apollonia was established on the coast of Libya in the seventh century BC and continued in occupation for over 1,000 years. The main city wall is Hellenistic, and on land, the southern part of the map, there are three Christian basilicas. The ruins of buildings in the water are much older, and the lowest layers probably date to the foundation of the city. Different parts of the city have sunk by 2.4 to 2.6 m. (Source: Flemming, 1971)

seafloor extending 900 metres alongshore and 350 metres offshore to two small islands (fig. 4). The most complete survey of the underwater structures was carried out by Flemming in 1958 and 1959 (Flemming, 1971, pp. 95–135). The ruins in the sea include roadways, city walls, fortress tower foundations, slipways for boats, jetties and docks, a fish tank, and numerous ashlar buildings, quarries and rock-cuttings. The city was founded in the seventh century BC, fortified and extended in the Hellenistic period, developed with several Christian basilicas during the Byzantine empire, and abandoned during the seventh and eighth centuries AD. The ruins underwater are submerged by 2.4 to 2.6 metres.

During successive visits in 1958 and 1959, the divers observed substantial damage to buildings caused by winter storms. (This is consistent with the rate of destruction observed at Plitra; see below.) There is also a measurable difference between the relative position of buildings and the shoreline as shown on the map by Beechey (1827) and that surveyed by Flemming (1971). Although the 1827 map may have been based on rough sketches, it appears accurate and suggests a shoreline retreat or erosion of several metres. It is difficult to reconcile the speed of modern storm damage with the survival of any structures in the sea for more than 1,000 years.

The subsidence and collapse of Apollonia can be envisaged as a probable sequence of events, although the timing and details are unknown. Early stages of subsidence may have occurred while the harbours were still in use, and this may account for several cases of superimposed buildings close to the harbour front, with one group of walls built over the slipways. During this phase the massive artificial rubble breakwaters still prevented waves from breaking into the harbours. Later, as many of the maritime constructions sank into the sea, most of the port became unusable for large trading vessels, but one can imagine the basins of the harbour still partly sheltered in most weather by the breakwaters. Only in severe winter storms did the waves break with white water into the harbour basins. The breakwaters, defensive walls and roadways then began to crack, and eventually the rubble breakwaters were overtopped whenever the wind blew and the rubble blocks were scattered landwards towards the harbour. It is possible that, after the Arab conquest of Cyrenaica, the breakwaters continued to provide some shelter for small fishing boats, but the economic basis was lacking for a complete reconstruction of the city and its expensive buildings.

Caesarea, Israel

Caesarea was built on the orders of Herod, starting in 25 BC, and was severely damaged by earthquakes and subsidence in the first century AD (Fritsch and Ben-Dor, 1961; Flemming et al., 1978, pp. 59–63; Oleson et al., 1984; Raban, 1992). In the late 1970s a series of surveys and test excavations showed that buildings on the shoreline, and out to a distance of a few tens of metres from the present shore, were situated at the correct vertical level in relation to the current sea level, with an uncertainty of less than +/- 50 centimetres. Further offshore the huge rubble breakwater, associated quays, public buildings and lighthouse were submerged by approximately 5 to 8 metres.

The discontinuity that runs parallel to the shore, and which has caused part of the city to sink underwater, has still not been fully explained, but there are a number of possible geological processes, combining earthquake tremors, faulting and sediment compaction or slumping, which can explain most of the observations. During the last

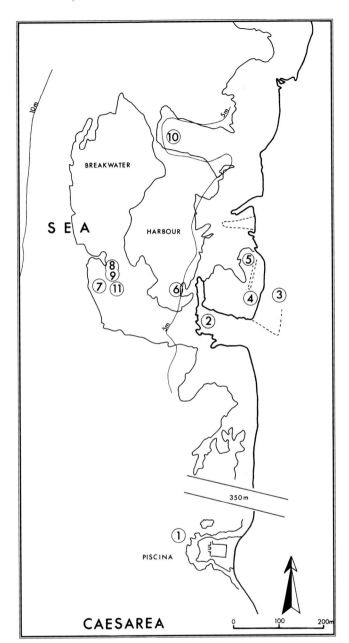

Fig. 5. The great port of Caesarea, Sebastos, was founded by Herod in 25 BC. The building along the coastline, fish tanks, sluice gates, walls and drains are at the correct relation to the present sea level, showing that there has been no measurable change of relative sea level. Offshore, large areas of rubble, concrete caissons and tower foundations are submerged by between 5 m and 8 m. (Source: Flemming *et al.*, 1978)

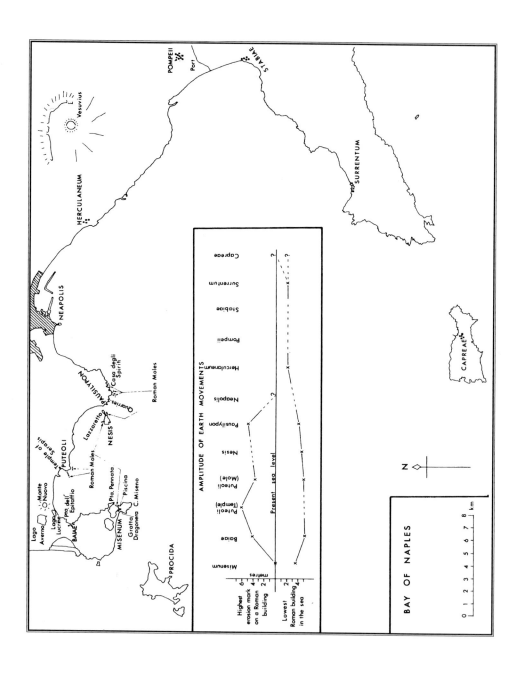

BAY OF NAPLES

0 1 2 3 4 5 6 7 8 km

N

POMPEII
Port
STABIAE
SURRENTUM
Vesuvius
HERCULANEUM
NEAPOLIS
PAUSILYPON
Casa degli Spirti
Quarries
Lazzaretto
Roman Moles
NESIS
PUTEOLI
Temple of Serapis
Monte Nuovo
Lago Averno
Lago Lucrine
Pro. dell' Epitaffio
BAIAE
Pta. Pennata
Piscina
MISENUM
Grotta Dragonera
C. Miseno
PROCIDA
CAPREAE

AMPLITUDE OF EARTH MOVEMENTS

Misenum · Baiae · Puteoli (Temple) · Puteoli (Mole) · Nesis · Pausilypon · Neapolis · Herculaneum · Pompeii · Stabiae · Surrentum · Capreae

metres
6
4
2
Present sea level
2
4

Highest erosion mark on a Roman building

Lowest Roman building in the sea

fifteen years the continuous underwater excavation at Caesarea, and the excavation of the inner harbour on land, have revealed one of the most astonishing technological achievements of the ancient world, including huge concrete caissons formed with wooden shuttering, and sunk into the sea to make the core of the breakwater (fig. 5). The work of Hohlfelder, Bull, Raban and others has shown that even after the earthquake and submergence or collapse of the outer breakwater the harbour continued in use for several centuries, and that warehouses on shore were kept in operation. In spite of the devastation of the outer harbour, which had been the whole reason for the construction of Herod's new city, the economic and social needs of the region were sufficient to justify continued investment in the city, though not the complete reconstruction of the main breakwater.

Campi Phlegreii, Italy

During the period of the Roman Empire, more trade reached Rome through the ports in the northern Bay of Naples than through Ostia. The Bay of Naples, with its commercial harbours, luxury villas and military port at Misenum, constituted the largest area of marine investment anywhere in the Empire. Günther and other early workers showed the general nature of subsidence and uplift along the northern shore of the Bay of Naples, known as the Campi Phlegreii. Günther (1903) described a submerged Roman thoroughfare winding along the coast linking the coastal cities from Naples to Misenum, bordered by the foundations of villas, harbour works, public buildings, fish tanks, jetties and breakwaters (fig. 6).

Flemming (1969, pp. 38–46) analysed the evidence prior to that date, combined with diving investigations, to produce a map showing varying magnitudes of subsidence followed by uplift of varying magnitude at all the sites from Naples to Misenum. The deepest submergence at present along this shoreline is between Baiae and Nisida, at a depth of 4 to 5 metres, and the greatest uplift is at Pozzuoli, with a magnitude of 6 metres. Since the submerged structures observed now are at their present depth *after* an uplift of 6 metres, the original subsidence was of the order of 10 metres. Dvorak and Mastrolorenzo (1990) examined the coast with geological, volcanological and archaeological analyses, and provided a regional explanation for the observed sequence of a basin-shaped subsidence, followed by a dome-shaped uplift, centred near the so-called Temple of Serapis at Pozzuoli.

The date of submergence of the Roman foreshore at the Campi Phlegreii is unknown. From the early sixteenth century AD there are reports of the foreshore drying up, and in 1538 a new volcano began to erupt near the coast close to Pozzuoli, producing the hill now known as Monte Nuovo. The sea retreated about 200 metres, and freshwater springs were observed bubbling up through the muddy ruins uplifted

Opposite: Fig. 6. The northern shore of the Bay of Naples is known as the Campi Phlegreii: the Fields of Fire. The coastal ruins and submerged buildings surveyed by Günther (1903), Flemming (1969) and Dvorak and Mastrolorenzo (1990) are shown in this diagram. The great uplift of the coast in 1538, which coincided with the eruption of Monte Nuovo, is shown by the upper line. Before 1538 the depth of submergence was even greater, so that the Temple of Serapis would have been about 10 m deep in the sea. (Source: Flemming, 1969)

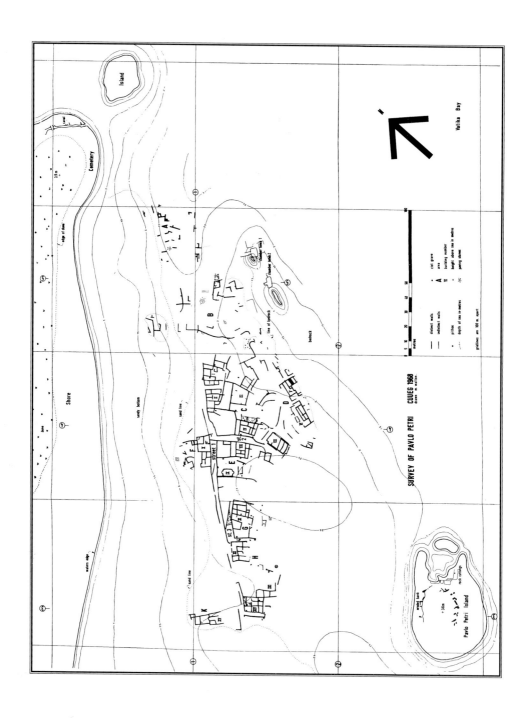

SURVEY OF PAVLO PETRI   CUUEG 1968
drawn in metres

Vatika Bay

distinct walls
indistinct walls
pillar
depth of sea in metres

cist grave
area
building number
height above sea in metres
paving stones

gridlines are 100 m. apart

Island

Cemetery

Canal

33 m

edge of dune

Shore

dune

sandy bottom

sand line

water's edge

sand line

line of bedrock

Number bank

bedrock

Pavlo Petri Island

rock cuttings

+3m

raised land

from the sea. The events of the next few centuries, including the discovery and excavation of the Temple of Serapis, were described by Hamilton (1776–9). Land movements in the area continue to the present day, and were particularly active in the 1970s.

Although the date of submergence of the Campi Phlegreii shore is unknown, the progressive discovery of more buildings and concrete constructions along the Roman shore is beginning to suggest that there was a massive investment in coastal defences against the rising sea during the middle to later period of the Roman Empire. The coastline was by this time largely artificial, consisting of an almost continuous chain of buildings, harbours and pools, all built as close as possible to the water, either for economic efficiency or for luxury and enjoyment. Given the economic and social importance of the coastal cities, and the huge investment already made over several centuries, it was logical and reasonable to maintain that investment, and protect the established military and civil installations. The precise extent of the defensive works against the sea is not yet clear, but the number of concrete pilae that have been found recently by divers is not compatible with earlier models of the development of the harbours on this coast.

The attempts by the Roman citizens of the Bay of Naples to fend off the encroaching sea – caused by subsidence of the shoreline – inevitably failed. No civilization, even today, could afford to combat a relative sea level rise of 10 metres over more than 10 kilometres of coastline. Future research will show to what extent engineering efforts were made to prevent the inundation.

When the land came up again in the sixteenth century, the response of local people was immediate. Because of the low gradient of the shoreline and the rich volcanic muds, vegetation colonized the new land quite quickly and the new land was swiftly occupied. During the 1970s, parts of the shore were again uplifted by about 1 metre, and coastal property owners immediately claimed any new land that appeared.

SUBMERGED BRONZE AGE SETTLEMENTS

Elaphonisos Pavlo-Petri, Greece

The submerged ruins of the Bronze Age site of Pavlo-Petri were first reported by Flemming (1968). A larger field survey with trial excavations was carried out in 1968 (Harding et al., 1969). The site was occupied from 2000 to 1000 BC, and the building foundations and roads surround a sheltered inner depression or basin that has its present floor at a depth of 2.5 metres below sea level. The buildings extend slightly deeper than 2.5 metres, where they disappear into the sediment, suggesting that the basin is a metre or more deeper below the sand and that the buildings may also go

Opposite: Fig. 7. The Bronze Age town of Pavlo-Petri was built over a ridge of rock projecting into the Gulf of Vatika, southern Greece. The town is submerged by more than 3 m, so every building is now under the sea. The ridge originally protected the town and its harbour from the wind and waves, but as it submerged the coast became exposed to storm waves and the site was abandoned. (Source: Flemming, 1971)

deeper below the current sea level. On the outer side of the ridge, which protects the harbour, the buildings continue almost to the 3 metre isobath (fig. 7).

The Bay of Vatika is exposed to the south and south-west, so the outer buildings at Pavlo-Petri must have been built a little way back from the water, suggesting a total submergence of the town by 4 metres. The ridge that protects the inner basin is now 1.5 metres below sea level, and would therefore have been 2.5 metres above the sea when the town flourished, providing excellent protection from storms.

The house pattern, roads, tombs, pottery and overall town plan of Pavlo-Petri are typical of a provincial town of the second millennium BC, and there is nothing to suggest that the sheltered basin was modified, protected or adapted to support the loading and unloading of vessels, or the building and repair of ships. The location of the town, the shape of the ridge, headland and basin, and the strategic position opposite Kythera and Crete demonstrate beyond doubt that the town was a trading centre. It is possible that there are special marine technological features beneath the sand, but none have been found at other sites of the Bronze Age. One concludes that boats were either pulled up on the sand, or anchored just offshore with a taut mooring rope to the beach. These techniques are widely used today, for example in Gaza, where fishing fleets operate with no shelter.

There are no buildings in the area of Pavlo-Petri that would suggest continued urbanization later than 1000 BC, although there are a few scattered tombs and rock cuttings related to saltpans of a much later date. The submerged town was abandoned and no attempt was made to rebuild or maintain occupation close by. The original usefulness of the site was provided by the topography of the ridge that protected the basin. As the land sank into the sea, the waves overtopped the ridge, and the buildings were exposed to the full force of the open sea. There was no point in reoccupying the adjacent shore since there was now no natural shelter for ships. The site became useless.

In the case of Pavlo-Petri, no investment in rebuilding the town could compensate for the loss of the protected harbour basin, and no technology was available at that date for building an artificial breakwater.

MEGALITHIC AND NEOLITHIC

Er Lannic, France

Crawford (1927) described and photographed the megalithic standing stone circle on the island of Er Lannic in the Gulf of Morbihan. The main circle covers the eastern slope of the small island, with one stone near the summit and the lowest half of the circle below mean sea level. Prigent et al. (1983) gave the date of the circle as 2500 to 3000 BC, and estimated that the lowest stone is 6 metres below mean high water springs. A second circle, or half-circle, touches tangentially against the one on the island, and is completely below mean sea level. The maximum depth of the lower circle is not known (fig. 8).

The Er Lannic circle is one example of numerous megalithic monuments and tombs on the coast of Brittany that are either in the sea or on such small islets or rocks that they cannot have been inhabited in their present topographic relation to the sea. Giot et al. (1979) and others have documented the scattered megaliths, which show that the submerged continental shelf off the coast of Brittany was occupied and exploited

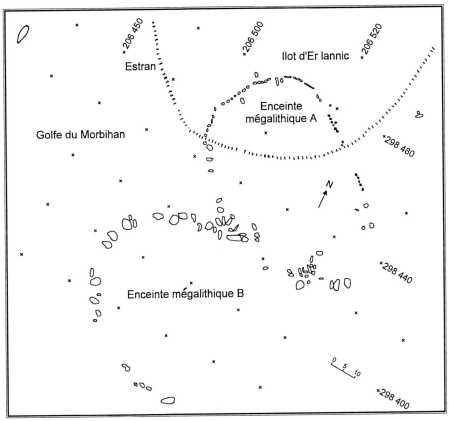

Fig. 8. Two nearly complete Megalithic stone circles lie on the island of Er Lannic in the Golfe du Morbihan. The upper circle 'A', or half of the 'W' shape, is partly on dry land and partly in the intertidal zone where it is covered by the sea at every high tide. The lower circle 'B' is entirely below the low tide level. Measurements of the exact depth of the lower circle have not been published. (Source: Le Gall and Gouezin, 1992).

intensively 4,000 to 6,000 years ago, but the process and stages of retreat from the shelf as the sea rose have not been analysed. Part of the submergence of the coast of Brittany in this period was caused by the last phases of the post-glacial rise of world sea level, and part is caused by a continuing land subsidence. Because of the large tidal range around Brittany, the study of these sites needs to be conducted very carefully in relation to land benchmarks and precise estimates of mean sea level and tidal amplitude.

Plitra, southern Greece

In 1967 I visited the site, making sketch maps (Flemming, 1973, p. 11; fig. 9) and taking photographs (Flemming, 1969) over the course of several days. In 1967 the site exhibited a graded stratigraphy with primitive walls of uncut stones standing 1 metre high from the seafloor at the southern limit of the site; ashlar and dressed masonry

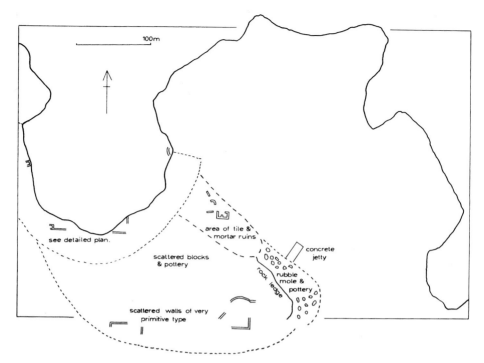

Fig. 9. Plitra, in southern Greece, includes buildings of all ages ranging from Neolithic or early Bronze Age through to late Roman or Byzantine. (a) The broad outline of the submerged headland extends south-east from the present shore, partly enclosing the bay. At the extreme south of the submerged area there are some very primitive walls. (b) The larger-scale drawing shows the buildings close to the present shore. The numbers in circles indicate the depth in metres below the present sea level. (Source: Flemming, 1973)

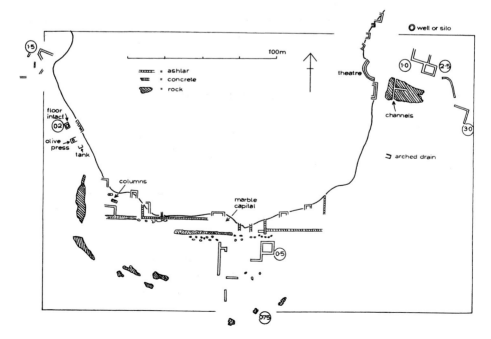

foundations close to the shoreline; and massive brick and mortar apsidal structures that are probably late Roman or Byzantine on the eastern side of the headland. Features in the very shallow water included an olive press, a small theatre on the beach and a circular well shaft just underwater. The primitive standing walls at the southern edge of the site were in 3 metres of water, and I originally thought that they were of the same date as the Helladic site at Pavlo-Petri (see above). I returned to Plitra in 1979 and found that the uncut stone walls had been completely destroyed by winter storms in the intervening twelve years. On the shoreline the small theatre had also been largely undercut by the waves and had collapsed.

Having worked on many Bronze Age sites since 1967, and having studied the photographs from 1967 very carefully, I conclude that nothing from the Bronze Age matches the walls, either in structure or in plan. They seem to be more primitive. If these walls were animal pens or field walls, their loose pattern of construction could be explained as compatible with a later period, but it is unlikely that animal pens made of poorly fitted stones would be built on the shore in an exposed location.

I conclude that Plitra illustrates a progressive retreat shorewards towards higher ground as an occupied site was inundated by the rising sea. The southern walls, based at 3 metres below present sea level, are in a very exposed position, and were probably used more than 5,000 years ago, when the land was higher and the world sea level was lower. The extreme exposure and fragility of the walls indicates that they must have been several metres above sea level when in use. A relative change of land–sea level of the order of 5 to 6 metres is compatible with the suggested Neolithic age for the walls.

At Plitra the rising relative sea level over a period of several thousand years did not destroy the topographic justification for occupying the headland. I do not suggest that the site was continuously occupied, and that successive generations literally built on higher ground. There does seem to be a cultural gap in the Bronze Age. Rather, the site was always attractive for settlers, and, although it may have been temporarily abandoned at times, people always moved back and reoccupied it.

The rapid destruction of the submerged ruins photographed in 1967 requires explanation. It is not possible that the fragile walls could have been standing exposed on the sea floor for centuries, or even many decades, and then have been flattened in twelve years. There must have been a metre or more of sand, sediment or terrestrial soil over the ruins, and supporting the primitive walls for thousands of years. This is consistent with a model of the site that suggests that the sea was originally at some distance from the southern walls. Wind-blown sand and soil covered the Neolithic walls, and the headland was reoccupied at a later date. As submergence continued, the southern shore was gradually eroded and the walls were exposed. As the height of exposed wall increased and the sediment was eroded away, the walls became more unstable and, some time in the 1970s, they collapsed.

Tokonami, Japan

Tokonami is a small port in the Japanese province of Kyushu, close to the narrowest point of the straits between Japan and Korea. It is on a small island off the coast of Kyushu, located on the landward-facing eastern side of the island, and sheltered from storm winds. Japanese diving teams reported by Araki and Hayakashi (1993) explored the drowned river valley, which prolongs the axis of the Tokonami river onto the submerged continental shelf (fig. 10). Excavating through sediments at a depth of 20

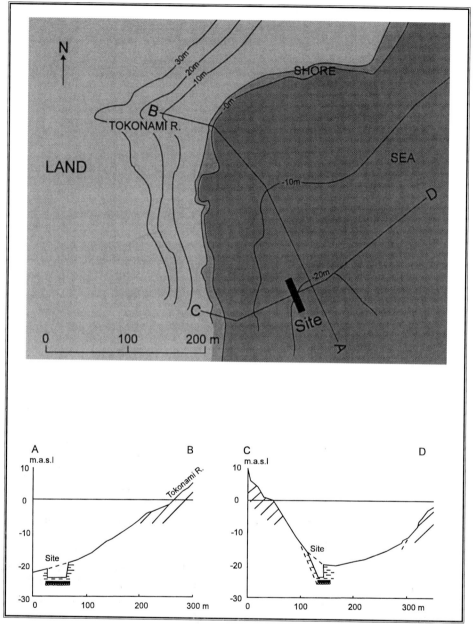

Fig. 10. The Neolithic settlement off the coast of Tokonami, Japan, is at a depth of 25 m below the present sea level and dates from the Jomon culture, 9,000 years ago. The top map shows the location of the site beside the drowned valley of the Tokonami river. The lower cross-sections show the excavated site in relation to the river bed and in relation to a section perpendicular to the river bed.

metres, they found a Jomon culture site 9,000 years old at a depth of 25 metres below present sea level. The excavation report shows acoustic penetration cross-sections of the site, and describes hundreds of artefacts, pottery fragments and stone tools. Excluding possible effects of local earth movements, the global sea level was about 40 to 50 metres lower 9,000 years ago, and so the Tokonami Jomon culture village would have been 15 to 25 metres above the sea in a sheltered river valley.

The Tokonami materials are covered in several metres of sediment and are well preserved. This is the deepest Neolithic settlement discovered so far. There is no evidence yet to indicate how the occupants of the site reacted to the rising sea level in terms of migration up the valley or abandonment of the area.

Florida – Gulf of Mexico

Dunbar *et al.* (1992) summarized the results of many years of work exploring drowned Indian settlement sites in the river beds and off the Gulf of Mexico coast of Florida. Human occupation materials, bones and food debris have been found to a depth of 25 metres in flooded sink holes on land close to the shore and connected to the sea by the water table (Cockrell, 1986). Offshore the 20 metre isobath is about 50 kilometres from the beach, and the so-called Clovis shoreline with a date of about 11,000 years BP is located at a depth of 40 metres and a distance of about 100 kilometres offshore.

Faught and Donoghue (1994) described the submerged karstic topography of the Florida shelf, with numerous drowned river valleys and submerged sink holes. Combining acoustic surveys and diving observations, they reported twelve rock outcrops with evidence of quarrying activities, and three sites with numerous human artefacts. Controlled coring and dredging has produced almost a thousand artefacts from the depth range 3 to 6 metres, and age of the order of 7,000 years BP.

It is too soon to evaluate the complete sequence of inundation of the Florida shelf and the process of human retreat. From the discoveries so far it will be a perfect type area to see how the gradual rise of sea level over the period 11,000 to 5,000 BP impinged on the scattered occupation sites and quarries, causing the people to retreat more than 100 kilometres onto higher ground. The horizontal rate of retreat of the order of 1 kilometre every sixty years indicates that every human generation would have had to make considerable adjustments.

Atlit, Israel

The Neolithic village just north of Atlit is in a water depth of 10.5 metres (Galili, 1987). The seasonal movement of sediments has alternately covered and exposed a range of artefacts, stone tools, organic materials, hearths and burials. A stone-lined well shaft descends 5 metres below the sea bed to a total depth of 15.5 metres below the present sea level. The house foundations are on the landward side of a low ridge, so the village was slightly protected from the direct impact of storms. As the sea level rose, the water table in the well rose and became saline, and the inhabitants responded by throwing stones and debris into the bottom of the well to prevent the bucket from picking up saltwater. Eventually the well had to be abandoned. There are so many Neolithic sites on land close to the present coast of Israel that it is not yet possible to deduce the movements of peoples when the Atlit submerged site was evacuated.

Aghios Petros, Northern Sporadhes, Greece

Flemming (1983) surveyed a submerged Neolithic site and carried out test excavations of 1 metre and 0.5 metre quadrats, off the island of Aghios Petros, which is in a bay on the island of Kyra Panagia, Northern Sporadhes (fig. 11). Pottery, flint tools, obsidian blades, and bones of goats and sheep were found to a depth of 9 metres. The archaeological stratum lay directly on the bedrock sloping seaward from Aghios Petros, and appeared to be a lag deposit from which all of the finer components of soil had been washed out by wave action. The location of the settlement is in the most protected corner of the bay, sheltered from every major fetch of wind and waves. This in itself confirms that the inhabitants chose the site to support seafaring.

When the village was occupied in about 8000 BP, the sea level was 20 to 30 metres

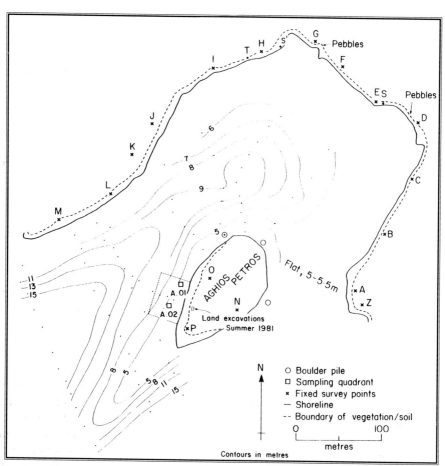

Fig. 11. The island of Aghios Petros lies in a bay on the coast of the larger island of Kyra Panagia, northern Sporadhes. The rectangle enclosed by a dotted line shows the areas of sea bed covered in gravels containing Neolithic pottery, obsidian and flint tools, and bones of goat and sheep. Two of the test quadrats are marked A.01, and A.02. Survey points on the coast are marked with capital letters. The isobaths were constructed by taking soundings with a weighted tape. The unlabelled dots indicate the sounding points. (Source: Flemming, 1983)

lower than it is now, and the village would have overlooked a steep narrow bay, with freshwater springs nearby on the shore. As the sea level rose at a rate of about 1 metre per century, the occupants could have retreated up-slope quite easily when required by building new houses on the landward side of the village. There is no evidence that this was actually done. In practice, the settlement was abandoned and there is no indication of later occupation.

PALAEOLITHIC

Palaeolithic sites found to date include artefact deposits in submerged peat off Cap Levi near Cherbourg, France (Scuvée and Verague, 1988) with an age of about 40,000 years BP; flint tools surveyed and retrieved from the sea floor off the west coast of Kerkyra, Greece (Sordinas, 1983; Flemming, 1985) with an age of about 45,000 years BP; charcoal and cave paintings found in the submerged cave known as the Grotte Cosquer, in the south of France (Clottes *et al.*, 1992), with an age of 19,000 years BP; and two Acheullian hand axes found in Table Bay, South Africa, by Bruno Werz (Werz and Flemming, in preparation) with an age of about 1 million years.

The Palaeolithic materials indicate that artefacts of this age were used on the continental shelf, were deposited on the continental shelf, and can still be retrieved and excavated stratigraphically in context. The Grotte Cosquer has a submerged entrance at a depth of 40 metres, and the sea level at the time of occupation would have been about 100 metres lower than at present (fig. 12). The two sites with ages of around 40,000 to 50,000 years BP occur during oxygen-isotope stage 3 (fig. 2), when the sea level rose to within 20 to 40 metres of present sea level (Richards *et al.*, 1994). Artefacts found at depths of 10 to 20 metres would therefore have been quite close to the sea on steep coasts.

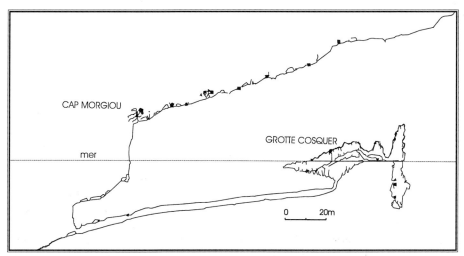

Fig. 12. The Grotte Cosquer at Cap Morgiou in the south of France can only be entered by a tunnel that is now submerged 40 m below sea level. The tunnel leads upwards to a cave that, in places, rises above the present sea level and contains cave paintings and datable charcoal. The oldest remains date from 19,000 years BP, when the sea level was more than 100 m below the present level. (Source: Clottes *et al.*, 1992)

The discovery of two Acheulian hand axes in Table Bay, South Africa, by Bruno Werz in the spring of 1995 suggests that artefacts deposited on the continental shelf below present sea level can survive *in situ* of the order of ten marine transgressions and ten marine regressions, being traversed by the surf zone each time. The stratigraphic context of the axes has been analysed for publication during 1996 (Werz and Flemming, in preparation).

Sites with an age of the order of 30,000 to 50,000 years BP are interesting because the sea level fell after the oxygen-isotope stage 3 to a depth of more than 100 metres (fig. 2). Rather than being inundated, these occupation zones would have experienced a falling sea level, and the population would have tended to migrate seawards. This hypothesis has not yet been tested, partly because 50 metres is close to the normal depth limit for compressed air diving.

The limited number of known submerged Palaeolithic sites is sufficient to show that the questions posed at the beginning of this chapter can, in principle, be answered some time in the future. Artefacts have already been found in situations and at dates where the sea level subsequently fell by tens of metres, and so we could investigate the process of colonization of the shelf. In time, submerged artefacts will be found from the relatively high-level stillstands around 100,000 BP, when one would expect the sea level to be only 10 to 20 metres lower than at present. The Klaseis river site in South Africa dates from the last interglacial high sea level a few metres above present sea level, and is thus probably the precursor of a number of offshore sites on the Aghullas Bank.

CONCLUSIONS

The human response to rising and falling sea level is conditioned by desire to stay close to known exploitable resources, by economic prosperity, technical competence, fear of piracy and changes in coastal topography brought about by the changing sea level. In some circumstances the coastal community will exert every effort to combat the damage caused by a rising sea level, and under other circumstances major ports and cities were abandoned, and the populations dispersed.

The response to falling sea level can only be studied for the Palaeolithic time zones preceding major sea level retreats, that is 130,000 years BP, 100,000 BP and 30 to 50,000 BP. Archaeological data are available from the first and third of these periods. The examples of the uplift of Phalasarna and the Bay of Naples described earlier are intriguing in the classical context and they show contrasting responses, but they cannot be taken as examples that provide any detailed insight into responses during the Palaeolithic. Consultation with Dutch hydraulic engineers who have worked on land enclosure and drainage programmes in the Netherlands confirms that the salt in freshly reclaimed land is washed out by rain and groundwater within a few decades. During Palaeolithic periods of falling sea level, assuming a descent rate of 1 metre per century and a land gradient of (for example) 1 in 50, there would be a freshly exposed strip of land 50 metres wide each century. Of this, approximately 40 metres would have been desalinated by rainfall and about 10 metres would remain saline for about 20 years. Since agriculture was not practised, the narrow strip of poor vegetation close to the shore during periods of falling sea level would not have been a disincentive to the exploitation of the sea.

This analysis does not suggest that the evidence has yet been obtained to answer all of the questions posed at the beginning of this chapter, but it does demonstrate that the evidence is preserved on the continental shelf, and can be found. The rate of discovery of sites is encouraging. The questions posed are important for understanding the early development of human cultures, technology and prosperity, and they can be answered in the next few decades.

REFERENCES

Allen, J., Golson, J., and Jones, R. *Sunda and Sahul*, London, Academic Press, 1977

Andersen, A.S.H. *Tybrind Vig, a Preliminary Report on a Submerged Ertebolle Settlement on the Little Belt*, Antikvariske Studier Vol. 4. pp. 7–22, 1980

Araki, S., and Hayakashi. *The archaeological materials from the Takashima seabed* (part II). Takashima Town cultural property research report. Educational Committee of Takashima Town, Nagasaki prefecture, 1993.

Bailey, G. Report on the First International Conference on the Palaeolithic of Greece and Adjacent Areas (I.CO.P.A.G), Ioannina, Greece, 6–11 Sept. 1994. *Palaeolithic Archaeology in Greece and the Balkans*, 1994

Beechey, F.W. *Proceedings of the Expedition to Explore the North Coast of Africa*, London, John Murray, 1827

Birdsell, J.B. *Some Population Problems Involving Pleistocene Man*, Cold Spring Harbor Symposium on Quantitative Biology, Vol. XXII., 1957, pp. 47–69

Blackman, D.J. *Evidence of Sea Level Change in Ancient Harbours and Coastal Installations*, Colston Symposium Papers, Butterworth, No. 23, 1973, pp. 114–37

Blanc, A.C. 'Low levels of the Mediterranean Sea during the Pleistocene glaciation', *Geological Society of London Quarterly Journal* 93, 1937

——. 'Industrie musteriane e paleolithiche superiore nelle dune fossile e nelle grotte litorannee del Cap Palinuro', R.C. Reale Academia d'Italia, Vol. 10, Ser. 7, 1940, p. 1

Chappell, J. 'Relative and average sea level changes and endo-, epi-, and exogenic processes on the earth' in I. Allison (ed.), *Sea Level, Ice, and Climatic Change*, Proceedings of the Canberra Symposium 1979, International Association of Hydrological Science, Publication No. 131, Washington, DC, 1981

Chappell, J. and Polach, H. 'Post-glacial sea-level rise from a coral record at Huon Peninsula, Papua New Guinea', *Nature* 349 (6305), 1991, pp. 147–9

Clark, J.A. and Lingle, C.S. 'Predicted relative sea-level changes (18,000 BP to present) caused by late glacial retreat of the Antarctic Ice Sheet', *Quaternary Research* 9, 1978, pp. 265–87

Clottes, J., Beltran, A., Courtin, J. and Cosquer, H. 'The Cosquer Cave on Cape Morgiou, Marseille', *Antiquity* 66, 1992, pp. 583–8

Cockrell, W.A., 'The warm mineral springs archaeological research project: current research and technological applications' in C.T. Mitchell (ed.), *Diving for Science* 86, American Academy of Underwater Sciences, 1986, pp. 63–8

Crawford, O.G.S. 'Lyonesse', *Antiquity* 1, 1927, pp. 5–14

Devoy, R.J.N. *Sea Surface Studies*, Bekenham and New York, Croom Helm, 1987

Dunbar, J., Webb, S.D. and Faught, M. 'Inundated prehistoric sites in Apalachee Bay, Florida, and the search for the Clovis shoreline' in L.L. Johnson and M. Stright (eds), *Paleoshorelines and Prehistory: an Investigation of Method*, Boca Raton, CRC Press, 1992

Dvorak, J.J. and Mastrolorenzo, G. 'History of vertical movement in Pozzuoli Bay, southern Italy: the result of regional extension related to evolution of the Tyrrhenian Sea and of local volcanic activity', Geological Society of America Special Paper 263, 1990

Emery, K.O. and Edwards, R.L. 'Archaeological potential of the Atlantic continental shelf', *American Antiquity* 31, 1966, pp. 733–7

Emiliani, C. 'The cause of the Ice Ages', *Earth and Planetary Science Letters* 37, 1978, pp. 349–52

Fairbridge, R.W. 'Eustatic changes in sea level', *Physics and Chemistry of the Earth*, London, Pergamon, Vol. 4., 1961, pp. 99–185

Faught, M.K. and Donoghue, J. 'Inundated archaeological sites and paleo-river channels in the Apalachee Bay of northwestern Florida', 59th Annual Meeting of the Society of American Archaeology, Annaheim, California, 1994

Flemming, N.C. 'Archaeological evidence for eustatic change of sea level and earth movements in the Western Mediterranean during the last 2,000 years', Geological Society of America, Special Paper 109, 1969

——. 'Holocene earth movements and eustatic sea level change in the Peloponnese', Nature 217, 1968, pp. 1,031–32

——. *Cities in the Sea*, Doubleday, New York, 1971

——. 'Archaeological evidence for eustatic and tectonic components of relative sea level change in the South Aegean', Colston Symposium Papers, Butterworth, D.J. Blackman (ed.) No. 23, 1973, pp. 1–66

——. Holocene eustatic changes and coastal tectonic in the north-east Mediterranean: implications for models of crustal consumption', *Philosophical Transactions of the Royal Society, (London)*, A 289, 1978, pp. 405–8

——. 'Preliminary geomorphological survey of an early Neolithic submerged site in the Sporadhes, North Aegean' in P. Masters and N.C. Flemming (eds), 1983

——. 'Ice Ages and human occupation of the continental shelf', *Oceanus* 28 (1), 1985, pp. 18–26

——. 'Predictions of relative coastal sea-level change in the Mediterranean based on archaeological, historical and tide-gauge data' in L. Jeftic, J.D. Milliman and G. Sestini (eds), *Climate Change and the Mediterranean*, London, Edward Arnold, 1993

Flemming, N.C., Czartoryska, N.M.G. and Hunter, P.M. 'Archaeological evidence for vertical earth movements in the region of the Aegean island arc' in N.C. Flemming (ed.), *Diving Science International*, London, British Sub Aqua Club, 1973

Flemming, N.C., Raban, A. and Goetschel, C. 'Tectonic and eustatic changes on the Mediterranean coast of Israel in the last 9000 years', *Progress in Underwater Science*, Underwater Association 3, 1978, pp. 33–93

Flemming, N.C. and Webb, C.O. 'Tectonic and eustatic coastal changes during the last 10,000 years derived from archaeological data', *Zeitschrift für Geomorphologie*, N.F. Supplement 62, 1986, pp. 1–29,

Flemming, N.C. and Woodworth, P.L. 'Monthly mean sea levels in Greece 1969–83 compared to relative vertical land movements measured over different timescales', *Tectonophysics* 148, 1988, pp. 59–72,

Fritsch, C.F. and Ben-Dor, I. 'The Link expedition to Israel, 1960', *Biblical Archaeologist* 24, 1961, pp. 52–5

Galili, E. 'A late pre-pottery Neolithic B site on the sea floor at Atlit', *Mitkufat Haeven* 20, 1987, pp. 50–71

Giot, P.R., L'Helgouac, H.J. and Monnier, J.L. *Préhistoire de la Bretagne*, Rennes, Ouest France, 1979

Günther, R.T. 'The submerged Greek and Roman foreshore near Naples', *Archaeologia* 58, 1903

Hadjidaki, E. 'Preliminary report of excavations at the harbour of Phalasarna in west Crete', *American Journal of Archaeology* 92, 1988, pp. 466–8

Hafemann, D. 'Die Nieveauveranderungen an den Kusten Kretas seit dem Altertum. Abhandlung math-naturwissenchaft', *Kl. Akad. Wiss. Mainz* 12, 1965, pp. 608–88

Hamilton, W. *I Campi Phlegreaei*, Naples, Peter Fabris, 1776–9

Harding, A., Cadogan, G. and Howell, R. 'Pavlopetri, an underwater Bronze Age town in Laconia', *Annual of the British School at Athens* 64, 1969, pp. 113–42

Inman, D.L. 'Applications of coastal dynamics to the reconstruction of palaeocoastlines in the vicinity of La Jolla, California' in P. Masters and N.C. Flemming (eds), 1983

Johnstone, P. *The Sea-craft of Prehistory*, Routledge, London and New York, 1988, pp. 7–43

Jones, R. 'Man as an element of a continental fauna: the case of the sundering of the Bassian Bridge' in J. Allen, J. Golson and R. Jones (eds), 1977

Le Gall, E. and Gouezin, P. 'Golfe de Morbihan, Er Lannic', Bilan Scientifique, Direction du Patrimoine, Département des Recherches Archéologiques Sous-marines, 1992, pp. 25–7

Louwe Kooijmans, L.P. 'Mesolithic bone and antler implements from the North Sea and from the Netherlands', *Bericht van het Rijksdienst Oudheikundig Bodemonderzoek*, Jaargang 22/21, 1970/1

Masters, P. and Flemming, N.C. (eds). *Quaternary Coastlines and Marine Archaeology*, Academic Press, London and New York, 1983

Oleson, J.P., Hohlfelder, R.L., Raban, A. and Vann, R.L. 'The Caesarea Ancient Harbour Excavation Project (CAHEP): preliminary report on the 1980–83 seasons', *Field Archaeology* 11, 1984, pp. 281–305

Pirazzoli, P.A. 'Les variations du niveau marin depuis 2000 ans', *Mémoire du Laboratoire Géomorphologique*, École Pratiques des Hautes Études, Vol. 3, 1976, pp. 1–421

——. 'Sea-level changes in the Mediterranean', in *Sea-level Changes*, Oxford, Basil Blackwell, 1987, pp. 152–81

Pirazzoli, P.A., Ausseil-Badie, J., Giresse, P., Hadjidaki, E. and Arnold, M. 'Historical environmental changes at Phalasarna harbour, west Crete', *Geoarchaeology* 7, 1992, pp. 371–92

Prigent, D., Vissent, L., Morzadec-Kerfourn, M.T. and Lautrido, J.P. 'Human occupation of the submerged coast of the Massif Armoricain and post-glacial sea level changes' in P.M. Masters and N.C. Flemming (eds), 1983

Raban, A. 'Sebastos: the royal harbour of Caesarea – a short-lived giant', *Int. J. Naut. Arch.* 21 (2), 1992, pp. 111–24

Riccardi, E., Chizzola, S. and Vicino, G. 'Considerazioni sul riliveo della parte immersa della caverna a mare di Bergeggi (SV)', *Rivista di Studi Liguri*, LII (1–4), Bordighera, Forma Maris Antiqui, 1987, pp. 403–11

Richards, D.A., Smart, P.L. and Edwards, R.L. 'Maximum sea levels for the last glacial period from U-series ages of submerged speleothems', *Nature* 367 (6761), 1994, pp. 357–60

Scuvée, F. and Verague, J. 'Le gisement sous-marin du Paléolithique Moyen de l'anse de la Mondrée à Fermanville (Manche)', Ministère des Affaires Culturelles, Autorisation No. 001740, CEHP-Littus, BP.306, Cherbourg 50104, 1988

Shackleton, J.C., Van Andel, T.H. and Runnels, C.N. 'Coastal paleogeography of the central and western Mediterranean during the last 125,000 years, and its archaeological implications', *J. Field Archaeology* 11, 1984, pp. 307–14

Shackleton, N.J. and Opdyke, N.D. 'Oxygen isotope and paleomagnetic stratigraphy of equatorial Pacific core V28–238: oxygen isotope temperature and ice volume on a 10^5 to 10^6 year scale,' *Quaternary Research* 3, 1973, pp. 39–55

Sordinas, A. 'Quaternary shorelines in the region of Corfu and adjacent islets, western Greece', in P. Masters and N.C. Flemming (eds), 1983

Spindler, K. *The Man in the Ice*, Weidenfeld and Nicholson, translated from the German edition (Bertelsmann Verlag GmbH, Munich), 1994

Spratt, T.A.B. *Travels and Researches in Crete*, Vols. 1 and 2, J. van Vorst, 1865

Tushingham, A.M. and Peltier, W.R. 'ICE–3G: A new global model of late Pleistocene deglaciation based upon geophysical predictions of post-glacial relative sea level change,' *J. Geophysical Research* 96, 1991, pp. 4497–523

van Andel, T.H. and Llanos, N. 'Prehistoric and historic shorelines of the southern Argolid peninsula; a sub-bottom profiler study', *Int. J. Naut. Arch.* 12 (4), 1983, pp. 303–24

Walcott, R.I. 'Past sea levels, eustasy and deformation of the earth', *Quaternary Research*, Vol. 2, 1972, pp. 1–14

Warwick, R.A., le Provost, C., Meier, M.F., Oerlemans, J. and Woodworth, P.L. (lead authors) IPCC Scientific Assessment Working Group 1, 'Sea Level Change' in Houghton *et al.* (eds), Cambridge University Press, 1996

Werz, B. and Flemming, N.C. 'Acheulian tools found in the sea off the coast of South Africa' (in preparation)

MARINE RESOURCES FROM ANTIQUITY TO THE PRESENT DAY

Anthony Laughton

INTRODUCTION

The exploitation of resources from the sea requires knowledge of their existence, and of the demand for the products, the technology to extract them and the right economic climate. They may be living, mineral, chemical or even intangible, such as energy or marine usage. In ancient times the marine resources used were those found on the shoreline and in shallow water, but as man ventured further onto the sea in ships, so more useful products were discovered and exploited. This discussion traces the impact of technology on the exploitation of marine resources throughout history and speculates about the future.

Just as the oceans are vast, so is the range of products in the oceans that can be used by humankind. Not only do the seas cover more than two-thirds of the surface of the globe, but in places they are nearly 11 kilometres deep. Now there is the technology not only to reach the bottom but also to penetrate another 2 kilometres below the ocean floor by drilling. The volume available in and below the oceans in which useful products could be found therefore hugely exceeds that of the surface and near subsurface of the continents.

Humankind looks to nature for food, medicines, shelter, building materials and minerals to satisfy the ever-increasing demands of a society that wants to improve its standard of living. When the immediately accessible land cannot provide these, we have turned to the seas. Marine resources can be defined as those products in or under the sea that can be used to meet the needs of society.

In the numerous recent debates and discussions on world resources, much has been written defining what is a reserve, what is a resource and what is a resource base (Archer, 1985; Tilton and Skinner, 1987). Knowledge, on its own, of the biological ecosystem of the ocean, of the chemistry of seawater, of the energy of the tides, currents and waves or of the geology of the ocean floor is not enough to define a resource. It is well known, for instance, that there is gold in solution in the sea, and because the seas are vast the total quantity of gold must also be large. After the First World War, Germany sought to repay its post-war debts by extracting gold from the sea and researched the potential on a major oceanographic expedition. However, the low concentrations and the high extraction costs proved it to be uneconomic, therefore it could not be described as a resource. It is also necessary to establish that products, to merit the term resources, are potentially exploitable. This in turn depends on whether there is a technology available to extract them and whether it is economic to do so.

For our purposes, I shall use the term resource to include those products that have been demonstrated to have been economically worthwhile because they have actually been exploited in the past, or those for which serious consideration has been given by industry for potential exploitation in the future.

Marine resources can be divided into living and non-living. The non-living can be further divided into solid, liquid and gaseous minerals, chemicals and the intangibles, which include energy and the utilization of ocean space (Laughton, 1994a). Among the intangibles are transport and warfare, which will be dealt with in other chapters, recreation, the use of the oceans for laying cables, and the storage or disposal of waste products, both intentionally and unintentionally (Laughton, 1994b).

In reviewing marine resources from antiquity to the present, I will restrict this discussion to the development of fisheries and the whaling industry, the exploitation of marine minerals and chemicals, and the extraction of energy from the sea. In all of these fields the growth of technology throughout history has been the determining factor in finding and exploiting new resources, and in some cases it is the very success of technology that has led to over-exploitation and the collapse of an industry. In other cases, alternative sources of the product or replacement by synthetic materials have led to their demise. Today it is widely recognized that many of the resources of the globe are finite and that over-exploitation is endangering the ability of the world to maintain a sustainable environment.

Technology has developed from the tools used by our distant ancestors for cracking nuts or killing animals, through to the incredibly complex machines of today. This development has not only enabled industries to grow and flourish but it has also, in some cases, led to their ultimate collapse. History can teach us some lessons.

LIVING RESOURCES

The living resources of the sea were gathered for food by the most primitive people from the shoreline and from the estuaries where many of them lived. Shellfish were easily collected because they could be harvested at low tide with no special skills or technology. The shores of Europe, America, Australia and Africa are dotted with shell heaps, or kitchen middens as they are called, from which archaeologists can deduce the diet of primitive man from the species of shell found. The archaeological evidence indicates that shellfish gathering preceded the hunting of fish.

The use of fish as a basic food and the techniques used by early hominid species between 1 and 2 million years ago have been reviewed recently (Stewart, 1994). Evidence from bone debris at African sites of habitation dating from 50,000 years ago suggests that fish were an important seasonal food.

It seems likely that fish were first caught by the extension to shallow water of the hunting technique of using spears, or even perhaps by hand. Fishing with baited lines can be traced back to at least 25,000 BC. Early man probably saw that larger fish ate smaller fish and so devised a bait armed with a primitive form of hook made from a thorn and later with a more solid toggle, known as a 'gorge', which became jammed in the throat of the prey. Many gorges have been found in different parts of the world, differing somewhat in shape and size but evidently performing the same function. They consisted of a narrow bit of horn, bone or stone sharpened at both ends and with a recessed waist to which the line could be attached (Daniel and Minot, 1954, p. 13). No doubt experience showed that curved gorges were more likely to get stuck and so the concept of a hook gradually evolved.

By 12,000 BC, harpoons plus bows and arrows had been added to the fishing technology, enabling the larger and faster fish to be caught. Paleolithic carvings depict remarkably accurate portrayals of fish.

The forerunners of nets were twisted barriers of branches and twigs set across a stream to trap fish in much the same way as is done today in the Dinka fishing festival in Africa, where barriers of reeds dam the river and fish are caught by hand or spear. Nets of knotted fibres, hair and thongs have been found in Neolithic lake dwellings and came into common use as dugouts, canoes and boats were developed, together with the invention of oars in about 8000 BC (Tannahill, 1988, pp. 9–10).

Thus all of the standard techniques used for fishing throughout the last ten millennia were already in use in Neolithic times and fishing was probably, even at that time, a collective activity to provide food for the clans. Thus the fishing industry was born.

The early Cretans in 2500 BC rated fish as a very high-quality food, 'fit for gods and kings', and there is some evidence, according to the interpretation of Sir Arthur Evans, that they were even catching tunny fish from the deep sea. Although the early Greeks appeared to have little interest in fish, Homer described in some detail how fish were caught with bent hooks, with net and spear, and even with a rod and handline (Daniel and Minot, 1954, p. 14). Throughout the classical period, fishing was a common practice that progressively improved as ships and trade developed and new fishing grounds were found.

However, the exploitation of the living resources of the sea in the ancient world was not limited to fish. Seaweeds were harvested for food and for medicinal purposes in ancient China. Shen Nung, who is said to have lived in 3000 BC and is considered to be the father of husbandry and medicine in the Orient, valued the medicinal properties of seaweed, and a poem in the *Chinese Book of Poetry* of about 800 to 600 BC describes a housewife cooking it (Humm, 1951, p. 47).

Today seaweeds are harvested in a large industry, principally to provide agar, which is a gel-forming agent used extensively in the food, drug, clinical and health industries. The first commercial agar production was started in Japan in 1670 and remained a Japanese monopoly for nearly two centuries (Firth, 1969, p. 10). Significant agar production elsewhere – in the USA, USSR, Australia, New Zealand and South Africa – did not start until the Japanese supplies were cut off in the Second World War.

In many countries, seaweed is collected, as in the past, to spread as a fertilizer on the fields, since it contains many valuable minerals. At one time it was the source of iodine and other elements, which were extracted from the ashes after it had been burned.

Sponges are marine animals that have long been valued for their resilience and their absorptive properties once they have been treated and dried. They have been gathered from the shallow waters in the Mediterranean at least since the time of Homer, who referred to them in his writings, and they are frequently mentioned elsewhere in Greek literature. Before the Christian era there was a thriving and lucrative trade in sponges, which were obtained by free diving to almost 100 feet in the clear and relatively warm water of the Mediterranean (Moore and Galtsoff, 1951, p. 733). The Greek islands bred a race of skilled and daring divers that gradually dominated the sponge industry throughout the Mediterranean and beyond. Aristotle described several groups of sponges, which were used not only for washing but also for padding the helmets of Greek warriors (*Encyclopaedia Britannica*, 1911). Roman soldiers carried sponges to lift water from streams for drinking, so it is not surprising that a sponge was used by a Roman guard to offer the drink of vinegar to Christ on the cross.

The principal sponge trade originated in the Mediterranean and stayed there until 1841, when a French sponge merchant, shipwrecked in the Bahamas, noted the fine quality of West Indian sponges and in time established a flourishing industry there. Free diving for sponges, with all of its risks, was replaced by hard-hat divers with air lines to the surface, and later by aqualung divers, and by hooking with rope loops from surface boats. Commercial cultivation flourished for a while but was overtaken by the rise of alternative synthetic products. In 1969 a quarter of the sponge production in the United States was used by amateur cleaners and housewives, a quarter by pottery, tile, shoe and miscellaneous manufacturers and half by professional painters, decorators and wall washers (Bergquist and Tizard, 1969, p. 670). Today the sponge industry is in serious decline as synthetic substitutes are cheaper and more easily produced.

Marine products were gathered in classical times not only for utilitarian purposes but also for decoration and personal adornment. It is fascinating to speculate who first appreciated the beauty of an abnormal concretion in an oyster, opened presumably for its food, and hung it around his neck. The earliest pearl fisheries were probably those in the Persian Gulf and the Red Sea in the time of the Ptolemies, some two thousand years ago. Indian Vedic literature indicates that pearls were known before 1500 BC, and in Sri Lanka there are records of pearling as early as 550 BC described by Pliny. The pearl divers of the Persian Gulf developed incredible skills of holding their breath for many minutes, swimming at 60 feet down and filling baskets lowered on ropes.

Pearls, and the shell of the oyster, which gives mother of pearl, have their principal charm in their appearance, which has been surprisingly highly valued over several millennia. In classical Rome, pearls were so highly esteemed that only people of specified rank could wear them. One famous pearl, 'La Peregrina' (the Wanderer), was found by a slave in the West Indies, in the sixteenth century, who sold it to buy his freedom. The 1 inch long pearl passed through the hands of various European rulers, including Mary Tudor, before it was bought for Elizabeth Taylor by Richard Burton in 1969 for $37,000. Another famous pearl from the French crown jewels, 'La Régente', which is egg-shaped and weighs 15 grams, was sold in 1988 for £460,000!

Legend has it that in the thirteenth century the Chinese discovered that a small object, such as an image of a Buddha, placed within a living freshwater mussel acquired a coating of nacre, a pearl-like substance (Alexander, 1951, p. 114). The idea of doing this with oysters to produce pearls was not exploited until the end of the nineteenth century, when Kokichi Michimoto produced artificially induced pearls and founded the Japanese cultured pearl industry, which dominates the world market today.

The use of precious corals for decoration and adornment also dates back to classical times, being described by the Greek philosopher and naturalist, Theophrastus, in the third century BC. In Roman times the finest coral was found in the Mediterranean, and Romans believed that it had beneficial medicinal effects, cooling the blood and reducing inflammation (Tresslor and Lemon, 1951, p. 141). It was highly prized by the ancient Gauls and used extensively for jewellery as it is today.

Let me now return to the development of the fishing industry. With the fall of the Roman Empire, the industry declined, and little is known about it through the Dark Ages. Fish eating was clearly encouraged by the early Christian church, so the harvesting of fish must have continued, but little is known about the development of fishing techniques. As ships became larger and the skills of seafarers increased, so fishing moved further from the coast into more distant waters. The great explorers of the fifteenth and sixteenth century discovered new lands and resources. In 1497 John Cabot landed at Cape Breton in Nova Scotia and explored some of the coast and the offshore islands of the Newfoundland shelf. He discovered huge schools of cod, which his crew caught merely by lowering baskets into the water. When word of these productive waters reached Europe, fisherman set off to exploit them, feeding not only Europe but also the infant colonies of the New World.

The hunting of whales for food is known to have been practised by the Vikings as early as the fifth century AD (Heizer, 1941), so when Ohthere voyaged to the White Sea in the tenth century, as recorded by King Alfred (*Encyclopaedia Britannica*, 1911), the Norwegians were already expert whale fishermen. From the tenth to the sixteenth centuries the Basques carried on a lucrative trade in whaling, going as far afield as Labrador, supplying Europe with whalebone and oil. When Barents discovered Spitzbergen in 1596, he also found the Greenland Right Whale, which was a species of much greater value than any previously hunted. This gave rise to a new phase in the whaling industry, which was exploited by the British and the Dutch, by this time the leading whaling countries. During the seventeenth and eighteenth centuries, these whalers roamed the northern Atlantic from Spain to Spitzbergen, and from Greenland to Hudson Bay.

In the early days, whales were caught for their meat, and for the oil, which could be obtained by reducing the blubber. Today, whale meat is eaten mainly in Japan and other far east countries, although, during the Second World War, those in the UK were almost persuaded by the Minister of Food to eat whale meat. The oil was used for burning in lamps, for the manufacture of candles, for the processing of sugar, for the treatment of leather and for lubrication. Whale blubber was in fact the principal source of a variety of oils before they were derived commercially from naturally occurring hydrocarbons early this century (Gilmore, 1951). Baleen, otherwise known as whalebone, which came from the horny filters in the mouth of the Baleen whale, was a valuable product used for dress stays, umbrellas, stiffeners for clothing, brush making and other purposes where advantage could be taken of its strength and flexibility. Of particular value was ambergris, a hardened accretion in the whale's stomach, which was used as a fixative for perfumes as well as having an attractive musty odour of its own. The Moslem people used to prize it as an aphrodisiac.

North American whaling started in the eighteenth century on the east coast, centred on Nantucket and New Bedford, and rapidly grew into a global whaling fleet in the middle of the nineteenth century. In 1846, 746 vessels out of a global total of about 1,000 were registered in American ports, mostly in New England (Gilmore, 1951). At this time, whales were harpooned by hand from small boats lowered from the whaleship. The magnificent seamanship, plus the dangers and the thrills of the chase, have been vividly described in Herman Melville's classic novel *Moby Dick*, and in the factual account by a crew member in *The Cruise of the Cachelot* (Bullen, 1898).

However, in 1866, the Norwegian Svend Foyn invented the explosive harpoon gun and at about the same time steam ships started to replace the sail. The combination of these two developments, of the increased effectiveness and range of the harpoon and of the increased speed and mobility of ships, enormously improved the efficiency with which whales could be caught, with the result that whale stocks started to dwindle. Whaling moved into the productive waters of the Antarctic at the turn of the century, using shore-based whaling stations for flensing and processing. Then, in about 1925, large whaling factory ships began to replace the shore stations and operated fleets of catchers working in teams. It was becoming clear that many of the whale species were being hunted near to extinction.

During the First World War the invention of the process of hydrogenation, which enabled whale oil to be converted into edible forms, and which then opened the way for it to be used in margarines and cooking fats, gave the whaling industry increased importance. In the UK, the Government, advised by an influential scientific and economic committee, decided to start a programme for the systematic investigation of the economic resources of the Dependencies of the Falkland Islands, with special reference to the whaling industry. It was soon realized that little was known about the life cycle of whales, their breeding habits, their eating and their migration. A scientific team was assembled using Scott's ship *Discovery* for their first investigations in the Southern Ocean and, later, RRS *Discovery II* was built specifically for this research (Coleman-Cooke, 1963).

It was soon apparent that in order to know about the ecology of whales, one had to know about their principal food supply of krill and squid, about the nutrients in the seawater and about the movement of the waters in the oceans around the Antarctic. From these beginnings was born the National Institute of Oceanography, later called the Institute of Oceanographic Sciences, where I spent my research career and which has now to become part of the Southampton Oceanography Centre.

Everyone is now aware of the dangers of overexploiting the whale populations. International discussions on how to control overfishing resulted in 1931 in the International Whaling Convention, which, in 1946, gave rise to the International Whaling Commission (Firth, 1969, p. 724). Commercial whaling has now virtually stopped, and thankfully whale stocks are beginning to recover.

Returning now to the fishing industry proper (for the whaling fishery is not really a fishery at all as whales are mammals), even in AD 1400 some legislation was attempted to prevent overfishing (Daniel and Minot, 1954, p. 23). However, it was not until the middle of the nineteenth century that there was serious concern over the depletion of some fisheries. Statistics began to be compiled and research started into the natural history of fish stocks (Deacon, 1990, p. 15).

During the last 150 years, four major technological developments have changed the face of the fisheries industry (Firth, 1969, pp. 225–60). First was the replacement of sail by steam, giving increased speed and manoeuvrability, and deck power to handle long lines and nets. Second, in the interwar years the use of echosounders gave a means of locating shoals of fish and thereby enormously improving the rate of catching. The more sophisticated sonar methods that have become available as a result of the needs of the Navy to detect submarines during the Second World War have readily been turned to commercial advantage by the fishing industry so that now not only can shoals be located but the species identified and quantities assessed. The fish hardly have a chance! Third, the quality of the nets and other gear has improved with the introduction of buoyant and long-lasting synthetic fibre, enabling huge nets to be made and deployed as seen in the 100 kilometre long drift nets now strung out in the Pacific Ocean. Fourth, the preservation of fish at sea, once caught, has improved from the salting that was necessary prior to the use of refrigeration, which was first used successfully in the late 1920s, and the storage and processing in attendant factory ships, which enable fishing fleets to roam the seas for many months without requiring port support.

The consequence of these factors has been that fewer ships and fewer men can catch greater and greater numbers of fish. Faced with declining fish stocks and the threat to large national industries, governments have increasingly subsidized the fishing industry and maintained artificially high prices. The extent of the catastrophe in world fishing is only now becoming apparent, although scientists gave clear warnings of this many years ago (Hardy, 1959, Ch. 13). A report by the Worldwatch Institute in July 1994 estimated that the industry would be decimated unless governments acted to curb overfishing (Weber, 1994). In this century the annual global catch has increased from 3 to 82 million tons, but now fish stocks in almost all of the major fishing grounds are seriously depleted and catches have fallen from the peak years of the 1960s and '70s by as much as 70 to 90 per cent. The report estimates that the current fishing capacity exceeds the sustainable marine catch by 100 per cent. The world marine fish catch in 1989 sold for $70 billion but cost $124 billion to catch. The difference of $54 billion was provided by government subsidies. How can this make sense?

The impact of reduced stocks is being felt in traditional fishing communities all over the world. In the maritime provinces of Canada, two-thirds of the fishing boats are being laid up. In Europe, conflicts based on fishing rights and quotas flare up as fishermen feel that their livelihood is threatened. Although farming of fish by aquaculture has grown considerably over the last few decades, it is unlikely that this can replace the lost fish stocks of the open seas.

In summary, then, the impact of improvements in technology and on the exploitation of living marine resources is amply demonstrated in the fishing and whaling industries, in both their growth and their decline. At the United Nations Conference on the Environment and Development in Rio in 1992, the major question was how to continue the development of the world's economies, especially those of the developing world, and at the same time ensure that global resources are not depleted at a rate that is not sustainable. Much remains to be done: there are no longer 'plenty more fish in the sea'.

NON-LIVING RESOURCES

So far I have discussed only the living resources from the sea, but from time immemorial humankind has also made use of the non-living resources. Sand and gravel, minerals from the outwash of rivers, salt, fresh water, chemicals and hydrocarbons are all resources that today are being actively extracted from the marine environment. Quantitatively, aggregates such as sand and gravel, shells and coral debris comprise one of the most important mineral resources being worked at this time – second only to oil and gas.

Aggregates are most obviously accessible on the beaches and on the foreshore. Doubtless in ancient times they were used to fortify paths and roads, to provide foundations for buildings and to make concrete when combined with lime or cement. Many splendid examples still exist of Roman concrete that was made with lime. It is not known, however, whether the aggregates were of land or marine origin. Marine gravel may have been useful for ballast in ships since it is often plentiful near ports.

Certainly in the UK the marine aggregate industry has its roots in the dredging of ballast for sailing ships in the sixteenth century (Ardus and Harrison, 1990. p. 113). By the eighteenth century the sale of aggregates for this purpose from the dredging necessary to deepen harbours and channels provided the main source of income for

Trinity House. In the last fifty years, the demand for aggregates by the construction industry the world over has exceeded the resources from land and has led to the exploitation of offshore sand and gravel banks, sometimes with unexpected consequences on the nearby beaches.

The ancient world recognized the value of salt from the sea and there is evidence that the deliberate production of salt (salt winning) was practised in Neolithic times. Doubtless, before that, salt was dug from naturally occurring deposits to flavour and preserve food (Tannahill, 1988, p. 179). Even before the glaciers had retreated from Europe, man had noticed that reindeer, feeding on mosses and ferns, migrated to naturally occurring salt licks or to the sea to compensate for salt deficiency in their diet. So salt was used as bait to lure the deer to the caves, where they could be killed (Tannahill, 1988, p. 17). Experience also showed that when meat was boiled in water to make it less tough, it lost its flavour (as a result of the loss of salts), and this deficiency was instinctively overcome by adding salt to the cooked food.

The first records of planned salt production by solar evaporation are in Chinese writings of 2200 BC (Charlier and Charlier, 1990, p. 2; Tresslor and Lemon, 1951, p. 12). Salt played a very important role in making food palatable, especially in hot climates where the loss of salt by sweating requires a high salt intake as well as being a valuable preservative. So important was salt that the control of supplies became an instrument of policy and a powerful political weapon. In the first millenium BC it was a significant feature of the administration in China and of the Ptolemies in Egypt. Salt became a vital factor in trade, and it influenced vocabulary and place-names: the word 'salary' is derived from the Roman for 'salt rations'. Cassiodorus, the fifth-century Goth administrator, put it succinctly: 'It may be that some seek not gold, but there lives not a man that does not need salt.' (Tannahill, 1988, p. 179). Even in twentieth-century India, all salt production was controlled by the British Raj, leading to the famous march in 1930 by Mahatma Gandhi to the seaside at Dandi to 'make salt' illegally as a political protest against the British.

As well as salt mines, the production of salt from the solar evaporation of seawater remains today an important industry supplying the needs of an ever-increasing world population, and with no risk of exhausting the natural resource.

The oceans contain a variety of other dissolved chemicals, several of which are extracted commercially. Bromine was discovered by the Frenchman A.J. Balard in 1825 by oxidizing seawater bittern (the mother liquor after the precipitation of salt) with chlorine, and his process is used commercially to provide an important component in anti-knock petrol (Tresslor and Lemon, 1951, p. 37; Moyer, 1969, p. 86). Magnesium, iodine and potassium are all extracted commercially from seawater.

By far the most plentiful component of seawater, and perhaps the least accessible on a commercial scale, is fresh water. Although Aristotle recognized that 'salt water, when it turns into vapour, becomes sweet; and the vapour does not form salt water again when it condenses', there is no record of creating fresh water by evaporation and condensation until the last few hundred years when simple evaporators were used to provide fresh water for sailors at sea (Othmer, 1969a, p. 162).

Modern desalination plants use solar power, fossil fuel or nuclear energy for evaporation, but at some cost in energy usage, so that desalination is most economic when it can be combined with electricity generation using the waste heat for evaporation. Nature performs a purification of water on a massive scale when it is frozen in the polar seas and elsewhere. Advantage of this was taken at the end of the nineteenth century when icebergs, which had been captured in the Southern Ocean, were towed from the Antarctic to Valparaiso in Chile to provide fresh water. There have been several proposals in this century to tow Antarctic icebergs up to Saudi Arabia, but none has been technologically and economically feasible (Charlier and Charlier, 1990, p. 11).

MINERALS FROM THE SEA BED AND BELOW

The shoreline and the continental shelves that extend seaward to depths of a few hundred metres are really extensions, in geological terms, of the land, and as such have many of the mineral deposits of the land. Rivers erode the land rocks and bring down with them sands and gravels containing minerals that accumulate as deposits along the shore or in depressions on the continental shelves. These are called placer deposits and include ores containing tin, gold, platinum, zircon, titanium and diamonds. All of these and many other placers are mined commercially today in a variety of ways (Cronan, 1992).

The identification and exploitation of placer minerals did not take place until the eighteenth and nineteenth centuries with the rise in the knowledge of chemistry and the demands of the Industrial Revolution, although the casual beachcomber may have noticed the concentration of different-coloured sands and gravel sorted by wave action because of their density differences.

Further offshore, other minerals grow *in situ* from the chemicals in seawater. The famous *Challenger* expedition of 1872 to 1876 discovered that there were accumulations of phosphorite ores in places on the shelves and on the continental slopes. These are currently being mined for fertilizer in some parts of the world, but land sources are generally more economic.

Useful minerals from the deep ocean were not discovered until the scientific expeditions of the nineteenth and twentieth centuries, and the development of the considerable technology needed to locate and sample them. Of particular interest has been the discovery of manganese nodules lying on the sediments of the deep ocean floor at depths of many thousands of metres. Although they were first dredged by the *Challenger* and *Albatross* expeditions at the end of the last century, it was not until the 1960s that huge fields of these nodules were photographed and sampled in the Pacific Ocean.

The nodules, which are about the size of a potato, are oxides of manganese and iron with significant amounts of copper, nickel and cobalt, and they grow *in situ* from chemicals in the seawater on a nucleus of a rock fragment and sometimes even on a shark's tooth. Photographs show them to occur in dense layers on, but not below, the seabed, looking rather like a cobbled pavement.

Data published in the 1960s on the abundance of manganese nodules (Mero, 1965) and the strategic requirements of the United States for copper, cobalt and nickel, led to extreme interest by industry and by governments to develop the technology to mine and to process them, and many foresaw the possibility of a new and highly profitable industry.

One important question, however, had to be addressed. As the deposits were far out into the deep ocean, to whom did they belong? In 1958 the mineral rights of coastal states to deposits on or below the continental shelf were settled by the UN Convention on the Continental Shelf, thus allowing the growth of the North Sea oil and gas fields. However, the convention was ambiguous about the seaward limits of national jurisdiction over mineral resources beyond the shelves. In 1970 the General Assembly of the UN declared that the resources of the sea bed and the subsoil beyond the limits of national jurisdiction were the 'common heritage of mankind'.

This grandiose declaration had to be translated into a practical and legally binding regime before substantial investment could be made, and this took two decades of international argument and negotiation. A new, and third, UN Conference on the Law of the Sea started in 1972 and did not conclude until 1982, when a convention was agreed and was available for signing and ratification. This convention (The United Nations Law of the Sea Convention – UNLOSC) covered all aspects of international law on maritime affairs, including the definition of zones of national jurisdiction; the rights and duties of states, in both national and international waters; the rights of passage of ships and of research; the protection and preservation of the marine environment; and in particular the control of mining in the international zone known as the 'Area'. It was not until November 1994 that sufficient countries had ratified the convention for it to come into force in international law.

However, by this time the interest in the manganese nodules had waned because of the changed economic and political climate. Some countries, notably Japan, India and China, are pursuing the possibility of exploitation largely for political reasons, but for most there are better sources elsewhere.

Other deposits of manganese and associated elements have since been discovered in crusts that form on the exposed rocks of underwater volcanoes. These are particularly rich in cobalt, a strategic element in the manufacture of high-grade steel. Many of these seamounts are found within the Exclusive Economic Zones of coastal states and so do not fall under the mining provisions of the UNLOSC.

During the last decade, much scientific attention has been given to a new potential mineral source in the deep ocean. Seawater penetrating deep into the cracks of the seafloor at the mid-ocean ridges, where new oceanic crust is continually being created by the addition of volcanic rocks from below, strips out minerals from the hot rocks before being forced by convective currents back to the seafloor. There it emerges as jets of hot water laden with metal sulphides, which precipitate out as clouds of black particles. Around these hydrothermal vents, or black smokers as they are called, metalliferous sulphides accumulate in mounds and hills. The deposits are rich in zinc, copper, iron, silver, cobalt, gold and other metals, and have been seriously considered as a mineral resource in spite of the difficulties evident in mining them.

The formation of these deposits has some similarity to that of the copper deposits in the Troodos Mountains of Cyprus, from which the name copper is derived. Cuprius was the Latin name for Cyprus, and Cu remains today the chemical abbreviation for the metal. These mountains are a slice of oceanic crust that has been pushed up above sea level by the northward movement of the African continent, so there is some expectation that the oceanic deposits will provide a similarly significant resource. In 1992 the international scientific Ocean Drilling Project drilled through 65 metres of a metalliferous sulphide ore west of Canada and estimated that the total body contained 100 million tons of ore. Exploitation, however, will require an expensive new technology.

The central valley of the Red Sea, formed by newly created seafloor separating Africa from Asia, contains metalliferous muds rich in copper, zinc, silver, gold and cobalt, which have been generated from the interaction of the seawater with the hot volcanic rocks and have not been able to escape because of the highly saline water suppressing convection. Ownership here is shared by the coastal states of the Sudan and Saudi Arabia, which have formed the Red Sea Consortium to consider their exploitation and the environmental consequences of mining operations.

I have so far not mentioned one of the most important resources from the sea, that of oil and gas from below the continental shelves. Although the hydrocarbon fields are now buried in the geological structures of the continental land mass, many were laid down as accumulations of organic matter in a marine environment and were subsequently buried by sediments. The first oil and gas fields exploited below the sea in the Gulf of Mexico and off the Californian coast in the post-war years were extensions of fields below the land, but new offshore fields are regularly being discovered in basins on the continental shelf far from the coastline.

Exploitation on the continental shelves, where there was not a clear legal claim to ownership, had to wait for the second UN Law of the Sea Convention on the Continental Shelf in 1958. It is now estimated that 40 per cent of the world's undiscovered oil lies offshore (Masters, 1985; Cook et al., 1991). Exploration has continued into progressively deeper water, and the techniques of test drilling and production have had to be developed to cope with the demanding environmental conditions.

In the deep water, some 2,000 metres below the sea surface, at the base of the continental slope beyond the continental shelves currently being exploited, huge quantities of sediment accumulate from the erosion of the mountains on land containing organic as well as inorganic matter. These deposits comprise the continental rise. Under conditions of high pressure and high temperature, the buried organic matter can be converted into hydrocarbons. If there are porous reservoir rocks capped by impervious rocks with suitable structures in which the hydrocarbons can become trapped, then there are potentially valuable resources. In the north of the Arabian Sea and the Bay of Bengal, the Indus and the Ganges rivers have brought huge quantities of the erosion products of the Himalayas to the sea and the sediments are more than 10 kilometres thick. A quarter of the entire sediment flow into the oceans comes from these rivers.

At present there is not the technology to verify the existence of these hydrocarbon resources on the continental rise by drilling, even though many scientific holes have been drilled into the deep ocean, since there is the constant danger of a blow-out of high-pressure gas or oil that could not, with the present technology, be controlled. Whether exploitation will ever be economic will depend on the availability of alternative sources and the price of oil. If it is economic, the engineers are confident that the appropriate technology can be developed. Industry is, however, already moving progressively to deeper water to the west of Scotland, and off Brazil production is already from a depth of 720 metres.

INTANGIBLE RESOURCES

Anyone sailing on the oceans or standing on the beach appreciates the enormous energy that is stored in water movements in the form of waves, currents, tides and, less obviously, as heat. In principle, these can be used as a source of energy that could be harnessed for humankind. The energy is derived, in the case of the tides, from the gravitational attraction of the moon and the sun, and in the case of the waves and currents, from the heat from the sun driving the circulation of the atmosphere, which causes winds. Solar heat warms the upper layers of the ocean, resulting in a temperature contrast with the deeper ocean, and from this temperature gradient, power can be generated.

The ancient Greeks tried to use the tidal currents that flowed through the Euripus Channel, between Euboea and the mainland, to power their mills, as they did also near Agostoli on Cephalonia, and the Romans were known to have harnessed water movement to drive impulse wheels for mechanical power (Charlier, 1982; Charlier and Justus, 1990, p. 500). In 1737, Bernard Forest de Belidor wrote a treatise on the energy potential dissipated by tides, since when there has been a great deal more written about harnessing tidal power resulting in a large number of small installations. The best known one working at present is that which dams the river La Rance in northern France, and generates 240 megawatts of power (Baker, 1986, p. 334). There have been serious proposals and designs for damming the Bristol Channel and the Mersey for tidal power, and even to dam the Bay of Fundy, where there are the world's largest tides and where the power generated could in principle be nearly 5,000 megawatts. However, the environmental impact and the cost would be enormous, and nothing is planned at present.

Wave power is considerable but is extremely difficult to tame. The first patents were taken out in 1799 by two Frenchmen, 'Girard et fils', who planned to convert the wave energy into the mechanical movements of a raft. There have been numerous devices designed since to extract energy from the waves, and some small installations are under trial today. However, they all face the problem of either too little energy in a calm or too much in a storm, giving extreme conditions that can, and have, destroyed installations.

Finally, use can be made of the difference in temperature between the surface waters of the ocean, typically 10 to 15°C, and the water several hundred metres deeper of 2 to 3°C. The system known as Ocean Thermal Energy Conversion (OTEC) uses this temperature gradient to drive an engine based on a low-boiling-point liquid, such as ammonia, just as a steam engine uses water and water vapour (Othmer, 1969b; Vadus, Bregman and Takahashi, 1992). Considerable engineering design work has been done on OTEC, and there is one successful installation off the coast of Hawaii where access to deep water is easily available. It is only economic because the water brought up from the deep is also rich in nutrients and is able to fertilize an algal farm on shore.

CONCLUSIONS

We have seen that, wherever there are products from the sea that are useful to us, they have been exploited. Curiosity about the oceans leads to discovery, which then requires exploration, research and surveying before products can be considered as potential resources. If the technology exists to exploit a resource and it is economically or strategically worthwhile, it will be exploited. If the demand and finance is there, but not the technology, then the technology can usually be developed.

However, new factors are emerging from the growing consciousness of the finite size of our planet and of its resources. We can no longer squander them, especially if they are not renewable or sustainable. The growth and decline of the fishing and whaling industries through the last centuries warns us of the dangers. We do not know how long hydrocarbon resources can last, but we do know that they cannot be renewed at the rate we use them, so policies have to be developed for the long term.

I have said nothing here about the pollution arising from the exploitation of marine resources. In the past there was an unacknowledged assumption that the oceans were large enough to absorb all of the waste products of civilization without being harmed. We now know that this is not the case. The UN Law of the Sea Convention spells out the duties of states to protect and preserve the marine environment. Any ocean exploitation, whether acquaculture or mineral mining, tidal power generation or desalination, must study the environmental impact, and the benefits must be weighed against any harmful effects.

We can only live in harmony with the seas if we treat them with respect, and if our use is sustainable and environmentally friendly. History can teach us the dangers of ignoring these principles and, together with a proper scientific understanding of how the oceans work, guide our policies in the future.

REFERENCES

Alexander, A.E. 'Pearls and the Pearl Industry' in D.K. Tresslor and J.M. Lemon (eds), 1951, pp. 107–23

Archer, A.A. 'Sources of confusion: what are marine mineral resources?' in P.G. Teleki, M.R. Dobson, J.R. Moore and U. von Stackelburg (eds), *Marine Minerals*, Dordrecht, Reidel, 1985, pp. 421–32

Ardus, D.A. and Harrison in D.A. Ardus and M.A. Champ (eds), *Ocean Resources*, Dordrecht, Kluwer Academic, Vol. 1, 1990, p. 113

Baker, A.C. 'The development of functions relating cost and performance of tidal power schemes and their application to small scale sites' in *Tidal Power*, London, Thomas Telford, 1986, p. 334

Bergquist, P.R. and Tizard, C.A. 'Sponge industry' in F.E. Firth (ed.), 1969, pp. 665–70

Bullen, F.T. *The Cruise of the Cachalot*, 1898

Charlier, R.H. *Tidal Energy*, New York, Van Nostrand Reinhold, 1982

Charlier, R.H. and Charlier, C.C. 'Ocean non-living resources: historical perspective on exploitation, economics and environmental impact' in H.N. Scheiber, *Ocean Resources: Industries and Rivalries Since 1800*, Working Papers on Ocean Resources History for the 10th International Economic History Congress, Center for the Study of Law and Society, University of California, Berkeley, 1990, pp. 2, 11

Charlier, R. and Justus, J.R. 'Ocean energy: historical development of its harnessing' in W. Lenz, and M. Deacon (eds), 'Ocean Sciences: their History and Relation to Man', Deutsche Hydrographische Zeitschrift, Reihe B, 22, 1990, pp. 449–503

Coleman-Cooke, J. 'Discovery II in the Antarctic', London, Oldhams Press, 1963

Cook, P.J., Haq, B.U., Heat, G.R., Hyland, J.L., Jennerjahn, T.C., Johnston, C.S., Sjei, J.M., Summerhayes, C.P. and Takahashi, P.K. 'Offshore petroleum hydrocarbon exploitation – reserves, impacts and alternatives' in K.J. Hsu and J. Theide (eds), *Use and Misuse of the Seafloor*, Dahlem Workshop Reports, 11, Wiley, 1991, pp. 337–56

Cronan, D.S. '*Marine Minerals in Exclusive Economic Zones*, London, Chapman and Hall, 1992

Daniel, H. and Minot, F. *The Inexhaustible Sea*, London, Macdonald, 1954

Deacon, M. 'State support for "useful science": the scientific investigations of the Fishery Board for Scotland, 1883–1889' in H.N. Scheiber, *Ocean Resources: Industries and Rivalries since 1800*, Working Papers on Ocean Resources History for the 10th

International Economic History Congress, Center for the Study of Law and Society, University of California, Berkeley, 1990, pp. 15–29

Encyclopaedia Britannica, New York, The Encyclopaedia Britannica Company, 11th edn, 1911

Firth, F.E. (ed.). *The Encyclopaedia of Marine Resources*, New York, Van Nostrand Reinhold, 1969

Gilmore, R.M. 'The whaling industry' in D.K. Tresslor and J.M. Lemon (eds), 1951

Hardy, A.C. *The Open Sea, Part II: Fish and Fisheries*, London, Collins, 1959

Heizer, R.F. 'Aboriginal whaling in the old and new worlds', unpublished PhD dissertation, Anthropology Department, University of California, Berekeley, 1941

Humm, H.J. 'The red algae of economic importance: agar and related phycocolloids' in D.K. Tresslor and J.M. Lemon (eds), 1951, pp. 47–93

Laughton, A.S. 'Exploitation or responsible use of the oceans?', *Underwater Technology* 20 (1), 1994a, pp. 32–40

——. 'Using the ocean wisely: the waste problem', *Marine Policy* 18 (6), 1994b, pp. 453–6

Masters, C.D. 'World petroleum resources – a perspective', U.S. Geological Survey Open-file Report, Reston, Virginia, 1985, pp. 85–248

Mero, J.L. '*The Mineral Resources of the Sea*', Elsevier, 1965

Moore, H.F. and Galtsoff, P.S. 'Commercial sponges' in D.K. Tresslor and J.M. Lemon (eds), 1951, pp. 733–51

Moyer, M.P. 'Bromine from the sea' in F.E. Firth (ed.), 1969, pp. 86–90

Othmer, D.F. 'Desalination of seawater' in F.E. Firth (ed.), 1969a, pp. 162–9

Othmer, D.F. 'Heat and power from seawater' in F.E. Firth (ed.), 1969b, pp. 298–302

Stewart, K. 'Early hominid utilisation of fish resources and implications for seasonality and behaviour', *J. Human Evolution* 27, 1994, pp. 229–45

Tannahill, R. *Food in history*, London, Penguin, 1988

Tilton, J.E. and Skinner, B.J. 'The meaning of resources' in D.J. McLaren and B.J. Skinner (eds), *Resources and World Development*, Wiley, Chichester, 1987, pp. 13–27

Tresslor, D.K. and Lemon, J.M. (eds). *Marine Products of Commerce*, New York, Reinhold Corporation, 1951

Weber, P. 'Net loss: fish, jobs and the marine environment', Worldwatch Papers 120, Worldwatch Institute, USA, 1994

Vadus, J.R., Bregman, R. and Takahashi, P.K. 'The potential of ocean energy conversion systems and their impact on the environment' in K.J. Hsu and J. Theide (eds), *Use and Misuse of the Seafloor*, Dahlem Workshop Reports, 11, Wiley, 1991, pp. 373–402

5

THE SHIP: CARRIER OF GOODS, PEOPLE AND IDEAS

Seán McGrail

In 1993 I visited China on an exchange scheme organized by the British Academy and the Chinese Academy of Science. The aim of the trip was to contact colleagues working in my field of maritime archaeology, or in related subjects such as nautical astronomy, naval architecture and maritime history. After some days in Beijing at the Institute of Astronomy, my wife, Anne, and I went on a memorable forty-seven hour journey by train to Fuzhou on the east coast, west of Taiwan. From there we went further south by car to Quanzhou (Marco Polo's *Zaitun*) to see maritime displays in the Museum of Overseas Communications History. This, to our ears, strange and overlong name was, in fact, most appropriate, for this was not simply a museum for ships and boats, but something far more wide-ranging: a museum dealing with the interchange of goods, people and ideas between China and the countries of the Indian Ocean and the Mediterranean. The displays included examples of the goods traded. People were represented by the possessions of seafarers, and by extracts from accounts written by medieval European and Arab explorers, such as Marco Polo and Ibn Batuta. The flow of ideas was represented by tombstones and other inscribed memorial stones set up by adherents to religions such as Zoroastrianism, Parsiism, Buddhism, Christianity and Islam who had been welcomed to China over the centuries.

The medium for that interchange of ideas, people and goods was the ship. There had been intermittent contact between China and the West along the overland Silk Road for many centuries (Blunden and Elvin, 1983, pp. 4–16), but from *c.* AD 1200, it was the Maritime Silk Route that became the most important cultural and trade link between East and West (Li, 1991, pp. 330; Snow, 1992, p. 58).

Other major examples of the transfer by sea of cargo, people and ideas are the peopling of Australia (Irwin, 1992, pp. 18–30) before *c.* 40,000 BC, and the ocean voyages of the late fifteenth/early sixteenth centuries AD, which resulted in the European 'discovery' of all the seas of the world (Parry, 1974; Arnold, 1983). It has been suggested that seamen from maritime cultures other than European could have become ocean navigators on a world scale in this late medieval period, and that it was mere chance that Europeans were the first. Certainly, in many regions of the world, Europeans were not the first to sail the high seas: the mariners of South-East Asia had explored and settled a vast expanse of the South Pacific by the eleventh century AD (Irwin, 1992) and sailed westwards as far as Madagascar before the ninth century AD (Manguin, 1980, 1996); the Chinese had sailed the breadth of the Indian Ocean and entered the Persian Gulf and the Red Sea by the early fifteenth century (Willetts, 1964; Snow, 1992); and the Arabs and their neighbours had done likewise but in the reverse direction, and probably earlier (Hourani, 1963; Tibbetts, 1971, p. 398; Aleem, 1980, pp. 586–8).

In their ship-building, seafaring and ocean-navigation abilities, the Austronesian-speaking Indo-Malaysians, the Chinese, the Arabs and the Polynesians at least equalled the Europeans. The reason for the explosive outburst of European activity in the late fifteenth/early sixteenth centuries AD, which resulted in the transfer of ideas (that is, aspects of European culture, material and metaphysical) to a large part of the world, must therefore be sought elsewhere. It may rest in European abilities in the financial and commercial fields (Fernández-Armesto, 1992, pp. 1–21), but perhaps it also lies in the realm of ideas, in European outward-ranging thought and speculation, the origins of which seem to lie in the early Eastern Mediterranean.

THE TRANSFER OF IDEAS BY SEA

The role of the sea in the transport of ideas in former times may become archaeologically visible as 'monuments', as 'ritual', and as technological innovations. In the absence of guidance from contemporary historical evidence, there are two main problems in the interpretation of such archaeological data:

- To decide whether this transfer was indeed by sea rather than overland: only in the case of islands can we be certain that water transport was used, although in other circumstances the sum of the evidence may point strongly in that direction.
- To decide in which directions ideas were transferred: for example, in the case of China and Europe, east to west or west to east.

It is sometimes possible to resolve this second problem by the accurate dating of relevant artefacts, documents and illustrations. However, dating in a general way, by attribution to the period of certain ruling dynasties, as has been done in some studies of China's past, can lead to difficulties as, for example, when attempting to decide priorities for the first use of the mariner's compass. Scientific dating, as is now used increasingly, and rigorous evaluation of documentary sources are necessary before the direction of the flow of ideas can be identified.

Boats and Boat Types

The question then arises whether the very idea of the boat could have been transferred by sea. After all, the boat is its own advertisement – like the wagon and other forms of transport. Was there, in other words, a unique time when – and a unique place where – the idea of a floating craft deriving its buoyancy from the displacement of water was first formulated, and from there spread outwards?

The total evidence for early water transport is minuscule: a handful of logboats from the eighth millennium BC onwards, and a scattering of plank boats from the third to the first millennium BC. Moreover, the overwhelming majority of these are from Egypt, the eastern Mediterranean or Europe, and it is therefore impossible to take a worldwide view of this matter – indeed, we may never know whether there was one origin of the boat or whether there was widespread independent invention. It may, however, be of value to consider not the general idea of the boat, rather specific types of boat, to see whether anything can be deduced about their origins. Boats can be built from different raw materials: bark, hide, waterproofed reed bundles, and logs, as well as the better-known plank boats (Hornell, 1970). Were there single centres of innovation for each one of these types from which the idea of the bark boat, the log boat, the plank boat and so on spread outwards?

Evidence from the Americas seems to contradict this hypothesis. It is generally agreed that the Americas were first populated in northern latitudes, from Siberia in north-east Asia eastwards to Alaska in north-west America. However, there is disagreement about the time of this migration: some scholars argue for *c.* 40,000 BC, while others prefer *c.* 20,000 or even 13,000 BC (Bray, *et al.*, 1989, pp. 1–5; van Andel, 1989).

Because of changes in sea levels, the date determines whether this journey, or rather series of journeys, could have been overland, or whether there was at least some sea to be crossed. Whatever the date, and whether such a journey was principally by land or by sea, some form of water transport was probably used, if only for crossing the northward flowing rivers when they were ice-free. In these cold northern latitudes, floats and rafts could not be used because the crew would be in direct contact with very cold water and would rapidly succumb to hypothermia. Furthermore, floats and rafts would have given no protection from the freezing wind (McGrail, 1991, pp. 91–2). For both of these reasons, boats that could give some shelter from wind and wave would have been necessary.

When the ancestors of the earliest migrants to America moved north-eastwards in Euro-Asia towards Siberia, into environments without suitable trees, they would not have been able to build bark boats, log boats or plank boats. They would, however, have been able to construct hide (skin) boats, possibly similar to the *umiak* or *baidara* (fig. 1) used in recent centuries by Asian and American Inuits (McGrail, 1987, pp. 173–87). Raw materials readily available in an Arctic environment can be used for hide boats and, technologically, they could have been built in Paleolithic times. I therefore think that, on present evidence, the hide boat was probably the type of water transport used by those early people who moved from Siberia to Alaska to become the first Americans.

There were later intruders into the American continent: proto-Inuit people in the north-west in *c.* 2000 BC (Bray *et al*, 1989, p. 75); Scandinavians in the Viking Age on the north-east coast (Clausen, 1993); possibly Polynesians on the south-west coasts at around the same time or later (Irwin, 1992, pp. 99–100); and there may have been others. Apart from the Inuit who settled in the Arctic north, these later visitors were only temporary and had no archaeologically detectable influence on the indigenous American cultures. Nevertheless, Europeans of the fifteenth and sixteenth centuries AD found, somewhere in the Americas, almost the entire range of water transport known to mankind (McGrail, in press).

The indigenous Americans used a range of floats, rafts and boats according to their environmental suitability. There were hide boats (fig. 1) in the high latitudes both north and south; bark boats (fig. 2) in the temperate latitudes, north and south; log rafts (fig. 3) in the tropics; and so on. The idea of such craft had presumably been visualized as the migrants moved generally southwards from Alaska, over millennia, into new ecological zones, to reach Tierra del Fuego in the far south by *c.* 10,000 BC. Indeed, in the case of the float raft, a variant form (fig. 4) was used on the coasts of Chile (Edwards, 1965, pp. 17–20; McGrail, 1987, pp. 187–91) that has no specific parallel anywhere in the world.

Fig. 1. Inuit *umiak* and *kayak* off Greenland in the twentieth century. (After Johnstone, 1988, fig. 9.9)

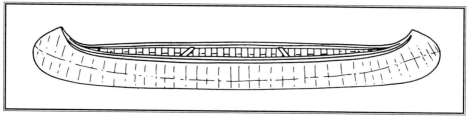

Fig. 2. A bark boat of the North American Ojibwa. (Institute of Archaeology, Oxford)

The plank boat was used in only two small regions: in the Santa Barbara Channel off the Californian coast and in the Cheos archipelago off the coast of Chile (Edwards, 1965, pp. 25–30; McGrail, 1981, pp. 80–1). These were stitched or sewn plank boats that, in the general order of things, both technologically and chronologically, precede boats with wooden fastenings and those with iron fastenings. This very limited use of the plank boat and its elementary form may seem strange to European eyes. In contrast, however, these indigenous Americans had perfected to the highest degree the hide boat, the bark boat and the seagoing sailing log raft.

This development of a range of raft and boat types within the Americas seems to be a clear case of independent invention, reflecting man's innate ingenuity. As circumstances (especially the environment) changed, as the early Americans moved southwards, so 'new' types of raft and boat were visualized and built. We should be aware, therefore, that similar inventions could have happened elsewhere, and not seek a unique time and place for the origin of the different types of raft and boat. The plank boat, for example, may have been conceived in different places at different times and from different bases: perhaps from bundle rafts in Egypt and in Mesopotamia; from the log raft in east Asia; the logboat in north-west Europe and south-east Asia; possibly

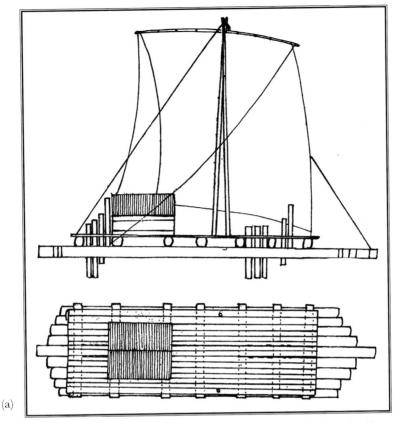

(a)

Fig. 3. (a) Nineteenth-century log raft with a square sail off Guayaquil, Ecuador (drawn by Admiral Paris); (b) Seventeenth-century log raft with fore-and-aft sails off Paita, Peru. (After Johnstone, 1988, figs 16.5, 16.7)

(b)

Fig. 4. Nineteenth-century sealskin float-raft drawn by Admiral Paris in Valparaiso, Chile. (After Johnstone, 1988, fig. 4.10)

the hide boat in northern Europe; and perhaps via the bark boat in the Americas. The idea of building the various types of water transport from logs, bark, reeds and hides, as well as planks, seems to have arisen wherever the environment and whenever the prevailing technology allowed. The worldwide distribution of floats, rafts and boats (Hornell, 1970; McGrail, 1985) testifies to common human characteristics.

The Transfer of Nautical Traits

A more restricted hypothesis and one that is intuitively more attractive, is that specific techniques used in, say, plank boat building had their origins in a unique time and place. There are numerous aspects of ships and seafaring that could be examined to see if there is evidence for invention and then dispersion, but here I shall limit myself to just four: hull shape; plank fastenings; and sail types – all of them important characteristics of ship-building traditions – and finally, navigation techniques.

Hull Shape

Here I am not thinking of shapes themselves, because optimum underwater hull shape is clearly related to the function of the vessel (for example oared warship; sailing cargo vessel; ferry boat) and to the environment it is to be used in (for example upper reaches of a river; tidal estuary; oceans). Evidence from around the world suggests that, where you have similar functional requirements and operating environments, you get similar shapes of hull, at least in the underwater parts (see, for example, Lewis, 1994, p. 313). This seems to me to be due not to diffusion from one central source, but to boatbuilders and boat users in different cultures seeking improvements through modification and experiment, and thereby converging towards similar solutions. On the other hand, how the shape of a boat was conceived and how, in the days before scale drawings and small-scale models, boatbuilders visualized the shape of the boat they were about to build, may be culturally related, as solutions to these problems seem to vary in time and place.

If we reduce the evidence, both archaeological and ethnographic, to the basic elements, it is apparent that there are two main methods:

- The builder visualized the shape he wanted to build in terms of the outer shell of the boat and, after he had created the shell, he inserted the framing (fig. 5).
- The builder visualized the vessel in terms of the inner framework and, when he had built that skeleton shape, he added the shell to it (fig. 6).

This distinction is probably clearest in the case of plank boats, but is not by any means restricted to them: it can also be seen in bark boats and in hide boats (McGrail, 1985). For example, builders of the simplest form of hide boat visualized their boat as a sort of leather bag: the hull shape was determined by the outside shell of the boat, that is by the shape of the single hide used. Subsequently, a framework of light timbers could be inserted to sustain that shape, although frameless hide boats are known (McGrail, 1987, pp. 178–9). Conversely, on the west coast of Ireland, builders of sea-going curachs, which are complex hide boats, visualize their hull shapes in terms of the internal framework of timbers, which they subsequently cover with hides (McGrail, 1987, fig. 10.1).

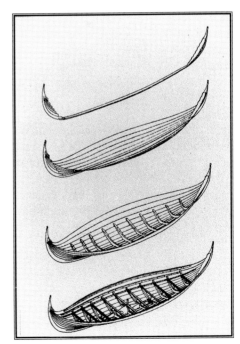

Fig. 5. The shell-first sequence of boat building.
(O. Crumlin-Pedersen)

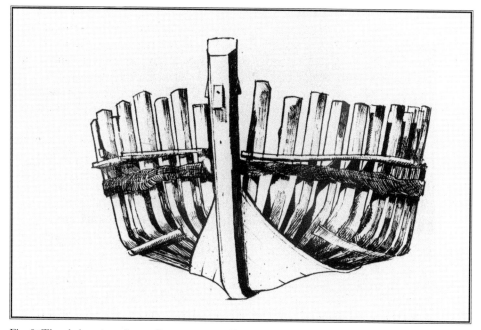

Fig. 6. The skeleton- or frame-first sequence of building. (National Maritime Museum, Greenwich)

It is the plank boat and ship on which I now want to concentrate. In earlier times, as in surviving, small-scale, pre-industrialized societies today, plank boats and ships were generally built (like the simple leather boat) by the shell-first method: that is, individual planks were fashioned and then fastened together to form the hull shape required. These hulls were plank-based, and frames were inserted only after the planking was fastened.

The evidence currently available strongly suggests that the earliest plank boats, worldwide, were built shell-first. The oldest plank boat known in the world to date is the royal burial ship of Cheops, who was Pharaoh in *c.* 2650 BC. Her hull shape was visualized by her builder in terms of the shell of planking, which was stitched together with ropes of halfa grass (Lipke, 1984).

The Ferriby boats of *c.* 1300 BC are among the oldest known plank boats in northern Europe, possibly *the* oldest. The remains of these three vessels were excavated from the tidal foreshore of the River Humber in 1946 (fig. 7) and in 1963, and they are now in the National Maritime Museum at Greenwich (Wright, 1990). These boats were also shell-built from stitched planks.

The oldest wreck so far excavated from the Mediterranean is from the same period as the Ferriby boats, that is the mid-second millennium BC. Although much of the cargo from this wreck at Kaş, off the south coast of Turkey, has been recovered and documented, insufficient of the ship's timbers have so far been excavated for the building methods to be documented in detail. Nevertheless, it is known that its planks were joined together with mortice and tenon (draw, or loose, tongue) fastenings (fig. 8). For this reason it is clear that the shape of the Kaş ship came from the planking – she was built by the shell-first method (Bass, 1985).

Fig. 7. Ferriby boat 1 during excavation from the River Humber foreshore. (E.V. Wright)

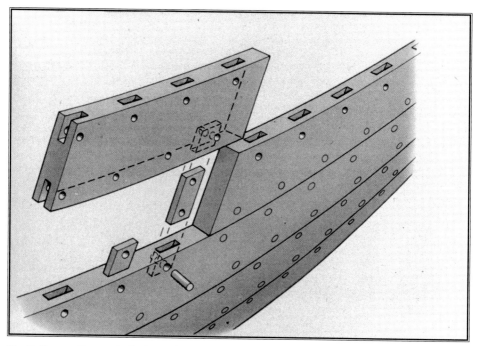

Fig. 8. Graeco-Roman locked mortice and tenon plank fastening. (John Coates)

Viking ships were also built by this method, the planking being built up by eye to the required shape before framing was inserted (McGrail, 1974; 1993, pp. 84–6): a skill that has now been lost in most of Europe. The earliest Arab, Indian, Indonesian and Chinese plank boats all seem to have been built in this manner (McGrail, in press). The plank-based, shell-first approach appears to have been used worldwide in early times, but whether there was a unique origin for this shell-first technique is impossible to say, at this stage.

The earliest evidence for the alternative technique, the frame-based approach, that is building plank boats and ships by the skeleton-first method, comes from late Roman north-west Europe. Remains of thirty or so ships and boats, with distinctive constructional features, have been excavated: some from the Swiss lakes; some from the Rhine and its tributaries; and others from Guernsey, London and south-east Wales (Marsden, 1994, table 16, fig. 146; McGrail, 1995b). These vessels date from the first to the fourth centuries AD and, as these sites are in regions occupied at that time by Celtic-speaking peoples, they have come to be known as Romano-Celtic craft. Most of these finds are flat-bottomed river and canal boats, but there are three sea-going or estuary vessels of a different form, the hull shape of which is derived from their framing: they are skeleton-first or frame-based vessels (fig. 9). The Celtic builders of these sea-going planked vessels are the first known who visualized their boats and ships in terms of the framing or skeleton, rather than in terms of the planking shell (McGrail, 1995b). Nevertheless, by that time, frame-based techniques had probably been used for centuries by the north-west European builders of sea-going hide boats, for which there is documentary but not yet excavated evidence (McGrail, 1990, pp. 36–9).

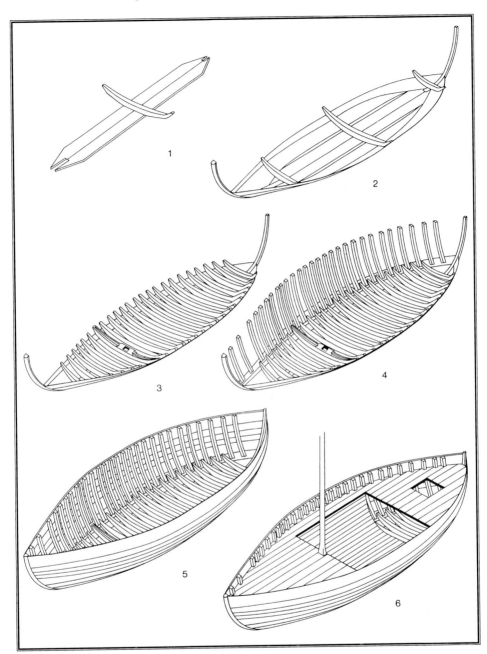

Fig. 9. The sequence of building Blackfriars ship 1. (Peter Marsden)

After the fourth century AD, this apparently innovative method of building planked boats and ships seems to disappear from the archaeological record of northern Europe until late medieval times. However, a late sixth-/early seventh-century Mediterranean wreck (*St Gervais 2*) from Fos sur Mer in the mouth of the River Rhone, off the south coast of France, had a hull that was almost entirely skeleton-first, that is frame-based (Jezegov, 1985; Parker, 1992, pp. 372–3). A near-contemporary vessel, the seventh-century AD wreck, *Yassı Ada 2*, from the south coast of Turkey, had a shell-built lower hull but was skeleton-first from the turn of the bilge upwards (Steffy, 1994, pp. 80–3). Furthermore, an eleventh-century wreck from Serçe Limanı in the eastern Mediterranean was frame-based throughout (Steffy, 1994, pp. 85–91).

Although the archaeological evidence is very limited, and the documentary evidence little better, it seems likely that this sixth- to eleventh-century Mediterranean trend towards a frame-orientated approach to ship-building subsequently spread westwards to Atlantic Europe where, from the fourteenth century onwards, sea-going ships of increasing capabilities were built. This development led to the frame-based three-masted, square- and lateen-rigged, ocean-going ships of the late fifteenth/early sixteenth century, in which Europeans sailed the seas of the world (Greenhill, 1988, pp. 67–76; Arnold, 1983). It can be appreciated, therefore, that this shift from shell-first to skeleton-first building methods was an important watershed in the history of technology, seafaring and European influence, albeit, on present evidence, a somewhat lengthy watershed of more than 1,000 years, from *c.* 100 to, say, 1400 AD. Indeed, it was not until the late seventeenth century, when ship-builders had mastered the skills of drawing to scale and building scale models, that the culmination of this revolution was achieved with the building of a full skeleton before any planking was installed (Greenhill, 1988, pp. 69–76).

During the fourteenth century the Chinese also seem to have begun to experiment with frame-based building methods. The evidence is not large: only five or six wrecks from the thirteenth to fifteenth centuries built in the Chinese tradition have been found (McGrail, in press), and detailed reports are not yet available in European languages. Nevertheless, it seems clear that the earlier ones (for example, the late thirteenth-century ship excavated in 1974 from Houzhou harbour in Quanzhou, Fujian) were built shell-first (Green, 1983; Li, 1989): the planking was joined in half-laps or rabbeted-laps, fastened together by angled nails. After the shell of planking had been built up in sections, the bulkheads and frames were inserted and nailed in position.

A ship from Peng-lai, Shandong, of the late fourteenth century, on the other hand, appears to have been built frame-first: two papers describing this ship contain information that strongly suggests this was so, but the authors do not make this absolutely clear (Yuan and Wu, 1991; Xi and Xin, 1991). The transom stern, the stem and several bulkheads were probably first built up to the shapes required and fastened to the keel. The planks were then fashioned to conform to this framework and were fastened to the framing by nails, scarfs in the planking being at frame stations (fig. 10): thus this ship appears to have been skeleton-built. The planking was also fastened together by dowels and angled nails. This unusual combination of frame-first building with edge-fastened planking is not unique (see Waters, 1947, on the twentieth-century Chinese twaqo; Greenhill, 1976, p. 65; and Coates, 1985). The result is a very strong ship. Three fourteenth- to sixteenth-century wrecks of sea-going ships from south-east Asia – *Ko Si Chang 3* and *Pattaya* in the Gulf of Thailand, and *Buket Jakas* off Sumatra –

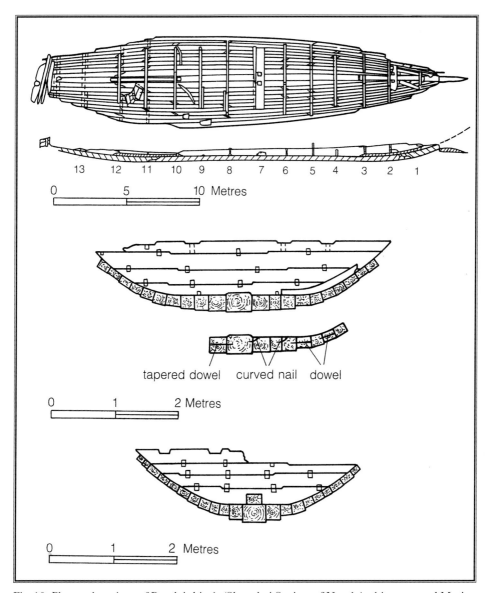

tapered dowel   curved nail   dowel

Fig. 10. Plan and sections of Penglai ship 1. (Shanghai Society of Naval Architecture and Marine Engineering)

also have scarfs in the side planking at their bulkhead stations (Green and Harper, 1983; Green, 1986; Manguin, 1982; 1996), suggesting that they too were built skeleton-first.

The archaeological evidence we have today suggests, then, that there were four separate 'outbreaks' of skeleton-first or frame-based building, which dated from:

- first to fourth century AD in Celtic Europe;
- Late sixth century onwards in the Mediterranean;
- fourteenth century onwards in Atlantic Europe;
- fourteenth century onwards, when skeleton-first methods appear to have been used in China and South-East Asia also.

There is no obvious direct connection between fourth-century Celtic north-west Europe and sixth-century Mediterranean, but the possibility of technological transfer through France cannot be ruled out.

A connection between sixth- to eleventh-century Mediterranean and fourteenth-century Atlantic Europe, on the other hand, seems more likely: the idea of building skeleton-first perhaps being carried to the Iberian peninsula by the ships themselves.

Although the 'outbreaks' in Atlantic Europe and China were evidently close together in time, these regions are widely separated in space, and direct transfer of the idea, although possible, seems unlikely. An alternative to be considered is that the skeleton-first idea spread to China from Byzantium in the eastern Mediterranean through the Arab world, which is known to have had overseas trading links with China from the seventh century onwards (Blunden and Elvin, 1983, p. 189; Scarre, 1992, pp. 190–1). However, there is, as yet, no evidence for this building method anywhere in the Indian Ocean region before the sixteenth century, as we would expect to find if Arabs had transmitted the idea.

In this case, the almost simultaneous appearance in Atlantic Europe (albeit after a long period of development) and in the seas of south-east Asia and southern China of ocean-going ships built skeleton-first is probably due to independent invention. It seems that in two widely separated cultures, with comparable technological capabilities – though different in detail – economic, environmental and political pressures encouraged the development of bigger ships that could be built from poorer quality timber by generally less-skilled labour and that were easier to repair (McGrail, 1981, pp. 42–3; Steffy, 1994, pp. 84–5). These are the main advantages of the skeleton-first method; as is the repeatability of good designs. Such desirable features could only be achieved by a marked shift in technology from shell-first to skeleton-first methods.

It should be noted that the conclusions reached above, about the diffusion and the independent invention of skeleton-based techniques, depend very much on the dates assigned to the wrecks with these characteristics. Future refinements in dating, especially of the south-east Asian finds, could cause some revision of these hypotheses; the discovery of earlier wrecks built skeleton-first would require a complete reappraisal of all the evidence.

Plank Fastenings

In the skeleton-first technology, generally speaking, planks are not fastened together but, rather, to the framework or skeleton. In shell-first building, however, planks are indeed fastened together, and different traditions and cultures have used different types of fastening. Sewn or stitched plank fastenings appear to have been the earliest; then came wooden fastenings; and finally metal. Sewn fastenings have not yet been recorded in sufficient numbers or in sufficient detail for patterns of similarities to be seen. Wooden and metal fastenings are, on the other hand, much better documented.

The double-dovetail wooden clamp (fig. 11a) was used to fasten planking in nineteenth-century France (Beaudoin, 1970) and Japan (Deguchi, 1991, pp. 204–5, figs 13, 14, 16), early medieval Germany (McGrail, 1978, fig. 162), second-century BC India (McGrail, 1981, plate 33), Britain in *c.* 1200 BC (McGrail, 1978, fig. 82) and Egypt in *c.* 2000 BC (Bartlett and Hobbs, 1897). These clamps were locked in position by treenails or pegs in medieval Germany and nineteenth-century France.

Flat tenons within morticed holes were used to fasten planking in third-millennium BC Egypt (Bartlett and Hobbs, 1897) and in nineteenth-century Japan (Deguchi, 1991, pp. 204–5). Similar tenons (loose tongues), but with locking pegs or treenails (fig. 8), were used in the Mediterranean from before 1500 BC to after AD 700 (Steffy, 1994, pp. 36–72). They were also used in nineteenth- and twentieth-century Malaya and Vietnam (Sieveking, 1954, pp. 229–30; Basch, 1972, p. 31; 1973, p. 337); in the

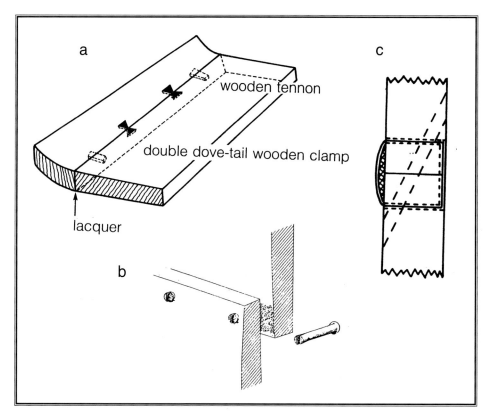

Fig. 11. Wooden plank fastenings: (a) Double-dovetail wooden clamp; (b) wedged treenail fastening; (c) oblique treenail fastening (combined with sewing). (Institute of Archaeology, Oxford)

thirteenth-century wreck *Butuan 2* in the Philippines (Clark *et al.*, 1993); in the eleventh-century AD *Wando Is* wreck off the coat of Korea (Green and Kim, 1989, pp. 39–41); and in one small boat-find of the first century BC/AD from Co. Westmeath, Ireland (O'h Eailidhe, 1992).

Treenails or pegs were used to fasten medieval and twentieth-century overlapping planking through the overlap in the Baltic region (fig. 11b) and in north-west Europe (Crumlin-Pedersen, 1969; 1981; Vlek, 1987; Marsden, 1994, pp. 170–4, fig. 150). They were also used, either vertically or obliquely, to fasten flush-laid planking in recent times in the Indian Ocean, from Madagascar and Somalia in the west to Indonesia in the east (fig. 11c), and on to Korea (McGrail, 1987, p. 136).

Metal nails have been used in a variety of ways to fasten planking (fig. 12). For example:

* Angled nails were used in Europe during the Roman period (McGrail, 1987, pp. 139–40); also in medieval China (McGrail, in press); and in recent times in Madagascar, Sudan, India, Vietnam, Malaysia, China, Japan and Russia (Basch, 1973, pp. 335–7).
* Clamp nails were used in recent times in Europe, India and China (McGrail, 1987, p. 141; Greenhill, 1971, p. 76).

Can the use of similar plank fastenings in vessels that are separated by thousands of miles and/or hundreds of years be due to independent invention? Or have there been, as yet unknown, transmissions of technological ideas outwards from a single source, or possibly from two or three sources? Since our knowledge of early building techniques outside Europe is meagre, it is very difficult to make sustainable deductions about the flow or otherwise of nautical ideas. Two specific cases may, however, be commented on, as they have some supporting evidence:

Plank-fastening tenons locked by treenails (fig. 8), which are characteristic of Mediterranean ships from *c.* 1500 BC to *c.* AD 700, have also been found in boats excavated outside the Graeco-Roman world: in first-century BC/AD Ireland; eleventh-century AD Korea; thirteenth-century Philippines; and nineteenth- and twentieth-century south-east Asia. Vessels with such fastenings have also been excavated from the Rhine region and in Britain, and are dated to Roman times (Marsden, 1994, pp. 168–70, fig. 147, table 15). The idea of mortice and tenon plank-fastenings may therefore have readily been transmitted from Britain, outside the Roman Empire, by sea to Ireland in the first century BC/AD. Some support for this hypothesis comes from the recently reported identification of a Roman 'trading town' dated to the first century AD at Drumanagh, 15 miles north of Dublin (*Sunday Times*, 21.1.96). Furthermore, Mediterranean traders of the later Roman Empire are known to have sailed to India in Roman ships, and probably further east occasionally (Casson, 1989). By these means, the idea for this type of plank fastening may have been transferred to south-east and eastern Asia, to become archaeologically visible in the eleventh, thirteenth and nineteenth centuries AD. Further finds in south-east and east Asian waters of such fastenings, especially from the period before the eleventh century, could help to substantiate this hypothesis.

There is also the unusual case of the fastening that involves clenching the nail by turning the emerging point back through 180° (a 'hooked' nail). This first appears in the archaeological record as a means of fastening the framing to the planking of early

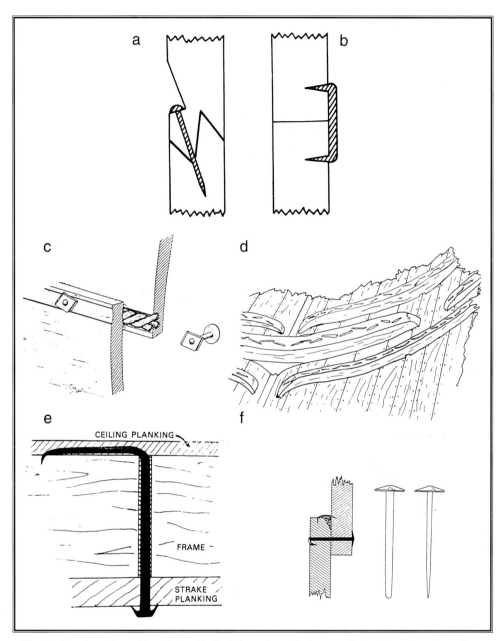

Fig. 12. Iron fastenings: (a) angled-nail plank fastening; (b) clamp-nail plank fastening; (c) nail clenched over a rove (washer); (d) hooked (turned through 180°) nails fastening framing to planking in the fourth-century BC Kyrenia ship; (e) hooked nail fastening planking to framing in second-century AD Blackfriars 1 ship; (f) hooked nail fastening clinker planking in the medieval cog. (Institute of Archaeology, Oxford)

Mediterranean ships built shell-first (fig. 12d), for example *Kyrenia* (see Steffy, 1994, pp. 47–9); then in the Celtic world it was used to fasten the planking to the framing of skeleton-first ships (fig. 12e) (McGrail, 1995b); and subsequently, in the medieval Cog tradition of north-west Europe, it was used to fasten together overlapping side-planking in shell-first hulls (fig. 12f) (Ellmers, 1994). In recent centuries this method has been used to fasten planking to framing in Britain (McGrail and Parry, 1991), and to fasten reverse-clinker planking together in Orissa, India (Blue *et al.*, in press). Apart from this Indian example, which could be a case of independent invention, the other instances of the use of this nail – all European – could be linked by the transmission of the basic idea of that fastening, but with changes in its method of use: successive adaptations of an original idea.

Before we can determine whether some of the other fastenings were independently invented in several places or whether ideas were transmitted widely by sea, we need evidence from further excavations and accurate dating of early boats and ships, especially outside Europe.

Sail types

Sails have rarely been excavated, and rigging is only slightly more evident archaeologically. There is, however, some useful representational evidence. The earliest form of sail seems to have been the square sail. Although these are square or rectangular in shape, they are called 'square' because they are laced to yards that lie square to the mast and are generally used across the ship, more or less at right angles to the vessel's fore and aft line (fig. 3a). When used singly they are set on a mast near amidships. The other main type of sail is the fore-and-aft sail, of which there are many

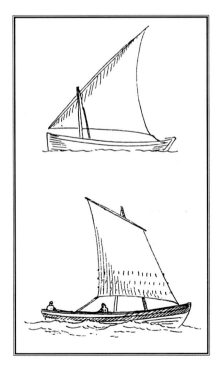

Fig. 13. Fore-and-aft sails: (a) lateen; (b) lug.
(Institute of Archaeology, Oxford)

and varied shapes: as a single sail, this has its leading edge (luff) close to the mast, and it is bent to a yard that is set more or less along the length of the ship on a mast positioned well forward of amidships (fig. 13). In general terms, the square sail is more effective in a following wind, the fore-and-aft sail when sailing closer to the wind.

There are *ad hoc* methods of using the wind to propel a boat by merely holding up a leafy bush, or a blanket or hide fastened to a paddle (McGrail, 1987, p. 218). Any such use in ancient times may never be detected archaeologically. The earliest evidence that we have for the use of sail anywhere in the world is depicted on an Egyptian pot, dated *c.* 3200 BC (Casson, 1971, fig. 6). There are many other Egyptian illustrations of such square sails throughout the second and first millennia BC (Landstrom, 1970). The earliest evidence for sails in the Mediterranean is on Cretan seals (fig. 14a), the earliest of which is dated *c.* 2000 BC (Casson, 1971, figs 34–6), while in north-west Europe the earliest artefactual evidence is the mast and yard on a small gold model of a boat from the north of Ireland, dated first century BC (fig. 14b). However, there is documentary evidence that suggests that sails were used in the seas between Ireland, Britain and Brittany in the sixth century BC (McGrail, 1990, pp. 36–9). In the Baltic region the earliest evidence (fig. 14c) is from *c.* 650 AD (McGrail, 1987, pp. 234–7).

The representational evidence for the sail east of Egypt shows a comparable chronological pattern: in Arabia, on seals from Falaika near Bahrein (fig. 15a), dated before 2000 BC (Casson, 1971, p. 23; Johnstone, 1988, figs 13.8, 13.9); in India, in a graffito on an Indus potsherd (fig. 15b) of *c.* 2000 BC (Johnstone, 1988, fig. 13.3); in China, possibly from before 1200 BC, depending on the interpretation of a pictogram (fig. 15c), but it may be as late as the Han dynasty, that is 200 BC to AD 200 (Needham, 1971, p. 601; Lin, 1991).

These two series of dates, from Europe and from Asia, seem to suggest a gradual dissemination of the idea of sail, both westwards and eastwards from Egypt – perhaps dispersed by the ship herself, due to the extraordinary mobility given by the sail. On the other hand, these date sequences flowing outwards, as it were, from an Egyptian centre may merely reflect the present state of research with a relative abundance of early evidence from Egypt. Or it may be that, in Europe and in Asia, sails were used from earlier times but that this use, along with other aspects of their culture, did not appear in their art until much later (see, for example, Westerdahl, 1994, p. 266). Once again, we need further well-dated evidence, particularly excavated evidence, before we can give substance to the hypothesis that Egypt invented the sail.

The evidence from the Americas shows, indeed, that Egypt was not the sole source of the idea of propulsion by sail, although Egypt may have been the first in the eastern hemisphere. The first Europeans in America found a range of sail types (fig. 3) on rafts and boats, on both east and west coasts, from the Arctic to Brazil and Peru (Edwards, 1965; Leshikar, 1988; Johnstone, 1988, pp. 224–31). This seems to be a clear case of the independent invention of sail in the western hemisphere.

So far I have dealt mainly with the square sail. The earliest evidence for fore-and-aft sails in European waters is said to be a second-century BC depiction showing a Mediterranean boat with a spritsail (Casson, 1971, fig. 176). There is comparable evidence for the Mediterranean use of the lateen sail from the second century AD (Casson, 1971, fig. 181). However, the fact that the mast-step of the Kyrenia ship was positioned well forward (Katzev, 1972), where a fore-and-aft sail is appropriate, rather than amidships, which is ideal for the square sail, strongly suggests that the lateen or sprit sail was used on the Kyrenia ship, which is dated to the fourth century BC.

a

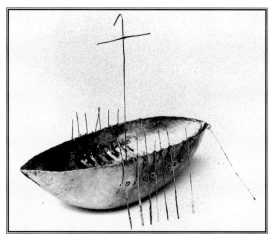

b

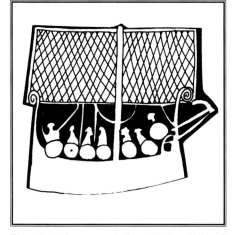

c

Fig. 14. (a) Cretan seal of *c.* 1800 BC. (After Casson, 1971, fig. 47); (b) first-century BC gold model from Broighter, County Derry, Ireland. (National Museum of Ireland); (c) carving on a seventh-century gravestone in Gotland. (Ole Crumlin-Pedersen)

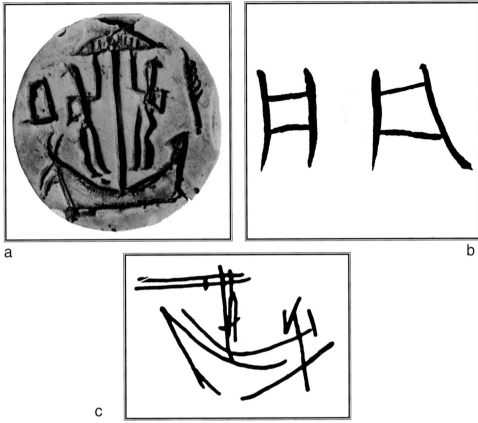

Fig. 15. (a) seal of *c.* 2000 BC from Falaika, new Bahrain. (After Johnstone, 1988, fig. 13.8); (b) graffito on an Indus potsherd of *c.* 2000 BC. (After Johnstone, 1988, fig. 13.3); (c) Chinese pictogram for 'sail'. (After Needham, 1971, 601)

A variant form of the lateen, with a short fourth side (the leading edge), is nowadays known as the Arab sail, but there is no clear evidence for its use by Arabs before the twelfth century AD (McGrail, in press).

The lugsail is generally associated today with the Chinese ship, but the earliest unambiguous evidence for such use is from the twelfth century AD (McGrail, in press). There is, however, the possibility of much earlier use of the lugsail in north-west Europe, strange though this may seem. Many of the excavated ships and boats of the Romano-Celtic tradition of the early centuries AD had their mast-steps well forward: on the canal and river boats, these were for towing masts; on the sea-going and estuary vessels they were for sailing masts. As there are illustrations of what may be lugsails on a contemporary Celtic mosaic and a gravestone (fig. 16a) in the Rhine region (Ellmers, 1978), it seems likely that such a fore-and-aft sail was used on sea-going Romano-Celtic ships off north-west Europe (fig. 16b) in the first to fourth centuries AD (McGrail, 1990; 1995b). If this hypothesis is correct, what happened to the fore-and-aft sail in north-west Europe after AD 400 is a mystery, for the square sail appears to have been ubiquitous there until the fifteenth or sixteenth century.

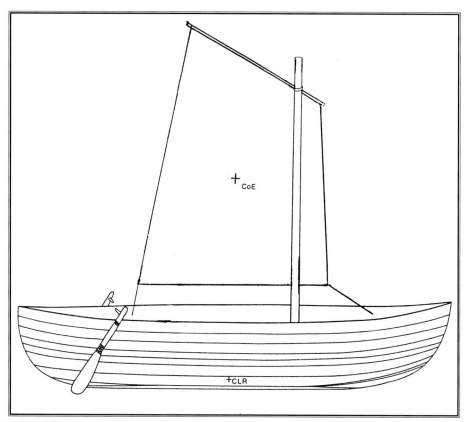

Fig. 16. (a) Carving on a second-/third-century AD gravestone from Junkerath, possibly depicting a lugsail. (Detlev Ellmers); (b) Reconstruction drawing of Blackfriars ship 1 with a lugsail. (After Peter Marsden)

Sails in other parts of the world are not so well documented. Nevertheless, what evidence there is (McGrail, 1981, pp. 47, 50, 55, 58–9, 62, 70–3, 78–9) seems to suggest that particular types of sail – that is the sprit, lateen, lug and the several others without European names (for oceanic sails, for example, see Doran, 1981; Horridge, 1986; Lewis, 1994) – were invented on more than one occasion, at different times and places, and were dispersed around their immediate region by the sailing ship herself. Some of these sails are unique and found only within a limited zone, others are to be found in several, not necessarily contiguous, regions. Needham (1971, pp. 605–17, table 72) has attempted to trace what he sees as the dispersal of the main types of sail, for example the lugsail from south-east Asia to east Asia and on to Europe. The evidence available suggests that aspects of his theories are no longer tenable. It is not possible, however, to replace Needham's ideas with well-argued hypotheses, as the evidence is not yet sufficient.

Navigational Techniques

How did early seamen find their way and keep their reckoning when out of sight of land? Studies of nineteenth- and twentieth-century seamen from small-scale, pre-industrialized societies show that they navigated without any instruments other than the sounding lead. This is environmental navigation, and aspects of it are known to have been used in recent centuries in the North Sea (McGrail, 1983), the Indian Ocean (Arunachalam, 1996), the China Seas (Yan, 1983) and the South Pacific (Lewis, 1970; 1994); and in some places it is still in use today. The methods used in these regions were very similar (McGrail, 1987, pp. 275–85). Directions were estimated relative to the wind; to the sea swell; to constellations and to individual stars; and to the sun at dawn, noon and dusk (fig. 17). The passage of time was estimated in relation to the sun's change of bearing, and to the relative position of circumpolar stars. Distances were estimated in units of a 'day's sail'; and relative speeds by the so-called Dutchman's Log, that is a stick was thrown into the sea, or a patch of foam was tracked, from the bows and timed to the stern by chanting the words of a standard sea shanty.

In the particular practice of measuring directions relative to the sea swell, which is known in the North Sea, the Indian Ocean and the South Pacific, there is the striking similarity that the predominant swell in both the Shetland and in the South Indian languages is known as the 'Mother Wave' (Lewis, 1972, pp. 86–92; 1994, pp. 124–33; Walton, 1974, p. 10; Binns, 1980, p. 20; Rajamanickam, personal communication).

We can trace the use of some of these non-instrumental navigational techniques back in time to the medieval period, in works by authors such as Chaucer, and in the lives of saints such as that of the Irish sailor, St Brendan. There are also corresponding clues in early Chinese and Arab sources, especially for the practice of nautical astronomy without instruments. Classical sources provide evidence for their use in the Mediterranean at an even earlier date, as far back as Homer of the ninth/eighth century BC (McGrail, 1987).

As all these methods are without instruments, archaeology can contribute little, except perhaps in a possible transitional stage, maybe in medieval times, when simple instruments similar to the post-medieval Arab *Kamal* (Tibbetts, 1981; Fatimi, 1996) may have been used to measure the vertical angle of the Celestial Pole to gain some idea of latitude (fig. 18). Such usage is, however, highly speculative until a *Kamal*-like object is excavated from an early context.

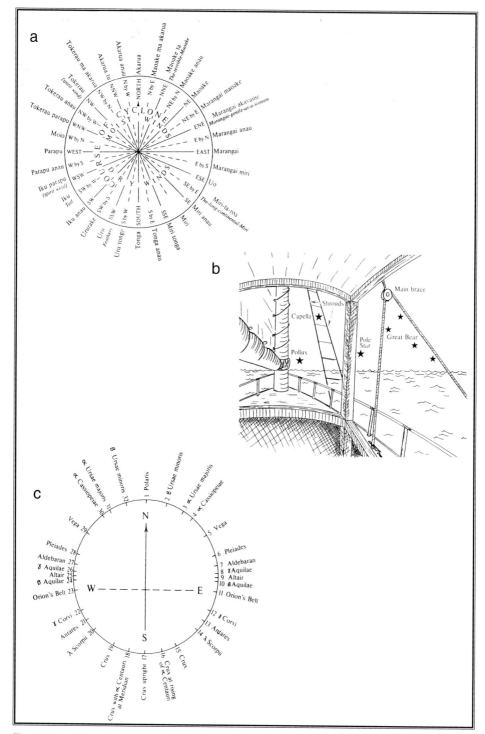

Fig. 17. (a) a Polynesian wind rose from Cook Island; (b) steering by the stars near the Equator; (c) a Micronesian star rose from the Carolines. (After Lewis, 1994, figs 14, 16, 19)

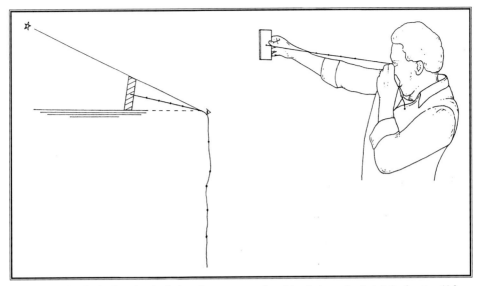

Fig. 18. Method of using the Arab *kamal* to measure the altitude (angular height) of a star. (After drawing by Capt. Søren Thirslund)

It seems to me that, in this worldwide use of similar techniques of navigation without instruments, we can see yet another aspect of the common heritage of humanity (Harris, 1994, p. 9): the tendency to arrive at similar solutions to universal problems. By detailed and perceptive observation of the maritime environment, especially the wind, waves and heavenly bodies, early seamen 'everywhere' evolved simple yet effective methods of navigation out of sight of land, which subsequently proved to be remarkably similar, worldwide.

THE CARRIAGE OF GOODS AND PEOPLE

Ideas travel free, either in the heads of the crew and passengers, or incorporated in the ship herself. The carriage of goods and people, on the other hand, has costs and creates problems in ship design. There are corresponding problems for maritime archaeologists when they try to interpret wreck remains. Let us first look at this problem from the viewpoint of the ancient ship-builder.

The list overleaf indicates the qualities that are needed by any sea-going craft, but all of these qualities cannot be maximized in one vessel. For example, if you want high speed, your boat must be relatively long; but if you want good stability, it must be relatively broad. Every ship and boat is thus a compromise. The builder of a vessel required to carry cargo would, I think, aim to maximize seaworthiness, stability and cargo capacity. If this vessel was also required to carry passengers, then a high rating in seakindliness would also be desirable. The other qualities of speed, manoeuvrability and closeness to the wind would then be residual ones, constrained by the requirement to maximize more desirable qualities.

DESIRABLE QUALITIES IN BOATS AND SHIPS

Safety
seaworthiness   –   buoyancy
                 –   strength and durability
stability

Performance
cargo capacity
speed
manoeuvrability and controllability
seakindliness and dryness
closeness to wind and minimum leeway (if sail)

Note: Economy of manning has been a desirable quality in recent centuries and may have been so from at least medieval times in Europe and comparable stages elsewhere.

If, on the other hand, a warship was required, the builder would undoubtedly choose to maximize speed and manoeuvrability and do the best he could with the other qualities. Different functions dictate a different blend of features and hence a different hull.

THE PURSUIT OF MARITIME ARCHAEOLOGY

Faced with a wreck, underwater, on land or in the intertidal zone, maritime archaeologists have to look at the boat and ship 'design' problem in reverse. The problem here is not how to build desirable qualities into a vessel, but how to deduce what qualities the wreck formerly had. Before tackling that set of problems, we must first work out how to visualize what an incomplete, shrunken, fragmented and distorted collection of timbers looked like in their former glory as a sea-going ship. To do that, we have to have a detailed knowledge of the remains; we have to know about the properties of the various timber species; we have to be familiar with the principles and the distinctive characteristics of the ship-building tradition of which the wreck was a member, and we must be aware of what might be called the 'technological environment' of those times. All this, so that we can reconstruct the wreck in as authentic a shape and structure as possible (McGrail, 1986; Steffy, 1994, pp. 191–234).

If we then want to go further and build up a picture of the performance of the ship – How much cargo? How many passengers? How fast? How stable? How close to the wind? – these are the sorts of question that historians, naval architects and the general public, as well as archaeologists, are interested in. If we are to assess the performance of the original vessel, we must come to grips with a range of sciences: environmental studies of former sea levels and climates, etc.; naval architectural questions of metacentric height and transverse stability; Bernoulli's theorum and the venturi effect of sails; freeboard, draft, ballast and stowage factors, and their effect on cargo capacity; and volumetric coefficients, one-wave speeds and the like (McGrail, 1987, pp. 12–22, 192–203, 258–66).

Moreover, if archaeologists want to know how these ancient mariners operated their ships, if we want to understand how early ships were sailed and navigated, then we must study and practise seamanship and nautical astronomy.

The eighth-century biblical author of the Numerical Proverbs tells us that:

> There are three things beyond my comprehension –
> The way of an eagle through the skies,
> The way of a snake over the rock,
> The way of a ship in mid-Ocean.
>
> (*Jerusalem Bible*, 1984, p. 851)

Unlike that landsman proverb-sayer, the maritime archaeologist must understand the way of a ship; technical studies cannot be an optional extra.

Furthermore, the maritime archaeologist must lay aside any ideas he or she might have about the romanticism of the sea and what can be called the 'messing about in boats' syndrome. Real life must be faced: the general harshness of life at sea in former times, and the stark reality of being lost at sea or of being wrecked. This was work, not recreation. John Millington Synge, in his descriptions of the life of the islanders of Arran off the west coast of Ireland, recorded one man saying:

> A man who is not afraid of the sea will soon be drowned for he'll be going out on a day he should not. But we *do* be afraid of the sea, and we do only be drownded now and again.
>
> (*Arran Islands*, 1907)

Maritime archaeologists should emulate the men of Arran: they must understand the way of a ship and the way of the sea.

Training Maritime Archaeologists

The would-be maritime archaeologist thus has to be trained in a range of disciplines, and also needs practical experience in boat-building, seafaring and archaeological work underwater or on an intertidal site (McGrail, 1995a). Such a course is probably best undertaken as a Masters degree, with a nice balance struck between theoretical and practical work. The courses this postgraduate student takes will include the humanities, as well as scientific and technical subjects. From my experience of recent students, I would say that the main gaps in knowledge and experience lie in the fields of the natural world, the night sky and, in such technical matters as hull structures, hydrostatics and sailing theory. These gaps need to be filled, for maritime archaeology is as much a science as an art – probably more so.

It has been said that facts do not matter in an undergraduate archaeological examination: the exam should be looked on as an opportunity to exercise debating skills. There is obviously some truth in this in a general educational sense. However, in the vocationally orientated, postgraduate training I have in mind for maritime archaeologists, facts *will* matter. An archaeologist's specialist expertise lies in the ability to understand and interpret material remains. Maritime archaeologists need scientific knowledge before they can undertake that task. As with any other discipline, the profession of archaeology must include the search for truth. In our case this is in the reconstruction of the maritime past. With the sort of training I have outlined, maritime archaeologists will be well-placed to dig out the facts and uncover the truth about ancient boats and ships, the carriers of goods, people and ideas.

Acknowledgement

I am grateful for the criticism of an earlier version of this paper by Dr John Coates and Dr Basil Greenhill.

REFERENCES

Aleem, A.A. 'On the history of Arab navigation' in M. Sears and D. Merriman (eds), *Oceanography: the Past*, New York, Springer-Verlag, 1980, pp. 582–95

Arnold, D. *Age of Discovery: 1400–1600*, Lancaster Pamphlets, Routledge, 1983

Arunachalam, B. 'Traditional sea and sky wisdom of Indian seaman' in H.P. Ray and J.F. Salles (eds), 1996, pp. 261–82

Bartlett, J. and Hobbs, X. 'Egyptian burial boat in the Field Museum, Chicago' (typescript in Field Museum), 1897

Basch, L. 'Ancient wrecks and the archaeology of ships', *Int. J. Naut. Arch.* 1, 1972, pp. 1–58

——. 'Golo wreck and sidelights on other ancient ships culled from Admiral Paris's "Souvenirs de marine conservés"', *Int. J. Naut. Arch.* 2, 1973, pp. 329–44

Bass, G. 'Construction of a seagoing vessel of the Late Bronze Age', TROPIS 1, 1985, pp. 25–36

Beaudouin, F. *Les bateaux de l'Adour*, Bayonne, 1970

Binns, A. *Viking Voyagers* Heinemann, 1980

Blue, L., Kentley, E., McGrail, S. and Mishra, U. 'The *pattia*: a seagoing fishing boat of northern Orissa with reverse-clinker planking', *J. Soc. South Asian Studies* (in press)

Blunden, C. and Elvin, M. *Cultural Atlas of China*, Phaidon, 1983

Bray, W.M., Swanson, E.H. and Farrington, I.S. *Ancient Americas*, Phaidon, 1989

Casson, L., *Ships and Seamanship in the Ancient World*, Princeton University Press, 1971

——. (ed.). *Periplus Maris Erythraei*, Princeton University Press, 1989

Clark, P., Green, J., Vosmer, T. and Santiago, R. 'Butuan 2 boat known as a *balangay* in the National Museum, Manila, Philippines', *Int. J. Naut. Arch.* 22, 1993, pp. 143–60

Clausen, B.L. (ed.) *Viking Voyages to N. America*, Roskilde, 1993

Coates, J.F. 'Hogging or "breaking" of frame-built wooden ships', *Mariner's Mirror* 71, 1985, pp. 437–42

Crumlin-Pedersen, O. *Das Haithabuschiff*, Neumunster, 1969

——. 'Skibe på Havbunden', *Handels og Søfartsmuseets Årbog*: 1981, pp. 28–65

Deguchi, A. 'Dugouts of Japan' in S. Zhang (ed), 1991, pp. 197–214

Doran, E. *Wangka: Austronesian Canoe Origins*, Texas, 1981

Edwards, C.R. *Aboriginal Watercraft on the Pacific coast of S. America*. Ibero-Americáná 47, University of California, 1965

Ellmers, D. 'Shipping on the Rhine during the Roman period' in J. du P. Taylor and H. Cleere (eds), *Roman Shipping and Trade* 24, CBA Research Report, 1978, pp. 1–14.

——. 'Cog as a cargo carrier' in R.W. Unger (ed.), *Cogs, Caravels and Galleons*, 1994, pp. 29–46

Fatimi, S.Q. 'History of the development of the *Kamal*' in H.P. Ray and J.F. Salles (eds), 1996, pp. 283–92

Fernández-Armesto, F. *Columbus*, Oxford, 1992

Green, J. 'Song dynasty shipwreck at Quanzhou, Fujian Province, People's Republic of China', 1983, *Int. J. Naut. Arch.* 12, 1983, pp. 253–61.

——. 'Eastern shipbuilding traditions: a review of the evidence', *Bull. Austr. Inst. Maritime Arch.* 12, 1986, pp. 1–6

Green, J. and Harper, R. *Excavation of the Pattaya wreck site and survey of three other sites* (Australian Institute for Maritime Archaeology Special Publication 1), 1983

Green, J. and Kim, Z.G. 'Shinan and Wando sites, Korea: further information', *Int. J. Naut. Arch.* 18, 1989, pp. 33–41

Greenhill, B. *Boats and Boatmen of Pakistan*, David & Charles, 1971

——. *Archaeology of the Boat*, A. and C. Black, 1976

——. *Evolution of the Wooden Ship*, Batsford, 1988

Harris, D.R. 'Pathways to world prehistory', *Proc. Prehistoric Society* 60, 1994, pp. 1–13

Hornell, J. *Water Transport*, David & Charles, 1970

Horridge, A. 'Evolution of Pacific canoe rigs', *J. Pacific History* 21, 1986, pp. 83–99

Hourani, G.F. *Arab Seafaring*, Beirut, 1963

Irwin, G. *Prehistoric Exploration and Colonisation of the Pacific*, Cambridge, 1992

Jezegov, M.P. 'L'épave 2 de l'anse St-Gervais à Fos-sur-mer', TROPIS 1, 1985, pp. 139–46

Johnstone, P. *Seacraft of Prehistory*, Routledge, 1988

Katzev, M.L. 'Kyrenia ship' in G. Bass (ed.), *History of Seafaring*, Thames and Hudson, 1972, pp. 50–2

Landstrom, B. *Ships of the Pharaohs*, Allen & Unwin, 1970

Leshikar, M.E. 'Earliest watercraft: from rafts to Viking ships' in G. Bass (ed.), *Ships and Shipwrecks of the Americas*, Thames and Hudson, 1988, pp. 13–32

Lewis, D. 'Polynesian and Micronesian navigation techniques', *J. Inst. Navigation* 23, 1970, pp. 432–47

——. *We the Navigators*, 2nd edn, Honolulu, 1994

Li, B. 'Notes on the design of replica models of Zheng He's treasure ship fleet' in S. Zhang (ed.), 1991, pp. 330–40

Li, G-Q. 'Archaeological evidence for the use of "chu-nam" on the 13th century Quanzhou ship, Fujian Province, China', *Int. J. Naut. Arch.* 18, 1989, pp. 277–83

Lin, H. 'On the origin of sails in China' in S. Zhang (ed.), 1991, pp. 320–9

Lipke, P. *Royal Ship of Cheops*. BAR, Oxford, S.225, 1984

McGrail, S. *Building and Trials of a Replica of an Ancient Boat: Gokstad Faering*, Greenwich, 1974

——. *Logboats of England and Wales*, BAR, Oxford, 51, 1978

——. *Rafts, Boats and Ships*, HMSO, 1981

——. 'Cross-channel seamanship and navigation in the late 1st millennium BC', *Oxford J. Arch.* 2, 1983, pp. 299–337

——. 'Towards a classification of water transport', *World Archaeology* 16, 1985, pp. 289–303

——. 'Experimental boat archaeology – some methodological considerations' in O. Crumlin-Pedersen, and M. Vinner (eds), *Sailing into the Past*, 1986, pp. 8–17

——. *Ancient Boats in North-West Europe*, Longman, 1987

——. 'Boats and boatmanship in the late prehistoric southern North Sea and Channel region' in S. McGrail, *Maritime Celts, Frisians and Saxons* (CBA Research Report 71), 1990, pp. 32–48

——. 'Early sea voyages', *Int. J. Naut. Arch.* 20, 1991, pp. 85–93

——. *Medieval Boat and Ship Timbers from Dublin*, Royal Irish Academy, 1993

——. 'Training maritime archaeologists' in O. Olsen, J.S. Madsen and F. Rieck (eds), *Shipshape*, Roskilde 1995a, pp. 329–34

——. 'Romano-Celtic boats and ships: characteristic features', *Int. J. Naut. Arch.* 24, 1995b, pp. 139–45

——. *Ancient Boats of the World*, Oxford (in press)

McGrail, S. and Parry, S. 'Flat-bottomed boat from the R. Usk at Tredunnoc, Gwent, Wales' in R. Reinders and K. Paul (eds), *Carvel Construction Techniques* (Oxbow Monograph 12) 1991, pp. 161–70

Manguin, P-Y. 'S.E. Asian ship: an historical approach', *J. SE Asian Studies* 11, 1980, pp. 266–76

——. *Bukit Jakas Wreck Site* (report of École Française d'Extrême-Orient), Jakarta, 1982

——. 'S.E. Asian shipping in the Indian Ocean' in H.P. Ray and J.F. Salles (eds), 1996, pp. 181–98

Marsden, P. *Ships of the Port of London*, English Heritage, 1994

Needham, J. *Science and Civilisation in China*, Vol. 4, pt 3, Cambridge, 1971

O'h Eailidhe, P. '"Monk's Boat" – a Roman period relic from L. Lene, Co. Westmeath', *Int. J. Naut. Arch.* 21, 1992, pp. 185–90

Parker, A.J. *Ancient Shipwrecks of the Mediterranean and the Roman Provinces*, BAR, Oxford, S.580, 1992

Parry, J.H. *Discovery of the Sea*, New York, Dial Press, 1974

Ray, H.P. and Salles, J.F. (eds). *Tradition and Archaeology: early maritime contacts in the Indian Ocean*, New Delhi, 1996

Scarre, C. (ed.). *Past Worlds*, Times Books, 1992

Sieveking, G. de G. 'Recent archaeological discoveries in Malaya', *J. Malayan Branch of Royal Asiatic Society* 27, 1954, pp. 224–33

Snow, P. 'Chinese Columbus: Zheng He and his predecessors', *Medieval History* 2, 1992, pp. 56–75

Steffy, J.R. *Wooden Shipbuilding and the Interpretation of Shipwrecks*, Texas A & M University, 1994

Tibbetts, G.R. *Arab Navigation in the Indian Ocean before the Coming of the Portuguese*, Royal Asiatic Society, 1981

van Andel, T.H. 'Late-quarternary sea-level changes and archaeology', *Antiquity* 63, 1989, pp. 733–45

Vlek, R. *Medieval Utrecht Ship*, BAR, Oxford, S.382, 1987

Walton, K. 'Geographer's view of the sea', *Scottish Geographic Magazine* 90, 1974, pp. 4–13

Waters, D.W. 'Chinese junks – the *twaqo*', *Mariner's Mirror* 33, 1947, pp. 155–67

Westerdahl, C. 'Maritime cultures and ship types', *Int. J. Naut. Arch.* 23, 1994, pp. 265–70

Willetts, W. 'Maritime adventures of Grand Eunuch Ho', *J. SE Asian History* 5, 1964, pp. 25–42

Wright, E. *Ferriby Boats*, Routledge, 1990.

Xi, L. and Xin, Y. 'Preliminary research on the historical period and restoration design of the ancient ship un-earthed in Peng-lai' in S. Zhang (ed.), 1991, pp. 225–36

Yan, D. 'Technique of maritime navigation' in Y. Mao (ed.), *Ancient China's Technology and Science*, Beijing, 1983, pp. 494–503

Yuan, X. and Wu, S. 'On the construction of the Peng-lai fighting sailship of the Yuan Dynasty' in S. Zhang (ed.), 1991, pp. 169–75

Zhang, S. (ed.). *Proc. Int. Sailing Ships History Conference*, Shanghai, 1991

6
SEA TRANSPORT AND TRADE IN THE ANCIENT MEDITERRANEAN

A.J. Parker

What is, in any defined period, the relation of maritime trade and exchange to political organization? The Mediterranean region in antiquity, in this as in other questions, offers the historian an especially well-focused overview. The very clarity, however, that is gained by distance from the subject and freedom from jumbled foreground detail is obtained at the price of that full information to which maritime historians of later periods are accustomed. For the ancient Mediterranean we have effectively no documentary statistics and, even in the Roman period, no economic history worth the name. What we do have is archaeology and, above all, shipwrecks – those closed, fine-grain assemblages that encapsulate episodic glimpses of larger processes.

Nothing, whether in historical or in documentary survivals from antiquity, could have prepared historians for the number or richness of wrecked ships and cargoes that lie, often in dense clusters, in most parts of the Mediterranean (Parker, 1992a). Since 1945, when self-contained compressed-air underwater apparatus first became widely available, some 1,200 shipwrecks (earlier than AD 1500) have been reported (fig. 1). The majority carried a cargo of amphoras – coarse pottery jars for wine, olive oil and other bulk goods – and many date from the Hellenistic and early Roman Empire period. The wrecks are, therefore, at first appearance a skewed sample; however, that even this apparent distortion in the evidence contains illuminating information is a subject to which I shall return.

The earliest maritime contacts on the Mediterranean are unknown; it is unlikely that traces will be found. The first crossings of straits will have been small-scale to serve immediate needs, such as pasture, food-gathering and migration, and offer no political historical insights. By the Mesolithic or the early Neolithic, sea voyages certainly took place, on a there-and-back basis, to obtain strategic materials and food. However, from those prehistoric times, maritime contacts are unlikely to have left archaeological traces other than as occasional finds of material on land.

From the Bronze Age, documents and pictorial sources from the Near East and Egypt offer an increasingly informative view of maritime exchange, which serves as a background to the first shipwreck sites. As one would expect, gift exchange and élite redistribution, rather than free commerce, are the characteristics of finds from this early phase. One site in particular, Ulu Burun (c. 1325 BC), is amazingly rich. The ship carried metal ingots and finished weapons, enough to equip a modest army. There were, however, also specialized materials for craft finishing, such as blue glass ingots, and finished pottery, as well as containers, including both flasks and coarse jars, the precursors of the classical amphoras. It is important to note that the assemblage of

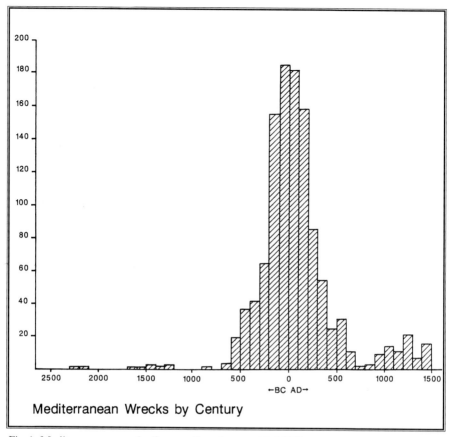

Fig. 1. Mediterranean wrecks (from earliest times to AD 1500).

goods on board is of varied origin, and that it is impossible to patch them into a single route. A simple model for the movement of ancient ships is thus inadequate, even at this early date. Neither 'coasting' nor 'random, opportune trading from port to port' will do. On the other hand, this is scarcely a 'bulk cargo' of a single product. Such are, in fact, rare at any date.

Between *c.* 1200 and *c.* 650 BC lies a 'dark age' of Mediterranean maritime exchange from which no shipwrecks are known, even though there is plenty of indirect evidence for raids and exploration by sea. This can only be due to the use of oared galleys for exploration, which, owing to their need to find water and rest except on a long reach, tended to haul out ashore when the weather turned bad. So it was only when substantial carriage by round ships became more frequent that wrecks, of a kind likely to be found in modern times, once more occurred. From Archaic times on, however, the archaeological record testifies to a gradual development of maritime exchange, which reached its height under the early Roman Empire. What fuelled this trade? In essence it was the variability of staple crops. Cereals, as grown in the ancient Mediterranean world, tend to fail from year to year, now in one area, now in another. If the people of one area are too numerous or too concentrated (that is, in cities) to migrate, food must be brought from another area in bad years. The central transport facility offered for this by the Mediterranean was a vital convenience throughout the Graeco-Roman period, and it was for this movement of foodstuffs that cargo ships were, in the final analysis, built and maintained. As such there existed an underlying economic structure, a 'merchant marine' in a way, on the back of which could ride movements of goods or people according to the demands of politics or markets.

This development is evidenced archaeologically by the appearance from the seventh and sixth centuries of cargoes, in the sense of groups of repeated items. These are coarseware wine jars at first, then fineware (as, for example, in the assemblage from Pointe Lequin). This was part of a real commercial development that flourished in the fifth and fourth centuries (Casson, 1991). At El Sec, of the mid-fourth century, for instance, items on board included sets of duplicates, and many bore owners' (or merchants') marks in both Greek and Punic. Of other cargo, neither the amphoras (identifiable as coming from a range of production areas) nor the millstones, which petrography shows came from several sources, could have been collected along a linear route from place to place, surprising though this at first seems (fig. 2). Even at this date the millstones must have been delivered to a dealer, who would have assembled lots and sold them on. The distribution of such items was, therefore, maritime. However, it was neither peripheral nor radial, but articulated by the invisible tracks of commercially determined voyages. Of course, maritime distribution was certainly vital for heavy goods, such as building stone or ceramic rooftiles, and then it might have been more direct, as can be inferred from the distribution of stamped tiles made at Aquileia (fig. 3). However, for most goods, including building materials, the pattern of distribution was usually more complicated. Thus, at Les Roches d'Aurelle, a first-century roof-load of about 300 tiles was taken on board, no doubt at Fréjus, from a local kiln, and set off perhaps for a coastal villa (fig. 4). Also on board were some fifty amphoras (presumably full of something, perhaps wine) and a collection of pottery

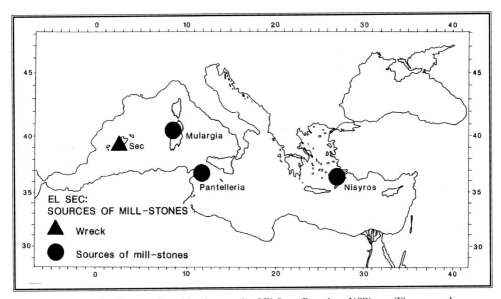

Fig. 2. Sources of millstones found in the wreck of El Sec. (Based on Williams-Thorpe and Thorpe, 1990)

Fig. 3. Distribution of tiles made at Aquileia. (After Matijašić, 1987)

made at or near Fréjus, including handmade cooking pots, the export of which along the southern French coast as far as Ventimiglia has been noted on terrestrial sites. Now it can be seen as part of a low-profile local traffic.

Who owned and captained the ships? There is no clear documentary evidence for this. Legal texts appear to distinguish western *navicularii*, ship owners or ship operators, from eastern *naukleroi*, ship captains, or *magistri*, ship's masters. The question is complicated by constraints of social law and custom. No doubt the wealthy social élites, especially of Rome, both invested (often covertly) and hired or leased and owned their ships, as they and others like them in other periods did with carriages or carts for land supplies. Many of the recorded shipwrecks carried 10 to 20 tons of cargo, equivalent to a container or an articulated lorry-load today. Sometimes this would have been in their own ship, at other times it would have been hired – one cannot always tell.

An example of this sort of traffic is the wreck of La Fourmigue C, sunk off the French coast in *c.* 70 BC. On board was a fine bronze vessel, a *situla*. There were also couches, all with Bacchic symbolism, bearing the marks of Greek makers, and about 100 amphoras (equivalent to 250 cases today) of different Italian wines. Small items included some samples of decorative marble from mainland Greece and the islands. It would be tempting to see this as the private property of someone being posted to the Province (Gaul), or as some kind of speculative venture. However, among the non-cargo finds were not only Italian black-gloss cups (Campanian B and C ware) but also a handmade pot of 'Gallo-Greek' type, from the Alpilles, a range of hills above Arles.

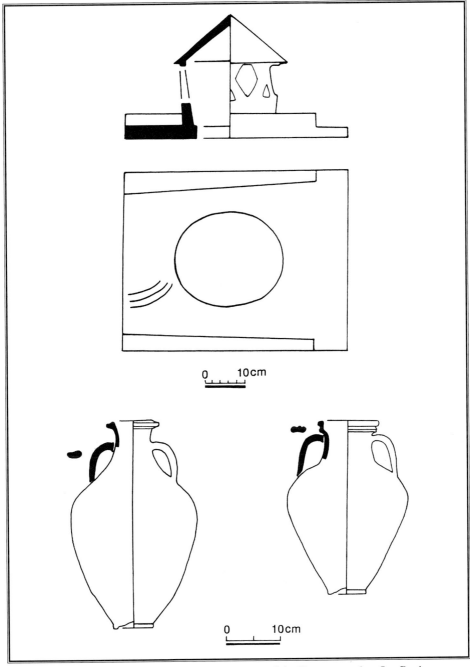

Fig. 4. Rooftile, amphoras and pottery from the cargo of the Roman wreck at Les Roches d'Aurelle. (After Berato *et al.*, 1986)

Arles must have been the home port of this modest ship. The material on board, however, indicates that it had travelled at least to Cosa or Ostia (for the wine), if not to Greece. The cargo constitutes much of a feasting kit. Whatever the precise ownership of the vessel, the cargo looks like a specific order for a Gallic or Roman colonial notable. Such private, command trade was obviously inevitably one element in a steeply pyramidal society.

On the other hand, traders and ships' owners can sometimes be the same. In the wreck of Sud-Lavezzi B (c. AD 20), southern Spanish amphoras were found together with about 10 tons of copper and lead ingots. The lead was counter-marked AP.IVN ZETH, the name of a merchant to whom they belonged, and AP ZE appeared on the anchor stocks, part of the ship's equipment. Similar links can be found in ships employed in the wine trade, so here we seem to be looking at merchants who used their own ships as well as contracting carriage from others.

Most categories of cargo have now been mentioned. Amphoras were, of course, especially frequent (fig. 5). These containers are characteristic of ancient maritime commerce (Grace, 1961; Peacock and Williams, 1990). Specially designed to stand up to the knocks of a long journey, maybe with several trans-shipments, these jars were the 'jerry-can' or 'bidone' of the ancient Mediterranean. There were scores of shapes, often derived from different techniques of manufacture and usually serving a specific purpose. Greek and Republican amphoras needed one porter, southern Spanish oil amphoras needed two and late Roman amphoras had to be lifted by tackle, but these had a more convenient weight-to-contents ratio. Whether they were carried by porters, carts or dinghies, the substructure needed to handle such containers was vast and labour-intensive. Where there were no pound locks on rivers, no mechanical power to manoeuvre ships in harbour and no alternative to laborious, craftsmanly building and repairing of ships, it is clear that even at a simple level of economics the sea transport and trade of classical antiquity were important in terms of income and demand for supplies.

Sea transport was particularly important for Italian wine of the late Republic. Agricultural manuals advised the élite on how to invest in wine estates and on the use of amphoras for marketing. There were no road links with Gaul, and Gaulish wine production was very restricted, while central and northern Gaul was the source of slaves, which bolstered the lifestyle of the élite and worked in trade and industry at Rome. Maritime commerce thus enabled Italian produce to be exchanged (no doubt by means of coins) for desirable Gaulish exports. The ships were the largest excavated from antiquity and carried thousands of amphoras, but the cargoes were often made up of consignments from different sources. There were also other goods on board. The wine identified in amphoras on board the wreck of La Madrague de Giens was red, but came from an area famous for its sweet white wine (*Caecubum*). All of this adds up to something more than personal goods and specific orders: perhaps to an operation targeted at more or less open trading. This traffic rose and fell with considerable abruptness, judging by wrecks. Italian exports were replaced, during Augustus' reign, especially by Spanish goods. This was associated with a gearing-up of wine traffic within the Mediterranean and an increased emphasis on bulk methods (Parker, 1992b). The role of amphoras as sea transport containers is emphasized by sculptural and mosaic scenes of stevedores pouring wine into a skin, or into large jars like tanks, at the port of Rome. Archaeologically, this development is seen in *dolium* wrecks such as that of Diano Marina, dating from the mid-first century AD (fig. 6). In this wreck there were

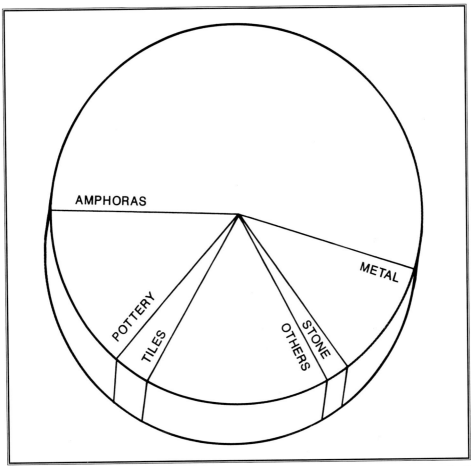

Fig. 5. Proportion of types of cargo in ancient shipwrecks. (From data in Parker, 1992a, pp. 20–1)

fourteen *dolia* (tank-like jars). The larger ones held 1,500 litres, that is about sixty amphoras, or sixteen cases in modern terms. One of them bears the stamps of a Campanian family that had considerable links, not only with pottery-making but also with the wine trade and ship-building at Minturnae. The jar has also been inscribed with the scratched name of Peticius Marsus, no doubt its owner or the owner of its contents. Very likely the same person appears in a dedication made at the sanctuary of Sulmona, where a statue bears the name of M. Attius Peticius Marsus on its base. These Campanians succeeded in profiting from the Augustan Peace to take over a traditional trade and become rich. This is the archaeological counterpart to the braggadocio of the comic upstart Trimalchio in Petronius' novel.

A rare document takes us back to the events of a spring day at Puteoli, the great harbour city of Campania. A writing-tablet (*Tab. Pomp.*, 13) dated 11 April AD 38 survives from the ruins of the nearby port of Pompeii. The writing is in Greek and refers to Puteoli as Dikarchêa. However, it is full of Roman law, recording a contract (the *traiecticius* or *naulôtikê*) made between Menelaos, son of Eurenaios, of Keramos (a city in Asia Minor) and Primus, slave of Publius Attius Severus. The last part of the

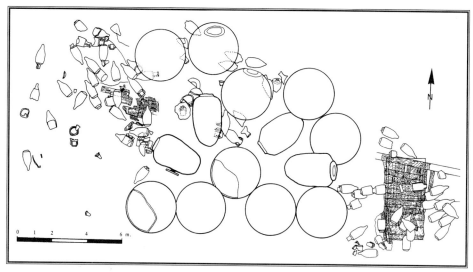

Fig. 6. The *dolium* wreck of Diano Marina. (After Pallarés)

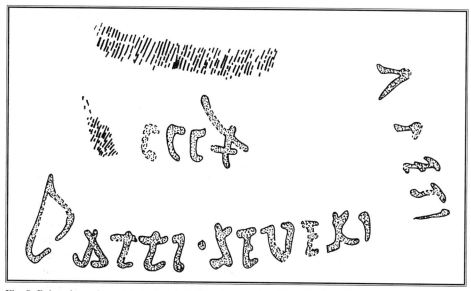

Fig. 7. Painted amphora label of P. Attius Severus. (After CIL XV 2 4748)

document, in Latin, repeats the lodging of a pledge for 1,000 denarii on behalf of Menelaos by a Roman, M. Barbatius Celer, who was illiterate. This document sets the scene and, with help from references in the collections of Roman law, emphasizes the importance of carriage contracts in this, the classical, world. Menelaos was to convey goods (their nature unstated here) from one place to another, not to go tramping around looking for bargains and sales. Of Capt. Menelaos from Keramos we know nothing, but the master of Primus (the slave who set the contract), P. Attius Severus, is known from another source (fig. 7). His name appears on amphoras from southern

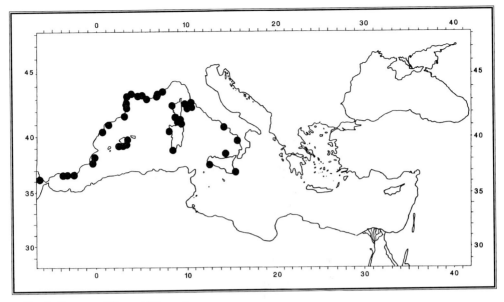

Fig. 8. Cargoes of Dressel 20 amphoras.

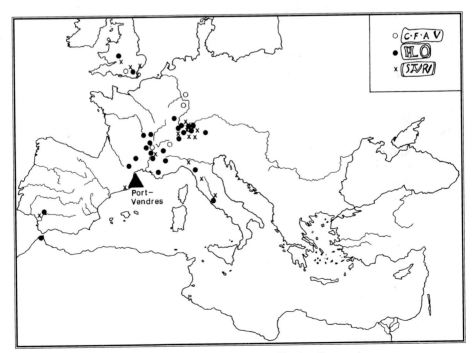

Fig. 9. Amphora stamps similar to those found at Port-Vendres B.

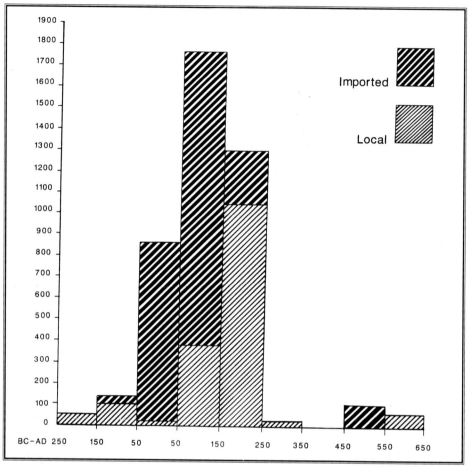

Fig. 10. Lamps at Berenice. (After Bailey, 1985)

Spain, both of olive oil and also for some other substance, found in a Roman deposit of the same period. Evidently he was one of the many merchants whose families or households, spread out around the Roman world, with junior relatives or servants in ports and trading centres, saw to the movement of goods. Our information on the trade of southern Spain is especially good, thanks to the preservation of thousands of painted inscriptions on amphoras. Labels on amphoras tend to be property markers rather than addresses. However, the same labels show that producing estates did not, in fact, send directly to their sister houses at Rome; rather, some sort of buying and selling went on.

Ships that sank, carrying olive oil amphoras from southern Spain, are shown in the map (fig. 8). Mediterranean traffic was obviously dense, but movements to continental Europe and towards the frontiers were significant, too. This may be confirmed from a map of identified stamps applied to amphoras by southern Spanish potters (as in the assemblage of stamped amphoras in the cargo that sank at Port-Vendres in the mid-first century; fig. 9). The role of the army was obviously important in this traffic but, in my view, as an influential purchaser. The tablets found at Vindolanda, and evidence

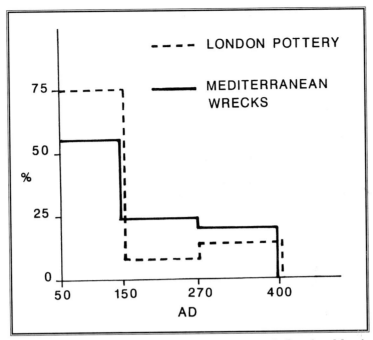

Fig. 11. London pottery finds and Mediterranean wrecks compared. (Based on Marsden and West, 1992)

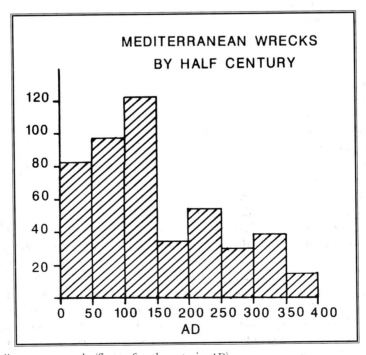

Fig. 12. Mediterranean wrecks (first to fourth centuries AD).

from elsewhere, increasingly show that this was the way the economy operated. Taxation provided for army employment, which necessitated expenditure on both staples and luxuries, which gave profits to producers and traders, who then paid taxes (Hopkins, 1983; Greene, 1986). This chain was broken by the loss of bullion, for instance to India (recognized by the Romans in one of the few economic analyses known to have been made in antiquity). Up until the end of Trajan's reign (AD 117) this loss of precious metal from the money system was made good by successive conquests elsewhere, and by the exploitation of imperial gold and silver mines, but such replacements thereafter declined. Into this framework we can set the so-called piggyback effect, in which products of every kind got to ride on board transport that was set up to supply the key demands. The corn supply of Rome (effectively bought by the emperors as an investment in public order) provided transport for St Paul; the oil for Romans' cookery or soldiers' baths provided a substructure for the carriage of pottery and other foods or products.

The decline of Roman trade during the later second century is well attested. A clear example (Bailey, 1985) is the incidence of imported lamps at Berenice (Benghazi), which were numerous until c. 150. Thereafter the finds are dominated by locally produced lamps (fig. 10). Another example, highlighted by Marsden and West (1992), is the incidence of pottery in Roman London (fig. 11). The same trend was previously highlighted at Ostia and at Settefinestre by Carandini and Panella (1981). From the second quarter of the second century AD the commerce of the Roman Empire fell away. The same trend is shown by the graph made from records of Roman shipwrecks in the Mediterranean (fig. 12). This might be the product, in part or whole, of a decline in the use of amphoras as containers; but, against the background I have reviewed, that in itself is an indicator of a changed commercial world. The commercial amphora belonged to a busy, profitable economy in which taxation, state expenditure and private enterprise all played their part. The decline of that economy, very likely imperceptible at the time, was due to factors beyond the control of Roman merchants and sea captains. That amphoras predominate among the surviving remains of ancient maritime trade, and that they became rarer in the late Roman and post-Roman Mediterranean, far from being a weakness and an irrational bias of the archaeological evidence is an important indication of the special nature of that trade and of the conditions in which it met so striking an apogee.

A statistic of economics it certainly is not, but as a demonstration with which to end one may highlight the Byzantine Wreck of *Yassı Ada*. This, effectively the last shipwreck of classical antiquity, dating from the seventh century AD, had a cargo of amphoras, but they were reused, possibly empty, something for which there is, to my knowledge, no firm evidence from the heyday of ancient maritime trade.

In conclusion, let us look at some questions that the historian might ask of the maritime archaeologist, and see what the latter can respond. In the case of the ancient Mediterranean world, what distinguishes trade from gift exchange, commissions placed by the state and so forth – that is to say, what is the definition of trade, and of successful trade? The answer, in short, is amphoras. What were the conditions for successful trade? Answer: a powerful demand that created a substructure. In what sort of political periods were these conditions met? Answer: the expansionist, consumerist world of the Roman Empire. From a global point of view, did states depend on maritime trade for their power and continuation, or was trade one result of the peace imposed by a strong military state? The latter, is the answer that seems to come to us from the sea.

Acknowledgements

The ideas, whether published or unpublished, of several friends and colleagues are included above; I am conscious of having borrowed from Mensun Bound, Teresa Clay, Pier Alfredo Gianfrotta, Kevin Greene, Keith Hopkins, Javier Nieto, Tina Panella, Jeremy Patterson, Gianfranco Purpura and André Tchernia. I am grateful once more to Susan Grice for drawing the illustrations.

REFERENCES

Bailey, D.M. 'The lamps of Sidi Khrebish, Benghazi (Berenice): imported and local products' in G. Barker, J. Lloyd and J. Reynolds (eds), *Cyrenaica in Antiquity* (British Archaeological Reports, Oxford; BAR Int 236), 1985, pp. 195–204

Berato, J., Boreani, M., Brun, J-P., Pasqualini, M. and Pollino, A. 'L'épave des Roches d'Aurelle', *L'exploitation de la mer: la mer, moyen d'échange et de communication*, VIèmes Rencontres Internationales d'Archéologie et d'Histoire, Antibes, Octobre 1985 (Éditions APDCA, Juan-les-Pins), 1986, pp. 191–216

Carandini, A. and Panella, C. 'The trading connections of Rome and Central Italy in the late second and third centuries: the evidence of the Terme del Nuotatore excavations, Ostia' in A. King and M. Henig (eds), *The Roman West in the Third Century* (British Archaeological Reports, Oxford, BAR Int 109) 1981, pp. 487–503

Casson, L. 'Maritime trade in Antiquity', *Archaeology* 34 (4), 1991, pp. 37–43

Garnsey, P., Hopkins, K. and Whittaker, R. (eds). *Trade in the Ancient Economy*, London, Chatto & Windus, 1983

Grace, V.R. *Amphoras and the Ancient Wine Trade*, Princeton, Agora Picture Books, 1961

Greene, K.T. *The Archaeology of the Roman Economy*, London, Batsford, 1986

Hopkins, K. in P. Garnsey, K. Hopkins and R. Whittaker (eds), 1983, pp. 84–109

Marsden, P. and West, B. 'Population change in Roman London', *Britannia* 23, 1992, pp. 133–40

Matijašić, R. 'La produzione ed il commercio di tegole ad Aquileia', *Antichità Altoadriatiche* 29, 1987, pp. 495–531

Parker, A.J. *Ancient Shipwrecks of the Mediterranean and the Roman Provinces* (Tempus Reparatum, Oxford; BAR S–580), 1992a

——. 'Cargoes, containers and stowage: the ancient Mediterranean', *Int. Journal Naut. Arch.* 21, 1992b, pp. 89–100

Peacock, D.P.S. and Williams, D. *Amphorae and the Roman Economy*, London, Longman, 1990

Williams-Thorpe, O. and Thorpe, R.S. 'Millstone provenancing used in tracing the route of a fourth-century BC Greek merchant ship', *Archaeometry* 32, 1990, pp. 115–37

7

NAVIGATION AND EXPLORATION IN THE MEDIEVAL WORLD

Sarah Arenson

L et us leave these calm surroundings and go on an exploration of the global maritime medieval scene. I am navigating in the timespan roughly between AD 500 and 1500. For the East – Byzantium, the Muslim Empire, India and China – these are no Middle Ages. Everywhere, we have evidence of the most audacious and far-reaching adventure into the unknown.

This period is the first for which we can attempt a well-documented historical study, as the exploits of the ancient mariners, like the Phoenicians and even the Greeks, are lost in the mists of time. This period is also the last in which maritime powers could act independently, for after 1500 the world's oceans were dominated by European sea power. My purpose is to review the maritime activity of medieval men (no women in this field!) – how far did they go, what were they looking for, which techniques did they use and what were the consequences? – and to learn something about these men, their culture and the meaning of the sea to them. The findings may have some relevance beyond that time and place.

It is a common feature of most modern, materialistic approaches to history to give undue importance to technical innovations, or to one major external event. Especially at the end of the twentieth century, with the explosion of knowledge, there is a strong tendency to take a short-cut and come up with a simplistic solution, usually in the technical field. This was common practice in dealing with the ancient world, which was divided and studied as the Stone, Copper, Bronze and Iron Ages.

Remaining within the framework of medieval research, there are excellent theses put forward concerning the impact of the heavy plough and later the stirrups on the development of feudalism (White, 1969) putting an emphasis on technical innovation as the vehicle of change. As to the '*deus ex machina*' external intervention approach, there is the famous though now passé thesis of Pirenne (1970; Havighurst, 1958) concerning the link between the Muslim conquests and the dawn of the Middle Ages. Coming closer to maritime affairs, we have the theses of Lombard (1958, pp. 53–106), explaining the maritime thrust of Muslim armies as a quest for ship timber, and that of Pryor (1988), blaming the mari-physical properties of the Mediterranean for the collapse of this thrust.

The maritime hegemony of the Medieval West was attributed in turn to the invention of the compass, to the introduction of the stern rudder, to the perfection of the combined rigging and to the improvements in ship design (carvel) (Parry, 1968; but see also Lane, 1968, pp. 331–44; Roërie, 1935, pp. 564–83). Luckily, not too much has been made of the betrayal of the Monsoon secret by an Arab pilot (Ibn Māgid? we shall return to him later) (Tibbets, 1971, pp. 9ff.). None of these can explain the most dramatic turning

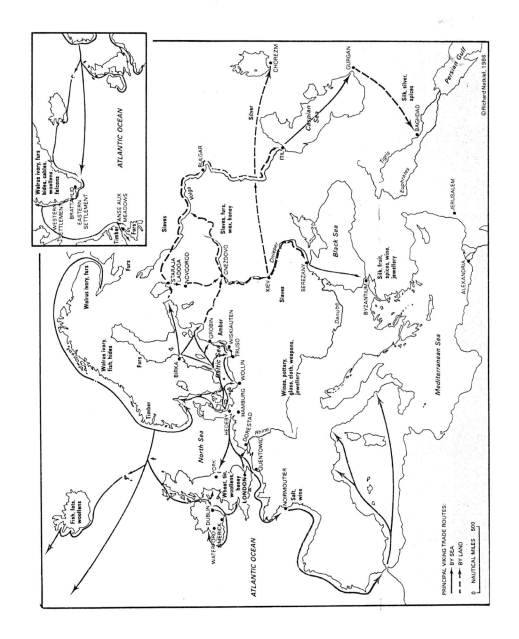

PRINCIPAL VIKING TRADE ROUTES:

--- BY SEA

→ BY LAND

0   NAUTICAL MILES   500

©Richard Natkiel, 1986

point in history, the great discoveries of the turn of the sixteenth century.

After Columbus's year in 1992, there is no need to go into great detail concerning the Viking achievement. What was until a generation ago determined wishful thinking, based on myths and fake evidence like the Vinland Map, the Kensington stone and the like (Washburn, 1971), has proved to be sound fact after the excavations of Helge Ingstad (1964) in l'Anse aux Meadows in Newfoundland.

The Basque, Portuguese and English fishermen have been across the ocean (again around Newfoundland), not realizing where they had been (Mollat du Jourdin, 1993, pp. 104, 143ff; Marcus, 1980, Ch. 22). The remains of their presence there have lately been discovered and studied (Grenier, 1988, pp. 69–84). I for one am sure that it will not be long before clear evidence of Phoenician presence in the New World will be discovered, as we cannot ignore Herodotus's trustworthy account of their circumnavigation of Africa, and their exploits on the Atlantic coasts of Spain, Morocco and south-west England (Gordon, 1971, pp. 170–4).

The ancient and medieval thalassocracies had a very reliable and seaworthy ship, but its size was small to medium in wooden ship terms (Unger, 1980, Introduction). Their rigging and steering devices were fairly simple too. Their navigational aids were primitive, if a sound astronomical observation can be called that, but this is true even for prehistoric man, of course (Taylor, 1956, Ch. I). As for the drive to explore and go beyond the known horizon, judging by the saga of Eric the Red, it was mostly drunkenness, ensuing quarrels and missing the point (Jones, 1984, pp. 290ff). The Greeks and Romans had much bigger ships (and needs), but except for a few legendary voyages (Pytheas 300 BC, Eudoxos 120 BC) they did not try to venture far into the Atlantic or Indian oceans (Taylor, 1956, Ch. II).

In connection with the Viking expansion, another factor, which has not been emphasized enough, in my opinion, should be mentioned, that is the climatic conditions. Le Roy Ladurie has shown (1971) the important changes in climate since AD 1000. There is no doubt that, during Viking times, the shifting ice line receded, and Greenland and Newfoundland were more hospitable.

However, the Vikings, or the Scandinavian people as they were called later, were not yet an integral part of Europe's cultural heritage (Sawyer, 1962, Ch. 9; Lopez, 1966, pp. 245–6) (which they have difficulty accepting even today; see the Norwegian vote on the Maastricht poll); Greenland's tragic story only became known recently, as the remains of the last community were discovered. It perished 200 years before Frobisher's landing in 1578. Greenland too had to be rediscovered! (Jones, 1984, pp. 306–11; Krogh, 1967)

For all intents and purposes, the great maritime explorers and navigators in the Middle Ages were the Italians. This may sound like an extreme overstatement, but in fact their systematic exploits laid the foundation for the oceanic discoveries, and as is well known, their role in these discoveries was outstanding, both on and behind the scene (Lopez and Raymond, 1955, p. 9). The Italians established regular shipping lines beyond Gibraltar to Flanders and south England, where they connected with the Hansa network, reaching all the way to the Baltic and beyond (Dollinger, 1970, Ch.10).

Opposite: Fig. 1. Principal Viking trade routes, from the coasts of Greenland and America far into the heart of Asia. (Source: Natkiel, R. and Preston, A. *The Weidenfeld Atlas of Maritime History*, London, 1986, by permission)

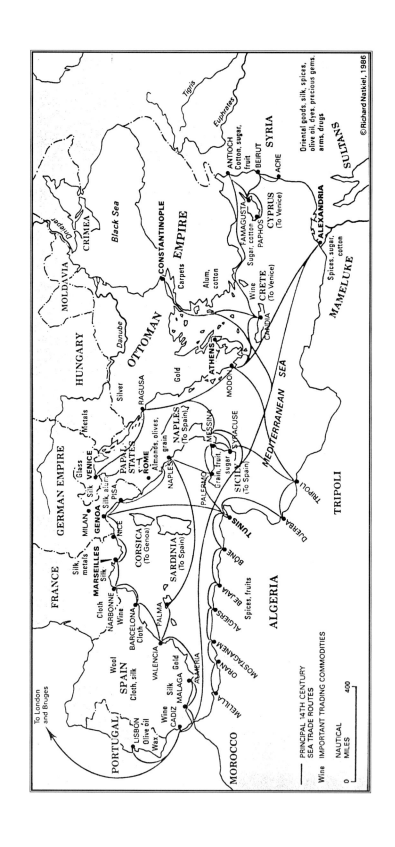

© Richard Natkiel, 1986

Oriental goods, silk, spices, olive oil, dyes, precious gems, arms, drugs

SYRIA

SULTANS

ANTIOCH
Cotton, sugar, fruit
BEIRUT
ACRE

ALEXANDRIA

MAMELUKE

Spices, sugar, cotton

FAMAGUSTA
Sugar, cotton
PAPHOS
CYPRUS
(To Venice)

Tigris

Euphrates

CRIMEA

Black Sea

Dnieper

CONSTANTINOPLE

EMPIRE

Carpets

OTTOMAN

Alum, cotton

Wine
CANDIA
CRETE
(To Venice)

MOLDAVIA

Danube

HUNGARY

Silver

Gold

ATHENS

MEDITERRANEAN SEA

RAGUSA

MODON

GERMAN EMPIRE

Metals

Glass

Silk
VENICE
MILAN

Silk, alum

GENOA
PISA

Silk

PAPAL STATES
ROME

Almonds, olives, grain

NAPLES
(To Spain)

NAPLES

MESSINA
SYRACUSE

PALERMO
Grain, fruit, sugar

SICILY
(To Spain)

TRIPOLI

TUNIS

DJERBA

FRANCE

Silk, metals

MARSEILLES
Silk
NICE

CORSICA
(To Genoa)

SARDINIA
(To Spain)

Cloth
NARBONNE
Wine

Wool

BARCELONA
Cloth

PALMA

SPAIN
Cloth, silk

VALENCIA

Silk
MALAGA
Gold

ALMERIA

MELILLA

BÔNE

BEJAIA

Spices, fruits

ALGIERS

MOSTAGANEM

ORAN

ALGERIA

MOROCCO

PORTUGAL

LISBON
Olive oil

Wax
CADIZ
Wine

To London and Bruges

PRINCIPAL 14TH CENTURY SEA TRADE ROUTES

Wine   IMPORTANT TRADING COMMODITIES

NAUTICAL MILES

0   400

They also went south and east. We know definitely of one attempt to circumnavigate Africa from the West: the Vivaldi brothers of Venice in 1291 (Lopez, 1936, pp. 1–60). Marco Polo was just one of a long list of merchants and missionaries, mostly Italian, who took advantage of the establishment of the Mongol Empire (Olschki, 1943; Dawson, 1955). The last testament of a merchant from Tuscany who died in Tabriz (south of the Caspian Sea) in 1264 has survived (Stussi, 1962, pp. 23–37). These Italians travelled mainly on land, but European maritime activity in the East started even earlier: in 1183, Renauld de Chatillon, the crusader prince of Transjordan, embarked in five galleys in the Red Sea and got as far as Gedda (Lebrousse, 1975, pp. 36–76). From that same fateful year, 1291, the date of the fall of Crusader Acre, there is evidence of several Genoese war galleys on the Euphrates, in service of the Mongols (Richard, 1970, pp. 353–63).

By the middle of the thirteenth century, the commercial revolution (a term coined by R.S. Lopez) had set in. The volume of trade dictated changes in ship design. The cogs entered the Mediterranean and bigger ships (of more than 1,000 tons), such as the carracks, were being built for the first time since Roman times (Singer *et al.*, 1964, Vol. II, Ch. 16, pp. 585ff.; Unger, 1980, pp. 220ff). Rigging and steering were perfected – the stern rudder came in together with sail combinations. Mainly there were new navigation tools – the compass, the portolani and their pilot books (English: rutters). The third factor is not directly connected with the economic field, but rather to the emergence of the new 'nation' states and the Hundred Years War: the appearance of firearms, which went onboard ship during the fourteenth century. By the middle of the fifteenth century the West was well into what Cipolla called 'the age of guns and sails', the agents of the great discoveries and of European domination of the world's oceans (1965; Villain-Gandossi, 1989–1992).

Here a perplexing puzzle arises. Most of these changes are attributed to Eastern origins, and there is no doubt that the East possessed the knowledge first, as in the case of gunpowder. However, even in Arabic and Turkish, the word for compass is the Italian *bussola* (Kahane and Tietze, 1958), while the first mention of the stern rudder, for example, was in the West (Anderson and Anderson, 1963, Ch. V). Undoubtedly, crucial areas, where different traditions interpenetrated, like the Bay of Naples in the case of the compass and the Bay of Biscay in connection with the stern rudder, play an important role (Lane, 1967).

The innovations, then, came from the West, and, relatively speaking, the eastern Mediterranean was quite conservative: new ship types, modern ammunition, improved packaging methods and new trends in trade organization were slow to penetrate. But what about the Muslims who had shores on two oceans, like Egypt with shores on the Mediterranean and Indian Ocean? Here there was no fruitful influence and merging of traditions. Until the end of the thirteenth century, Muslim ships and navigation aids in the Mediterranean were almost indistinguishable from the Christian types, but the innovations in ship design, navigational tools and artillery, transforming the West in the later Middle Ages, did not penetrate the declining Muslim shipping world (Arenson, 1994, pp. 37–42). The ship became another manifestation of the technical decadence of the East, treated so aptly by Eliyahu Ashtor (1983, 1976, 1978). This decadence started at that time, and came to include many sectors of the economy, such as the production of industrial crops, textiles and chemicals. The Ottoman Turks are a

Opposite: Fig. 2. Italian sea-lanes, spread all over the Mediterranean and beyond, connecting the three then known continents. (Source: *The Weidenfeld Atlas of Maritime History*, by permission)

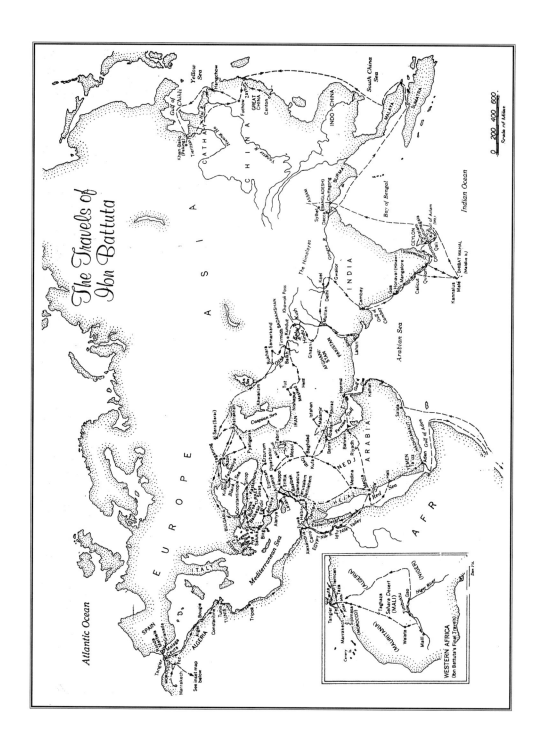

different story, of course, but since they rose to prominence at the end of the period, they were not a medieval power (Hess, 1970, pp. 1892–1919). When I refer to the Muslims, I have in mind the Mamluk Empire of Egypt and what used to be the Abbasid Empire centred in Bagdad until the Mongol invasion (Ayalon, 1965).

Moreover, the Indian Ocean, including the Persian Gulf and the Red Sea, remained unchanged and uninfluenced even by the first stage of Muslim maritime achievement. It took the European powers no more time to dominate global waters than it took the followers of Genghis Khan to make their conquests and establish their empire (Boxer, 1969, Ch. II; Nowell, 1954, Ch. IV). The consequences, though, are on an entirely different scale. Coming into eastern waters, the Portuguese encountered a maritime world basically unchanged for thousands of years. Why?

Islam has accomplished what the Persian Darius and Alexander the Great failed to do in their conquests: it unified the region conquered by it and created a lasting link between the Far East, India and China, and the Mediterranean region, as far as the Atlantic coasts of Spain and Morocco (Christides, 1985, pp. 75–82; 1987, pp. 87–99). Because of the Haj obligation, Islamic society created a whole group of people who can be classified as explorers and travellers – *raḥḥāla*, *tulāb al'ilm* (Ziadeh, 1980; Trapier, 1937). Among these were Ibn Jubair in the twelfth century (Broadhurst, 1952) and Ibn Battuta, one generation after Marco Polo, who gave the most detailed and accurate description of Chinese craft (Ibn Battuta, 1879–1893), and the sealore centred on the figure of Sindbad, who is rather more Persian in character and genre (Langles and Reinaud, 1845, p. 87). From the turn of the fifteenth century and immediately after, we have great Arab navigational treatises, like Ibn Māgid (mentioned above) and Sulaiman alMahri (Khoury, 1970). They represent a very advanced naval tradition, with at least the same 'discovery potential' as the Western one. They belong to the milieu of the Kārim merchants who, according to the Geniza documents and other sources (Goitein, 1958, pp. 175–84) were as important economically in the western Indian Ocean in the twelfth to fourteenth centuries as the Hansa merchants were in northern Europe at the time, but without the political power wielded by the Hansa League.

Now, history is made of events, which did happen; but it is as important to look into the whole array of negative events that did not happen. One can ask 'Why not?' in the same fruitful manner as in treating the positive facts (Squire, 1972, ff. vii–xiii). So why did this potential not assert itself in the East?

The Muslim world was basically self-sufficient – it was so vast and diversified. The style of commerce in the Indian Ocean seems completely different from that of the Mediterranean–Atlantic World. Lewis has already stressed this point (Lewis, 1976). International maritime relations were based on diplomacy and economic power, and trade was free to all. The violence characterizing the Western world was almost absent here, except for some piratical activity, as in the case of the Crividjava, that pirate state of the Archipelago (Toussaint, 1975, pp. 703–43). In fact, it seems that the Indian Ocean, at least its western part, lacked a specialized fighting ship of its own, and whenever there was an urgent need to fight on the water, Mediterranean-type ships were transported there. We cannot go further into this amazing phenomenon, but to

Opposite: Fig. 3. The itinerary of Ibn Battuta, the indefatigable Moroccan traveller of the mid-fourteenth century. (Source: McDonald, L. *The Arab Marco Polo: Ibn Battuta*, New York, Nelson, 1975)

illustrate the mentality that lay behind it I should like to quote an eloquent passage by a Persian sage, talking about the differences between terrestrial and naval tactics (AlHimawi, 1945, p. 112):

> Chess is similar to land-battle, while backgammon represents a sea battle. The backgammon player places his pieces in choice positions and stays on guard, but the dice come up with what does not agree with his plan, so there is no use for his watchfulness, and his stratagem comes to nothing, as with the shifting winds and the everchanging sea.

Fig. 4. Muslim medieval eastern craft: note the stern rudder, the iron anchor, the travellers' compartments, the captain and the person in the crow's nest. (Source: AlHariri, Maqamat, Bagdad, thirteenth century)

In other words, the sea arena is for fortune seekers and common people, who are unworthy of playing noble chess.

To complete and confirm the picture, let me describe now, very briefly, another maritime horizon: that of the Far East, China and south-east Asia. Under the Sung (tenth to twelfth centuries), there was a major economic revolution that was almost unknown in the West (Yoshinobu, 1970; Lo, 1969, pp. 57–101). Commerce and finance flourished, and transportation, mainly by inner waterways, reached enormous proportions. State revenues came mainly from taxation on commerce. There were huge exports and imports, but with a prohibition on the export of rice! The imperial order was collapsing, and a broad middle class was formed that did not share the bureaucratic disdain of business and profit but still had a lot of prejudice against conspicuous consumption. Five cities at least reached a population of more than a million, with first Canton and then Zeitun serving as world centres of maritime commerce. At this time the Chinese used inventions like the printing block, the mechanical clock and paper money. Celadon ware was spreading all over. During this period it is probable that Chinese trading colonies, or at least naval bases (supplies for the merchant marine), were established along the East African coast between today's Rhodesia and Mozambique (Filesi, 1972, Ch. VII). Speaking of Chinese–African relations, it is worthwhile noting that already in the first centuries of the common era, Madagascar was settled by whole communities from Malaysia, the Waqwaq of the Muslim sources (Hourani, 1951, p. 80). Black slaves were sold by the Muslims in China, and the Chinese were especially fascinated by African animals, like the giraffe, as much as they were afraid of 'black magic' (Filesi, 1972, Ch. IV).

Under the Ming, in the first quarter of the fifteenth century, a spectacular maritime *tour de force* took place (Filesi, 1972, Chs V, VII). Under the leadership of the eunuch Cheng-Ho, seven expeditions left China in a period of about 30 years. There were about 250 'Pearlships' accompanied by a host of other vessels, with around 250,000 crew. They visited the coasts of Malaysia, Ceylon, India, the Persian Gulf and East Africa. The pearl ships of Cheng-Ho probably had stern rudders, as found at the site of a Ming shipyard (Chou-Shih-te, 1962/3, pp. 30–5). They also used a compass, and, according to the descriptions of Marco Polo and Ibn Batuta, the ships were of great tonnage and divided into separate compartments, hundreds of years before they were in the West. They also had excellent maps and sailing directions. All of these innovations in the same century as Columbus and Vasco da Gama!

Let us ask again 'Why not?' Why did the 'discovery and domination potential' not assert itself here, as was the case in Islam? By way of an answer, let me touch on mental attitudes, summarized so aptly by Joseph Levenson (1957, pp. 59–60). I would add that these attitudes, which seem to be changing only today, make our topic all the more relevant:

Liang Sou-ming defined civilization as a way of life and outlined three types of civilizations in the world. First, there is Western civilization, the basic spirit of which is a 'forward moving will'. Science, democracy and the desire to conquer nature all are derived from this will. Secondly, there is Chinese civilization, the basic spirit of which is characterized by the will to contemplate, harmony and the golden mean . . . it looks sideways. When confronted with a problem, it does not aim at changing the situation, but attempts to readjust its own desires to gain harmony. The Indian civilization tends to cancel both the problem and the desires. It turns backwards . . . to asceticism, withdrawal and retreat.

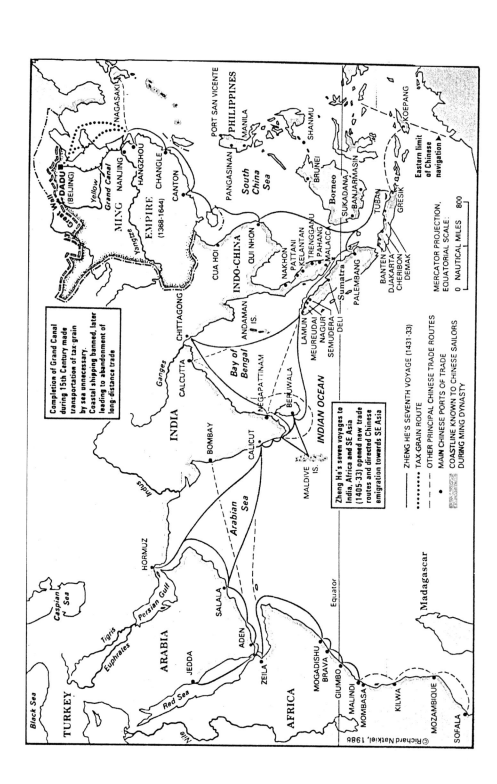

Completion of Grand Canal during 15th Century made transportation of tax-grain by sea unnecessary. Coastal shipping banned, later leading to abandonment of long-distance trade

Zheng He's seven voyages to India, Africa and SE Asia (1405-33) opened new trade routes and directed Chinese emigration towards SE Asia

———— ZHENG HE'S SEVENTH VOYAGE (1431-33)

············ TAX-GRAIN ROUTE

———— OTHER PRINCIPAL CHINESE TRADE ROUTES

– – – – COASTLINE KNOWN TO CHINESE SAILORS DURING MING DYNASTY

• MAIN CHINESE PORTS OF TRADE

MERCATOR PROJECTION, EQUATORIAL SCALE:

0   800

NAUTICAL MILES

Eastern limit of Chinese navigation ▶

© Richard Natkiel, 1986

Black Sea

TURKEY

Caspian Sea

MING EMPIRE (1368-1644)

DADU (BEIJING)

Great Wall

Yellow

Grand Canal

NANJING

HANGZHOU

CHANGLE

CANTON

Yangtze

NAGASAKI

PORT SAN VICENTE

PHILIPPINES

MANILA

PANGASINAN

SHANMU

KOEPANG

South China Sea

BRUNEI

Borneo

SUKADANA

BANJARMASIN

TUBAN

GRESIK

BANTEN

DJAKARTA

CHERIBON

DEMAK

PALEMBANG

Sumatra

DELI

NAGUR

SEMUDERA

MEUREUDAI

LAMUN

MALACCA

PAHANG

TRENGGANU

KELANTAN

PATTANI

NAKHON

QUI NHON

CUA HOI

INDO-CHINA

CHITTAGONG

Ganges

CALCUTTA

Bay of Bengal

ANDAMAN IS.

NEGAPATTINAM

BERUWALA

INDIAN OCEAN

INDIA

BOMBAY

CALICUT

Arabian Sea

MALDIVE IS.

Indus

HORMUZ

Persian Gulf

SALALA

Tigris

Euphrates

ARABIA

JEDDA

ADEN

ZEILA

Red Sea

Nile

AFRICA

MOGADISHU

BRAVA

GIUMBO

MALINDI

MOMBASA

KILWA

MOZAMBIQUE

SOFALA

Equator

Madagascar

Fig. 6. Chinese war-junk: note the rudder and auxiliary oar, the great sail and the weather band, the internal division and the workmanship on the hull. (Source: Filesi, T. *China and Africa in the Middle Ages*, D.L. Morrison (trs), London, F. Cass, 1972)

Finally, let me discuss briefly an unheralded component of these developments: the role of the Jews in the story of medieval exploration and navigation (Tolkowsky, 1964, Chs V, VI). The year 1992 was the 500th anniversary not only of Columbus's landing, but also of the expulsion of Spanish Jewry. It seems that the last word in this connection has not yet been said. As we have seen, the areas of mixed traditions and interpenetrating cultures, like Spain and Portugal, were of crucial importance to maritime progress. The Jews there were a major vehicle by which this occurred. But this pattern had started many centuries earlier.

A precious description of their role in world communications comes to us from the Abbasid master of the post, Ibn Khurdādhabeh, from *c.* 880. He wrote of the 'routes of the Jewish merchants called alRadhāniyya' (Lopez and Raymond, 1995, pp. 31–2):

These merchants speak Arabic, Persian, Roman, Frankish, Spanish and Slavonic. They travel from the East to the West and from the West to the East by land as well as by sea. They bring from the West eunuchs, slave girls, boys, brocade, beaver skins, marten furs and other varieties of fur, and swords. They embark in the land of the Franks on the Western Sea, and they sail toward al-Farama. There they load their merchandise on the back of camels and proceed by land to al-Qulzum, twenty five parasangs distant. They embark on the Eastern Sea and proceed from al-Qulzum to al-Jar and al-Jidda; then they go to Sind, Hind, and China. On their return from China they load musk, aloe wood, camphor, cinnamon, and other products of the

Opposite: Fig. 5. Chinese maritime expansion under the Ming Dynasty, in the Pacific and Indian Oceans. (Source: *The Weidenfeld Atlas of Maritime History,* by permission)

eastern countries, and they come back to al-Qulzum, then to al-Farama, and from there they embark again on the Western Sea. Some of them sail for Constantinople in order to sell their merchandise to the Romans. Others proceed to the residence of the king of the Franks to dispose of their articles.

Jumping back to the great age of exploration in the fifteenth century, suffice to mention a few well-known Jewish contributions to the art of navigation (Tolkowsky, 1964). The cross-staff or Quadrans Judeus was devised by Yaacov ben Machir ibn Tibon and Levi ben Gershon between 1300 and 1330; the Catalan Atlas was drawn in *c.* 1377 by the Majorcan Jewish family of cartographers, the Cresques. Yehuda Cresques later became the director of the newly founded naval academy at Sagres, under his new Christian name: Jaime Ribes. Finally, the astronomical tables known as the Toledo and Alfonsine tables were the work of Jewish scholars like Avraham Zacut, whom Columbus had met, and whose work had also helped Da Gama's expedition.

The much debated question of the Jewish origins or contacts of Columbus remains undecided, but there seems to be strong evidence of the connection between him and Don Yizhaq Abravanel, the mystic philosopher, treasurer of Castille and an associate of Santangel, who may have been the financier of the first trip (Feuerstein, 1993).

To sum up: exploration and navigation in the Middle Ages, in contrast with the Ancient world, can be studied in a fairly detailed fashion. This study shows that technical progress is not a precondition to successful performance, but rather a parallel consequence of the same complex set of factors, both material and spiritual, that lie at the base of any human achievement.

Since the *Odyssey*, western people have gone in quest of adventure. Since monotheism they have been imbued with the awareness of humankind being the crown of creation, bound to take possession of the world and its riches, which is the true original sin (Shahar, 1985, pp. 85–93). Since the Crusades, the 'blessed island dream', in the form of legends of Prester John or the Ten Lost Tribes, was becoming an obsession (Richard, 1957, pp. 225–42). Indeed, side by side with the technical development mentioned at the beginning, and against a complex political and economic background that is beyond our scope here, western Europe at the end of the Middle Ages burst the ancient physical and psychological horizons to create a new world, for better or worse.

REFERENCES

AlHimawi, M.Y., *A History of the Arab Navy*, Damascus, 1945, (in Arabic), quoting AlHasan ibn `Abd Allah, *Athār alUwal fi Tartīb adDuwal*

Anderson, R. and Anderson, R.C. *The Sailing Ship*, New York, Norton, 1963

Arenson, S. 'The Mystery of the Oriental Warship' in S.R. Rao (ed.), *The Role of Universities and Research Institutions in Marine Archaeology*, Goa, National Institute of Oceanography, 1994, pp. 37–42

Ashtor, E. *Levant Trade in the Later Middle Ages*, Princeton University Press, 1983

——. Two collections of articles, London, Variorum Reprints, 1976, 1978

Ayalon, D. 'The Mamluks and Naval Power', *Proceedings of the Israel Academy of Sciences and Humanities*, Jerusalem, 1, 1965

Boxer, C.R. *The Portuguese Seaborne Empire, 1415–1825*, Berkeley, 1969

Broadhurst, R.J.C. (ed./trs.). *The Travels of Ibn Gubair (1145–1217)*, London, Cape, 1952

Chou-Shih-te 'Notes on the great ships of Cheng-Ho – the rudder found at the side of a Ming shipyard', *Wen-Wu*, 1962/3, pp. 30–5 (mentioned by Filesi)

Christides, V. 'Some remarks on the Mediterranean and Red Sea ships in Ancient and Medieval times: A preliminary report', TROPIS 1, 1985, pp. 75–82

——. 'Some remarks on the Mediterranean and Red Sea ships in Ancient and Medieval times: A preliminary report', TROPIS 2, 1987, pp. 87–99

Cipolla, C.M. *Guns and Sails in the Early Phase of European Expansion*, London, Collins, 1965

Dawson, C. *The Mongol Mission*, London, 1955

Dollinger, P. *The German Hansa*, Stanford, 1970

Feuerstein, E. *Columbus, the Jew*, Tel-Aviv, 1993 (in Hebrew)

Filesi, T. *China and Africa in the Middle Ages*, D.L. Morrison (trs.), London, F. Cass, 1972

Goitein, S.D. 'New light on the beginning of the Kārim merchants', JESHO 1, 1958, pp. 175–84

Gordon, C.H. *Before Columbus – Links between the Old World and Ancient America*, New York, Crown, 1971

Grenier, R. 'Basque Whalers in the New World: The Red Bay Wrecks', G. Bass (ed.), *Ships and Shipwrecks of the Americas*, London, 1988, pp. 69–84

Havighurst, A.F. (ed.). *The Pirenne Thesis – Analysis, Criticism and Revision*, Lexington Heath, 1958

Hess, A.C. 'The evolution of the Ottoman seaborne empire in the age of the oceanic discoveries', *American Historical Review* 75, 1970, pp. 1,892–919

Hourani, G.F. *Arab Seafaring in the Indian Ocean in Ancient and Early Medieval Times*, Princeton, University Press, 1951

Ibn Battuta *Rihla*, C. Defremery and B.R. Sanguinetti (ed./trs.), Paris, 1879–93

Ingstad, H. *Westward to Vinland, The Discovery of Pre-Columbian Norse House-sites in North America*, New York, St. Martins, 1964

Jones, G. *The Norse Atlantic Saga*, London, 1964

——. *The History of the Vikings*, Oxford, 1984

Kahane, H. and R. and Tietze, A. *The Lingua Franca in the Levant, Turkish nautical terms of Italian and Greek Origin*, Urbana, 1958

Khoury, I. *Sulaiman alMahri's Works*, Damascus, 1970 (in Arabic)

Krogh, K.J. *Viking Greenland*, Oslo, National Museum, 1967

Lane, F.C. 'Le navi raffigurate nello zibaldone', *Zibaldone da Canal*, Venice, Fonti, 1967

——. 'The Economic Meaning of the Invention of the Compass' in F.C. Lane, *Venice and History – Collected Papers*, Baltimore, Johns Hopkins, 1968, pp. 331–44

Langles, M. (ed.) and Reinaud, M. (trs). *Relation des voyages faits par les Arabes et les Persans dans l'Inde et la Chine dans le IXe siècle de l'ère Chrétien*, Paris, 1845

Le Roy Ladurie, E. *Times of Feast, Times of Famine – A History of Climate since the year 1,000* New York, Doubleday, 1971

Lebrousse, H. 'La guerre de course en mer rouge pendant les croisades' in M. Mollat (ed.), *Course et Piraterie, Travaux du quinzième Colloque International d'Histoire Maritime*, Paris, CNRS, 1975, pp. 36–76

Levenson, J.R. (ed.). *European Expansion and the Counter-example of Asia, 1300–1600*, Cambridge Mass., 1957

Lewis, A.R. 'Les marchands dans l'Océan Indien, AD 1100–1500', *Revenue d'Histoire Économique et Sociale* 54, 1976

Lo, J.P. 'Maritime Commerce and its relation to the Sung Navy', *JESHO* 12, 1969

Lombard, M. 'Arsenaux et bois de marine dans la Méditerranée Musulmane (VII–XI siècles)' in M. Mollat (ed.), *Le Navire, travaux du Deuxième Colloque International d'Histoire Maritime*, Paris, SEVPEN, 1958, pp. 53–106

Lopez, R.S. *Studi sull'economia genovese nel medio evo*, Torino Lattes, 1936

——. *The Birth of Europe*, New York, Evans, 1966

Lopez, R.S. and Raymond, I.W. *Medieval Trade in the Mediterranean World*, New York, Columbia University Press, 1955

Marcus, G.J. *The Conquest of the North Atlantic*, Suffolk, Boydell Press, 1980

Mollat du Jourdin, M. *Europe and the Sea*, Oxford, Blackwell, 1993

Nowell, C.E., *The Great Discoveries and the First Colonial Empires*, Cornell University Press, 1954

Olschki, L. *Marco Polo's Precursors*, Baltimore, Johns Hopkins, 1943

Parry, J.H. *The Discovery of the Sea*, Berkeley, 1981

Pirenne, H. *Mahomet et Charlemagne*, Paris, PUF, 1970

Pryor, J.H. *Geography, Technology and War-Studies in the Maritime History of the Mediterranean, 649–1571*, Cambridge University Press, 1988

Richard, J. 'L'Extrême Orient légendaire au M.A. – Roi David et Prêtre Jean', *Annales d'Éthiopie* II, 1957, pp. 225–42

——. 'Les navigations des occidentaux dans l'Océan Indien et la Mer Caspiènne' in M. Mollat (ed.), *Sociétés et compagnies de commerce en Orient et dans l'Océan Indien, Travaux du huitième Colloque International d'Histoire Maritime*, Paris, SEVPEN, 1970, pp. 353–63

Roërie, G. de la. 'Les transformations du gouvernail', *Annales d'Histoire Économique et Sociale*, 1935, pp. 564–83

Sawyer, P.H. *The Age of the Vikings*, London, Arnold, 1962

Shahar, S. *The Legacy of the Middle Ages*, Tel Aviv, Open University, 1985

Singer, C. *et al* (eds.). *History of Technology*, Oxford, Clarendon, 1964

Squire, J.C. (ed.). *If It Had Happened Otherwise*, New York, St. Martin's Press, 1972, pp. vii–xiii

Stussi, A. 'Un testamento volgaro scritto in Persia nel 1263', *L'Italia dialettale*, Pisa n.s. II 25, 1962, pp. 23–37

Taylor, E.G.R. *The Haven-finding Art, from Odysseus to Captain Cook*, London, Hollis and Carter, 1956

Tibbets, G.R. *Arab Navigation in the Indian Ocean Before the Portuguese*, London Royal Asiatic Society, 1971

Tolkowsky, S. *They Took to the Sea, A Historical Survey of Jewish Maritime Activities*, New York, Barnes, 1964

Toussaint, A. 'La course et la piraterie dans l'Océan Indien' in M. Mollat (ed.), *Course et Piraterie, Travaux du quinzième Colloque International d'Histoire Maritime*, Paris, CNRS, 1975, pp. 703–43

Trapier, B. *Les Voyageurs Arabes au Moyen Age*, Paris, Gallimard, 1937

Unger, R.W. *The Ship in the Medieval Economy, 600–1600*, London, Croom-Helm, 1980

Villain-Gandossi, C., Busuttil, S. and Adam, P. (eds.). *Medieval ships and the birth of technological societies*, Malta Foundation of International Studies, 1989–92

Washburn, W.E. (ed.). *Proceedings of the Vinland Map Conference*, Chicago University Press, 1971

White, L. Jr 'The Expansion of Technology, 500–1500', *The Fontana Economic History of Europe*, Vol. I, Ch. IV, 1969

Yoshinobu, S. *Commerce and Society in Sung China*, Ann Arbor, Michigan Abstracts no. 2, Mark Elvin (trs.), 1970

Ziadeh, N. *Geography and Travel of the Arabs*, Beirut, 1980 (in Arabic)

8

THE DEVELOPMENT OF THE COMMAND OF SEA POWER IN THE NINETEENTH AND TWENTIETH CENTURIES

James Eberle

I am neither a historian nor an academic, but I want here first to trace a little of the history of the command of sea power in the nineteenth and early twentieth centuries; secondly, in the light of my own experience, to bring this history up to date in the post-Second World War era, in the field that we now refer to as C3I (command, control, communication and intelligence – to which a fourth C – for computers, and even a fifth C for consultation, are now sometimes added); and then to attempt very briefly to outline a few major concerns for the future. My subject is that command of sea power, but the interdependence of land, sea and air operations today is such that considerations of naval command can only sensibly be made within a tri-service context.

I think understandably this discussion is skewed towards the modern rather than the ancient and, in preparing it, I became acutely aware of the enormous extent and comprehensive nature of the subject, and, more seriously for me, and perhaps you too, the inadequacies of my knowledge of it. It is one of my deepest regrets that my study of history at the Naval College at Dartmouth was somewhat lacking in depth and understanding. I don't think I got much beyond memorizing the names of famous admirals and the dates of their notable sea battles! It is perhaps not surprising that for a young boy in 1940 the idea that the pen might be mightier than the sword seemed totally absurd, and that I therefore concentrated nearly all of my efforts on the science of my newly chosen profession. It was very much later in my career that I fully realized the extent of my inadequacies in this respect, which were only partly rectified when as a naval captain, I spent a very pleasant year at the university as a Defence Fellow.

Nevertheless, I am in little doubt that the problems of the command of sea power, though influenced by history, are dominated by advances in technology, particularly communication technology. But technology cannot be expected to solve every problem. Admiral Lord Mountbatten, when he was the national and NATO Commander-in-Chief in Malta, once put it this way:

In the time of one of my great predecessors in the Mediterranean, when Lord Nelson had an urgent matter on which he required a response from the Admiralty Board in London, a letter was written in longhand and given to the coxswain of a small boat for it to be rowed across and given to the hand of a frigate captain, together with his orders to proceed with all despatch to England. The frigate would set sail, pass through the straights of Gibraltar, across the Bay of Biscay and up the Channel. With reasonably fair winds, the ship would arrive at Portsmouth several weeks later. The letter would then be given to a man on a horse who would gallop up to London and deliver the letter for the consideration of the Lords of the Admiralty, sitting in that lovely Admiralty board room in London that the Board still uses.

Their Lordships would consider their response, which would be written out by the secretary, and the process would be reversed. And if the westerlies in the Channel were not too strong, and the captain did not forget to turn left at Gibraltar, some six months later, Nelson received his reply. 'How different things are today'. 'If I have an urgent matter upon which I need a decision from their Lordships, I can have a message on their desks in London within minutes. And six months later, I get the reply!'

Let me start in a general sense by trying to draw two distinctions. I believe it is helpful to distinguish between what I like to call 'political direction' and 'military command'. I do not wish here to attempt to establish rigorous definitions, although definition is of course necessary where precision is required. (The armed services also have different ways both of doing things and of saying things. If you tell the Army to secure a building, they will post an armed sentry at the front door, place a machine-gun on the roof and sandbag the rear approaches. If you tell the Navy to secure a building, they will close the windows, turn out the lights, lock the doors and go home. If you say to the Air Force, secure a building, it means take out a twenty-five year lease with an option to buy after ten years!) However, in agreed UK and NATO terminology, command is 'the military authority and responsibility of a superior office to issue orders to subordinates. It covers every aspect of military operations and administration, and exists only within national services.' Thus, although our sovereign has 'command' of the British armed forces, ministers of the Crown do not. Command as a personal authority to issue orders and have them obeyed is a military function vested only in those who wear uniform. It is, in Britain, a special authority, backed by its own parliamentary law, the Armed Forces Act.

Nevertheless, today the Chief of the Defence staff is accountable to the Secretary of State for Defence for tendering advice on military operations and on the military implications of defence policy, and it is through this accountability that the primacy of civil control over the military is exercised. Thus, in operational terms, the Secretary of State has the power of 'direction', not the power of 'command'. This seemingly rather arcane distinction is based on the very special nature of military service, under which a serviceman can be required to risk or even to lose his life without the option of lawful refusal. This applies throughout the uniformed services, in which there is the fundamental principle that all ranks share the same risks and rewards. Thus, if mutual confidence is to be maintained, operational orders – that is command – can only come from a uniformed officer.

The second distinction that it is necessary to make is between the strategic level of command and the tactical level. At the tactical level at sea, the process is concerned with the manoeuvring and fighting of ships of a task force to complete an assigned operational task, which in modern parlance is described as 'tactical control'. At the strategic level, there is clearly a much wider field in which military judgement is required to determine the pattern of naval operations required to meet declared political objectives, to decide the allocation of forces, to assign operational tasks and to decide priorities.

There is a further politico-strategic level that is concerned more with defence policy and the conceptual aspects of sea power than with operational strategy and the command of sea power. However, we will find that it is not easy to draw firm lines of demarcation, for military judgement must be a factor in determining defence policy at the strategic level; and political considerations can impact even at the tactical level.

A very early example of this can be found in the battle of Toulon in February 1744 when a combined Spanish and French fleet under the command of the French Admiral de Court was ordered by the King of France to sail from Toulon and to seek out and attack the British ships under Admiral Mathews, which were attempting to blockade the combined fleet in Toulon. Britain was at war with Spain, but France was not directly involved and a formal state of war between Britain and France did not exist. Admiral de Court's orders read thus:

> His Majesty wishes his ships to be employed only as auxiliaries to the Spanish in this expedition, and desires M. de Court when he is in range of the English ships – if they do not commence the action – to cause them to be attacked by the Spanish ships, which should engage them in such a manner that it cannot afterwards be said that hostile acts have been committed by His Majesty's ships before the declaration of War.

In the years leading up to the nineteenth century, the source of the strategic direction of Britain's naval power was the Sovereign. It was the King who issued directives to his admirals. Sometimes these were delivered direct, but at other times through a Secretary of State, and occasionally through the Board of Admiralty. These directives often came as the result of a recommendation from the Cabinet, a body that obtained its professional advice on maritime matters from the First Lord of the Admiralty, who was sometimes an admiral and sometimes a politician. Their content was often unclear and muddled.

Because of this, reinforced by the complexities of eighteenth-century politics, the lack of a clear intelligence picture in London and the slow speed of communication, particular to ships at sea, such directives were the subject of much necessary local interpretation and re-interpretation. Frequent councils of war, sometimes at sea, were held in which available local authorities took decisions of both a political and a military nature, based on their most up-to-date information and local circumstances. As Nelson wrote to his wife in 1795, 'Political courage in an officer is as highly necessary as military courage.' Nevertheless, the existence of a formal declaration of war did provide a welcome degree of freedom of action for commanders at sea, although the prospective rewards of both fame and fortune, which could result from a successful engagement, were at any time a powerful incentive for individuals to seek the initiative, to be audacious and to take bold, decisive action.

At the tactical level, the characteristics of engagements between the clumsy, sail fighting ships of the time provided little opportunity for tactical innovation. The integrity of the line of battle was fundamental, and superiority in numbers and fighting skills were the key to success. As the ability of the admiral to issue orders to his other ships immediately before, and in the course of, the battle improved with the use of flag signals, so the sailing and fighting instructions for the fleet grew in complexity and sophistication. (An alphabet-based flag hoist system, which enabled a commander to pass messages to other ships, rather than just initiate prearranged fighting instructions, such as 'close the enemy', was only introduced on a navy-wide basis in 1805. At a later date such local signalling was done by morse code using a signal light. Today it is, of course, almost all done by voice radio.) As the complexity of the fighting instructions grew, so gradually the rigidity of the eighteenth-century 'rules of battle' began to give way to the modest encouragement of a degree of personal initiative on the part of individual captains, marked perhaps by Nelson's manoeuvre at St Vincent, which clearly broke the rules, but was subsequently warmly approved by Jervis, and more popularly by his use of his blind eye at Copenhagen. This general rigidity in set piece naval engagements was in some contrast to the land battle, of which the Duke of Wellington wrote during the Peninsular war:

Nobody in the British army ever reads a regulation or an order as if it were to be a guide to his conduct or in other manner than as an amusing novel; and the consequence is that when complicated arrangements are to be carried into execution . . . every gentleman proceeds according to his fancy.

Each admiral also promulgated his own instructions, which laid down the way he expected his captains to handle their ships in battle, and reflected his personal convictions with regard to such issues as whether, once close action had been joined, it was better to fight from the windward or the leeward side of one's opponent. From this particular issue there arose the one innovative tactic that Nelson (as most every schoolboy used to know) employed with such success at Trafalgar – that of deliberately breaking through the enemy line of battle.

With the end of the Napoleonic Wars, British naval power went through a period of decline, when the Navy was more involved in the support of the army in native wars abroad than in countering the threat of another ocean-going navy. Thus it was not until the latter decades of the nineteenth century, with technical innovation, the replacement of sail by steam, the use of steel rather than wood for ship-building, the invention of the torpedo, and spurred by the threat of German and Russian naval expansion, that the field of naval tactical development and ideas about the use and control of sea power once more became issues of importance and dispute.

While the introduction of steam gave rise to a great deal of discussion and intellectual argument about evolving concepts of sea power, and to the strategy and tactics of the great new navy that was being created, there was little opportunity to test or practise these effectively at sea, and with the innate conservatism that was a hallmark of the Royal Navy of this period, real progress was slow. The conservative nature of mariners is not confined to the British. Franklin D. Roosevelt once noted of the US Navy Department:

The Treasury is so large and far flung that I find it almost impossible to get the action and results I want . . . But the Treasury is not to be compared to the State Department. You should go through the experience of trying to get any changes in the thinking, policy and action of the career diplomats and then you will know what a real problem was. But the Treasury and the State Department put together are nothing compared with the Navy. To change anything in the Navy is like punching a feather bed. You punch it with your right and you punch it with your left until you are exhausted; and then you find the darn bed just as it was before you started punching.

If intellectual progress was slow, technical progress was not. New developments, driven chiefly by new science and new technology and its application by the ship-builders and armament producers, came apace. With the dawn of the new century, the increasing speed of ships driven by the new steam turbines; the increasing range, accuracy and rate of fire of naval gunnery that followed the introduction of breech-loading guns; the letting of electrical transmission systems; the advent of wireless telegraphy; the invention of an effective ocean-going submarine; the introduction of class-building all required a revolution throughout the navy, a revolution for which its earlier mastery of the seas had ill prepared it. For was it not Edmund Burke who wrote:

Of all the public Services, the Navy is the one in which tampering may be of the greatest danger, which can be worst supplied in an emergency, and of which failure draws after it the largest and heaviest train of consequences.

The Navy was not prepared to be tampered with. Thus the intellectual 'push' for new ideas came principally not from within the Navy but from a small group of intellectuals and Members of Parliament.

I remember being surprised, when I was Commander-in-Chief of the Fleet, to discover the comment of a predecessor of mine. It was Admiral Sir Arthur Wilson who, at the time of the arguments in 1911 that led up to the introduction of a Naval Staff at the Admiralty, said: 'The Service would have the most supreme contempt for any body of officers who profess to be specially trained to think . . . Officers are judged by what they can do when afloat.' Other contemporary comment on the utility of the fleet submarine as a weapon of war was similarly blinkered. There was, however, some conspicuous precedent. In 1828 the then First Lord of the Admiralty wrote:

Their Lordships feel it their bounden duty to discourage to the utmost of their ability the employment of steam vessels, as they consider the introduction of steam is calculated to strike a fatal blow at the supremacy of the Empire!

The formation within the Admiralty in 1879 of a Naval Intelligence Division was an early and important development, which was, and continues, to have a vital influence on the development of the control of sea power. Indeed, it was the Naval Intelligence Division that was later to become the embryo of the Naval Staff.

Intelligence is about information – information about your own side as well as about the enemy. One of my favourite interchanges of signals between the Admiralty and the Fleet went as follows:

Admiralty to Destroyer: 'Raise steam and proceed with all despatch. Acknowledge.'
Destroyer to Admiralty: 'Your . . . Acknowledged. What destination?'
Admiralty to Destroyer: 'Your destination is Aden.'
Destroyer to Admiralty: 'I am at Aden.'

The characteristics that define intelligence as a special subset of information merit a study in their own right. I would merely note here that the very highly classified intelligence that was brought out of Russia under extraordinarily difficult and dangerous conditions at the time of the Bolshevik revolution, by secret agents such as Sydney Reilly, was no more than one would today expect to read as political commentary in a daily newspaper. It is also important to recognize that intelligence is not just about what you know, but also about how you use and organize information.

I will digress for a moment to comment on the more sturdy operational independence that had by this time gripped the individual naval officer. Lt Walter Cowan, who was later awarded the VC and became an admiral, but then commanding a torpedo boat in support of the newly fledged MI6 intelligence operations in the Baltic, came across the Red Cruiser *Oleg* bombarding one of the White Russian Ports. Having telegraphed London for instructions, he was told to confine himself to his intelligence duties. He interpreted this as giving him, the man on the spot, the right to define what his intelligence duties were, and promptly torpedoed and sank the *Oleg* to the considerable embarrassment of the British Government. It is difficult to imagine a parallel today!

It was principally the availability at the Admiralty of special intelligence, derived from radio intercepts of the worldwide network of communication that was becoming the hallmark of naval operations, and the navy's ability to use this in support of the defence of the rapidly growing global network of maritime trade routes, that brought about an important difference between the First Sea Lord as Chief of the Naval Staff and his Army and later his Air Force counterparts. While the latter were empowered to issue directives to their appropriate military commanders, the First Sea Lord was also responsible to the First Lord for the 'issue of orders to the Fleet affecting war operations and the movement of ships, which orders may be issued in his own name in his capacity as Chief of the Naval Staff'. The Chief of the Air Staff and the Chief of the Imperial General Staff had no similar function or authority.

This direct operational control function of the Admiralty carried with it two clear disadvantages. First, it created uncertainty in the Chain of Command to ships at sea. Who was driving the task force: the First Sea Lord or the Commander-in-Chief? The consequences of such uncertainty were sadly illustrated in the Second World War by the tragic events concerning the Arctic convoy PQ17. Second, it confused the matter of principle as to whether the Admiralty (and later the Ministry of Defence) was a Department of State for the administration of the armed forces, or a military headquarters for the conduct of military operations in peace and in war. That question remains to be satisfactorily answered to this day.

Nevertheless, and particularly in the field of anti-submarine operations, the part played by the Admiralty's Operational Intelligence Centre made a vital contribution to Britain's success in both world wars. Somewhere in the post-Second World War period the naval operational intelligence organization rather lost its way. The Admiralty concentrated its intelligence efforts on obtaining technical data about Soviet ships and their weapons. The Naval Staff and the material divisions concentrated on the improvement of the various very successful radio direction-finding devices that had proved so valuable against the German Second World War submarines. Others concentrated on the improvement of action data systems. However, nobody began seriously to develop the idea of intelligence as a tactical weapon of warfare at sea.

With the introduction of the nuclear-propelled submarine, the whole character of naval warfare changed radically. No longer could the submarine's role as a 'fleet unit' be seen to be little more than that of a mobile and reloadable mine. The conventionally powered submarine still represented a major threat to the supply lines of maritime trade and of military re-enforcement, but the speed, endurance, weapon potential and difficulty of detecting and effectively counter-attacking the nuclear submarine, now also comprising an element of the nuclear deterrent force, posed a new and severe threat to the operations of the surface navy, in which the aircraft carrier had replaced the battleship as the major unit. The main thrust of tactical development, which, under the impetus of the Second World War carrier operations in the Pacific had been concentrated on the protection of the carrier from air attack, and which had led to the development of several generations of new surface-to-air and air-to-air guided missiles, now turned towards countering the nuclear submarine.

Let me now backtrack. Setting aside the operational role of the Chief of Naval Staff ashore at the Admiralty in London, to which I have already referred, the control of maritime operations had traditionally been in the hands of a Commander-in-Chief of a Fleet, operating from his flagship at sea or in harbour, as the situation demanded. The system was well tried and trusted. Despite the disaster in the First World War of the Dardanelles, there was little enthusiasm in the interwar period for inter-service cooperation. While the committee of Imperial Defence, both in the First World War and thereafter, could have been an effective instrument of political direction of military operations and of inter-service cooperation, it was not in practice used this way and achieved little beyond some success in coordinating the mobilization of the country's resources for the forthcoming conflict, and in considering the machinery of Government that would be required in war. The responsibility for coordinating the direction of operations after the outbreak of war remained loose and poorly defined. It was not adequate for a new type of warfare that demanded for success the closest possible cooperation of the land, sea and air forces. Lord Ismay wrote of the Norwegian Campaign of 1940: 'The chief of the General Staff and the Chief of the Naval Staff appointed their respective commanders without consultation with each other; and worse still, they gave directives to those Commanders without harmonising them.'

After 1940, gradually and almost informally under the personal leadership of Winston Churchill, and with the formation of the Defence Committee (Operations), Whitehall grew into a highly efficient organization for the direction of the war. Lord Ismay wrote:

With all the powers and authority which attach to the office of Prime Minister, Winston Churchill exercised a personal, direct, ubiquitous and continuous supervision, not only of military policy at every stage, but also over the general conduct of military operations. . . . All the considerations affecting any problem, political and economic as well as military, could now be brought into focus more readily, and thanks to Mr Churchill's personal exercise of the wide powers given to him by the war cabinet, and to his astonishing drive, firm decisions could be reached and translated into action far more quickly than had hitherto been the case. For the first time in their history, the Chiefs of Staff were in direct and continuous contact with the head of the Government, and were able to act as a combined battle headquarters – a superchief of a war staff in commission – as had always been contemplated.

In Mr Churchill's own words:

The key change on my taking over was, of course, the supervision and direction of the Chiefs of Staff Committee by a Minister of Defence with undefined powers including selection and removal of all professional and political personages. Thus for the first time, the Chiefs of Staff Committee assumed its due and proper place in direct contact with the executive head of Government and in accord with him had full control over the conduct of the war and the armed forces.

At the operational end it took rather longer to reach a satisfactory unity of command. Throughout the war in the Eastern Mediterranean, operational command was exercised by three service commanders, each separately responsible to Whitehall. There was no supreme commander. This system worked with a degree of success which varied according to the circumstances and with the individual personalities of the commanders involved. Nevertheless, even during the periods when cooperation was at its closest, one cannot help but be struck in reading the memoirs of this period by the time and effort that was involved in discussion and argument over who controlled what.

With the entry of the Americans into the North African Campaign, with the setting up of the South-East Asia Command and the preparations for Operation Overlord, the concept of a supreme theatre commander with commanders of the ground, air and naval forces directly under his command, and the formation of an inter-service, inter-allied planning staff, became a reality, although not without some initial difficulties.

Unfortunately the success of this Supreme Command organization did not spread into the British post-war organization, either in Whitehall or in the field. Despite a recommendation from Admiral Mountbatten that a Supreme Command organization should be retained in the Far East Command in peacetime, the political and military coordination of overseas defence was placed in the hands of Military Coordinating Committees, on which sat the senior local British political representatives and military commanders. Such committees were set up in the Far East, the Persian Gulf, East Africa and the Middle East.

From the naval point of view it became increasingly clear that, despite the symbolic disadvantage of the fleet being separated from its commander-in-chief, the proper place of the fleet commander was ashore alongside his two other service colleagues. The necessity of this 'move ashore' was further emphasized by the increasing complexity of administration and of logistics. The numbers of staff to deal with them just could not reasonably be accommodated afloat. Thus all of the fleet commanders moved ashore.

In due course the concept of the 'Unified Command' became accepted. This was a significant step along the road from 'Joint Command', in which no single point of final decision or authority existed, to 'Supreme Command', in which there was a comprehensive command structure with full authority over subordinate single service or functional commands. The first Unified Commander, to whom the single service commanders were responsible in matters of the operational efficiency and training of the forces under their control and the detailed conduct of their operations, was set up in Aden on 1 October 1959. (The single service commanders nevertheless retained a direct line of responsibility on administrative matters to their own authorities in London.) Unified Command in the Far East was formally established in 1962, and proved itself thoroughly competent in dealing successfully with operations during the years of 'confrontation' with Indonesia – operations in which the Navy was heavily involved.

At this same time in London, Admiral Mountbatten was working progressively towards the setting up of a unified Ministry of Defence under the military charge of a chief of defence staff with authority over the three single service chiefs of staff, a process that has only recently been completed but is still evolving.

It has to be noted that, in the formation of NATO, the need for political compromise overcame the military lessons of the Second World War in the matter of Supreme Command. NATO was not given one supreme commander; it was given three (major NATO commanders as they were formally and more properly designated). They were the Supreme Commander Europe (SACEUR), the Supreme Commander Atlantic (SACLANT), and the Allied Commander in Chief Channel (CINCHAN), the latter being of equal status to SACEUR and SACLANT, despite having limited forces and a limited task compared with those of his two fellow major NATO commanders (MNCs). The origin of the Channel Command was the result of Churchill's insistence that the command of the vital sea areas of the western approaches and the North Sea, and of the major part of the British Fleet, could not be entrusted to an American admiral seated 3,000 miles away in Norfolk, Virginia.

These three MNCs all had allocated naval forces. While they were, in theory, responsible to the chairman of the NATO Military Committee, it was not practicable for the Military Committee to act as an effective coordinating authority in the chain of operational command. This was a serious weakness of the system. It still exists today, although the number of supreme commands has been reduced to two. While in the early days of NATO it was often said that SACEUR and SACLANT were preparing to fight entirely different wars, under later personalities there was good coordination between the supremos. In my day the three MNCs met regularly together and with the Secretary General and the Chairman of the Military Committee to keep each other in touch with developments. As well as wearing the hat of a supreme commander as CINCHAN, I was, in a different hat, a subordinate commander to SACLANT in my role as Commander-in-Chief Eastern Atlantic. Such overlaps greatly assisted good coordination. Nevertheless, good coordination is no substitute for short clear lines of command.

Let me again digress slightly. In the Falklands (Malvinas) war a very short chain of command led from the prime minister, supported by a small 'war cabinet', direct to the chief of defence and thence to the overall operational commander, the Commander-in-Chief of the Fleet at his headquarters at Northwood. This permitted the crisp decision-making that was essential to success. That there was no overall commander in the operational area (Admiral Woodward only commanded the carrier forces that operated in support of the inshore operations) is a matter of some contention, and I will leave detailed investigation of its impact to some aspiring modern historian when in due course all of the records become available. There was, however, one notable failure of command that has curiously attracted little public attention. Some of the lessons of joint warfare planning, learned at such cost in the Second World War and subsequently maintained in currency by the Joint Warfare School until its closure, were forgotten. The consequences could have been disastrous. Briefly, what happened was this.

There was confusion as to the role of 3 Brigade and 5 Brigade. Having seized the bridgehead, the 3 Brigade commander was expecting 5 Brigade to land and take on the next phase of the operation – the break out from the bridgehead. London, however, was not prepared to accept the delay that would have resulted, so 3 Brigade had to be ordered to move, even though its commander did not consider that he had sufficiently consolidated his position and was therefore not yet ready to move. There followed very shortly afterwards the attack at Goose Green, where British forces prevailed only through the remarkable bravery and spirit of the Paras. This command misunderstanding was the result of inadequate joint planning. The consequences of it could have been very serious indeed.

Thus the recent announcement of the setting up of a standing joint force operational headquarters at the headquarters of the Commander-in-Chief of Fleet at Northwood is much to be welcomed.

Let me return to NATO and illustrate the sort of command problems that were faced as a result of divided command by a story of my own experience during a visit to North Norway.

I was talking with the NATO commander, N. Norway, whose operational area extended 50 miles to seaward of North Cape. He was responsible to the Supreme Commander Europe for the control of this sea area. He commanded some well armed coastal vessels and submarines. As the NATO Commander-in-Chief Eastern Atlantic, I was responsible to the Supreme Commander Atlantic for the adjacent sea area. I said to him:

Let us assume that war has broken out and we see a Soviet Amphibious Face sail from the Northern Fleet base. It is now passing some 60 miles North of North Cape. We know from signals intelligence that its destination is Iceland – and not North Norway. The weather is good and your naval forces are not otherwise engaged. Can I assume that you would send your forces to attack, even though the target is in my area and not yours? Or do I have to send a formal request to you via SACEUR? What would you do?

He thought for a few moments and then replied: 'I would feel very sorry for the Icelanders'!!

There will, of course, always be problems when it is necessary to establish any command boundary, and much effort was expended within NATO in arguing about the appropriate demarcation of operational boundaries, particularly at sea. These arguments often rested more on political than on military grounds. However, the harmonization of procedures that minimized the operational impact of a unit crossing from the command area of one authority to that of another did much to reduce these problems.

Another major weakness of the system, and a regular item for discussions with the Secretary General, then Joseph Luns, was the lack of any definition of who was to be the supreme political authority directing the war. The Defence Planning Committee, comprising the fourteen ambassadors to NATO in Brussels, and chaired by the Secretary General, was clearly not a suitable body. In practical terms, power lay in Washington.

However, following the demise in 1966 of the 'Standing Group' in Washington as a consequence of the French withdrawal from the military structure of the Alliance, there was no organization there for effective and timely politico-military consultation in the event of war. The best that we could get from the Secretary General was the contention that, after the outbreak of war, it was all up to us, the military commanders, to which our response was that there was no way that we were going to allow our political masters to 'opt out', just when things were getting hot! Our NATO command exercises failed to highlight this problem because they almost invariably stopped at the moment of the outbreak of hostilities. The best we managed to do was to investigate some of the problems of de-escalation and of stopping the war once it had run at least part of its course. As far as I am aware, the situation remains equally unsatisfactory today, although it can be argued that the resolution of this problem is of less importance.

Let me return to matters of intelligence. Ships on the high seas are out of sight and, from the public perspective, also out of mind. For generations, proponents of sea power have declaimed the ability of a naval force to remain 'hull down' over the horizon in international waters, undetected but ready to engage in action at very short notice. To a very large degree the ability of surface ships to remain undetected on the high seas has gone. The combination of improved methods of active and passive detection, together with the ability of satellites to carry the appropriate sensors and to relay their information back to fixed and mobile stations, means that for today's major powers the surface warship has 'no place to hide'. Under the sea surface, the picture is more complex. Passive acoustic detection devices in fixed arrays such as the US SOSUS system, and mobile arrays carried by submarines and surface ships, have lifted much of the veil of opacity that once made the presence of a submarine so difficult to detect. A technological battle has been waged, and still goes on, between measures to quieten the submarine and thus reduce the chance of its detection, and others to improve the acoustic sensors and the computer processing of their information, thus improving detectability. However, it still remains difficult and costly to detect and localize the position of a well handled submarine.

Perhaps the most important development in the intelligence field that has a profound effect on the control of maritime operations has been the linking of strategic and tactical intelligence into computer-based systems that communicate automatically with each other by secure high-speed data links, thus allowing ships and shore headquarters to share a common, comprehensive, real-time intelligence picture. Strategic intelligence has, at least in the public mind, mainly been associated with radio interception, code-breaking and traffic analysis. These matters are principally handled by GCHQ Cheltenham. In the UK we were slow to appreciate that advances in these techniques, which provide the basic inputs to strategic analysis, could also provide valuable information at the tactical level.

We were also slow to appreciate that the techniques that had been developed for strategic intelligence could also be adapted for direct tactical use in shipboard systems. Let me tell a story from my personal experience.

Some years ago I was in command of a NATO task group in the Mediterranean due to carry out an exercise involving the largest-scale amphibious landing since D-Day. The command facilities of my flagship, HMS *Hermes*, were not well suited to the control of such a large force. I therefore requested the US Commander-in-Chief for permission to fly my flag and command the operation from a US warship. It was quickly approved.

To my surprise I then received a visit from a US officer who gave me a detailed briefing on some then highly secret and sensitive equipment, of which I had never heard, that was fitted in the US command ship. That equipment provided tactical intelligence of a sophisticated nature that was entirely novel to me. As the exercise proceeded, I was enormously impressed by its performance and potential, and very soon after sent an urgent report to the First Sea Lord. As a result of one of the quickest major equipment programmes that the Navy has handled, that equipment became fitted in British warships.

It subsequently transpired that the US Navy had tried to 'lift the curtain' on what it was doing in this vital field, but the Royal Navy had failed to appreciate the importance of what the Americans were trying to tell it. Fortunately, we did not 'drop this pass', and a very important step was taken towards improving our command capability at sea.

There have been two other developments to which I would like to refer that have had a major impact on the UK's ability to make the most effective use of its sea power. The first is the development of simulators for tactical and strategic war gaming. During the Second World War was witnessed for the first time the significant application of scientific method to the development of anti-submarine warfare tactics. These were played out on a 'tactical floor' ashore, where ships' captains in a 'cubicle', supported by their principal tactical advisers, manoeuvred their ships in set moves in accordance with the latest doctrine. They received and transmitted action information so as to defend a convoy, as an offensive surface action group, or to counter the moves of enemy submarines. It was sometimes expensive for a captain to make a tactical blunder, for fines were raised in aid of the Royal National Lifeboat Institute (RNLI), but to be sunk sometimes had its reward in allowing the shipwrecked crew to peep behind the curtain, where the Women's Royal Navy Service (WRNS) was busy maintaining the floor plot, and to select the prettiest member to chat up and get advice on how to do better next time, for the WRNS became very expert in the appropriate tactics. Perhaps they ought then to have been employed at sea!

The tactical floor was not only a very valuable training ground but also a valuable tool of tactical development. This value was recognized by the post-war formation of the Royal Naval Tactical School at Woolwich, which is now housed at HMS *Dryad* near Portsmouth. The advent of computer simulation has permitted games of much greater complexity to be played in real time and with a far greater degree of realism. Training courses are interspersed with periods allocated to the investigation of tactical problems and to the refinements of operational tactics and techniques.

There have been parallel developments of gaming at the strategic level. The US War College at Newport has played a major part in introducing the techniques of war gaming, and permitting senior national and NATO commanders to rehearse possible scenarios of East–West military confrontation. At another level, command exercises, using the 'real live' headquarters, have been principally aimed at rehearsing the routines of the transition to war and have been valuable in identifying problem areas, and in improving procedures and techniques. One of the most daunting problems is posed by the sheer mass of information that has to be moved round the system. At peak periods, my NATO headquarters at Northwood were dealing with more than 3,000 signal messages a day. Even with good organization and computer assistance, it is not difficult for a commander, ashore or afloat, to become overwhelmed with information. I used to tell my staff that they had to have a ready appreciation of what it is that the captain at sea really needs to know. I used to illustrate this with the story of the escort at sea in the Atlantic in December 1941 when the senior officer of an Atlantic escort force, protecting a convoy from Halifax to Liverpool, was in deep trouble. An attack by a German submarine 'wolf pack' had resulted in a number of the merchant ships being sunk and the remainder scattered. His own corvette had been damaged and his captain injured. He was trying against great difficulties to reform the convoy since it was reported that another 'wolf pack' was gathering in its path. The weather was bad and deteriorating.

At that time of tension, he was informed that a most urgent, secret and important signal had arrived in the ship and was being decoded. When the plain language version of the signal was rushed to him he read: 'Commence hostilities against Japan.' This was not a thought that was then uppermost in his mind.

The other development of great significance is that of what we call 'Rules of Engagement'. These were a British invention, sold to NATO, designed to improve the ability for crisis management. They were a response to the growing post-war awareness that there was no longer a clear dividing line between peace and war – a line that was once provided by the formal declaration of state of war. Rules of engagement were established as a formalized set of instructions as to the limits of action that a commander was authorized to take. They took the form of positive and negative instructions to the man on the spot. Some were of the form 'You may . . .', and others 'You may not . . .'. Like many good ideas they rapidly developed a life of their own and were expanded to cover almost every readily conceivable situation; and some others that were not. They became popular with politicians, for they permitted a degree of fine political control that had never before been available. They were less popular with commanders at sea because they inhibited their freedom of action. My own fear was that they could as easily become a factor for instability as for stability. Let me explain. It is the task of the commander on the spot to seek appropriate rules of engagement to meet a particular situation; and to request changes to them as the situation develops. The approval by military and political authorities ashore inevitably takes time. On the assumption that a particular change of rules is approved, then it might be that, by the time this approval had reached the commander on the spot, the situation would have moved on to an extent that the change was no longer appropriate. As with any closed-loop system, the imposition of delay is a cause of instability. I campaigned vigorously for simplication of a system that, in my view, had become overcomplicated and self-defeating. With a measure of overstatement, I argued that the man on the spot in a fast-moving situation required only one piece of information from his political masters: he would wish to know whether they wanted him to escalate the confrontation, to de-escalate the situation, or to retain the status quo. It was then up to the commander on the spot to make the military judgements that would fulfil this basic instruction. I did not win, but did succeed in making some important simplifications, which remain.

Where does this leave us today? We need to recognize that, with the ending of the cold war and the break-up of the Soviet Empire, the western powers face a situation somewhat akin to that of the middle of the nineteenth century – there is no immediate prospect of a major war involving large fleets on the high seas. However, we cannot discount the possibility that such a situation might again arise in the future. At present it is not within our time horizon. Nevertheless, there are plenty of 'native wars' around the globe that can become a threat to global peace and security, the preservation of which is the responsibility of the United Nations in general and the permanent members of the UN Security Council in particular. Such wars can involved large-scale operations at sea, as in the Gulf war. However, unlike the native wars of the nineteenth century, those of today may involve the use on both sides of modern, powerful and sophisticated weaponry. The days when peacekeeping could effectively be conducted with the use of sidearms and sympathy are probably gone forever.

There is one particularly important point related to command and control in general that I would like to make here. Probably the greatest restraint on UN peacekeeping operations is the reluctance of member governments to provide the resources necessary for the effective conduct of such missions – many men and equipment. Member governments are, rightly, influenced by public opinion. If the price of participation is paid in the form of casualties (body bags), then public opinion can very quickly turn towards the cry 'bring our boys back home'. Such a movement will be greatly aggravated if it is believed that the casualties have arisen through political or military incompetence, through bad or inadequate command and control. Considerable progress has been made in improving the UN's procedures and structures for military command and control, but there is much still to be done.

Returning to the maritime scene, we also face increasing pressures, for a variety of reasons, for a greater degree of regulation on the high seas. The coming into force of the Law of the Sea Treaty in December 1995 has brought to conclusion a negotiating process spanning some twenty-five years. This treaty, however, deals mainly with the waters contiguous to member states. The attention of the maritime community, it seems to me, will now inevitably turn to matters of the high seas to ensure their peaceful use, to meet the needs of global environmental protection and to preserve the fisheries stock as we have recently seen in the Canadian–Spanish dispute over fishing in the Grand Banks.

In every situation there is a clear need for good intelligence, and for the global, rapid, secure and two-way exchange of information. This is what the modern C4I system provides. Such systems are, however, very sophisticated and very expensive, and their effectiveness requires us to maintain the very closest possible relationship in these matters with the United States. However, I believe that their very sophistication carries with it three particular dangers. The first danger is that everyone is working from the same database. That is fine and to be welcomed, provided that the database is accurate. If it is inaccurate, then everyone will make the same mistake. That could be fatal. In the past, the very fragmentation of the system introduced checks and balances that made such an event highly unlikely. Where in the system can we build in those vital checks and balances?

Secondly, the capability of modern communication systems encourages the process of centralization. It has been a fundamental tenet of twentieth-century naval operational philosophy to leave the commander on the spot a high degree of freedom of action. Because it is now possible to control naval opertions from remote headquarters ashore, are we sure that we are right to do this, and is there not a danger of remote micro-management?

Finally, have we blurred too much the distinction that I drew at the beginning of this discussussion between political direction and military command? It may be that a full analysis of the way that operations in the former republic of Yugoslavia have been conducted will give us a better feel for the answer. At this time the stream of political directives emanating from the Security Council in the form of UN resolutions, which have not been effectively enforceable in military terms, does not give me confidence that we have yet, certainly in global terms, got the political–military relationship right for the effective command of military power, of which sea power is still a major ingredient, in the complex and uncertain world that is the aftermath of the cold war.

9

THE SEA AND THE ENGLISH

John Keegan

Nowhere in England, geographers tell us, is more than 80 miles from the sea. Nor, it might be said, is anywhere in Ireland or Scotland or Wales, or indeed Sicily or Corsica or peninsular Italy. Yet it is not of the sea that one thinks at the mention of Ireland or Scotland – great ship-building country though it was – and certainly not Wales or Sicily or Corsica or even Italy. All those places mean quite different things altogether to outsiders: mountains, lakes, great cities, past civilizations, Celtic mist – but not the sea. The sea is English, to outsiders and insiders alike. To insiders the sea usually has particular rather than general significance. It is the rare English person who does not have his or her seaside, if not of the here and now then certainly of childhood memory. In our part of the world, west Wiltshire under the lip of Salisbury Plain, the seaside of the here and now is at Poole or Bournemouth. A few miles further north, inside Somerset, it is Minehead or Weston-super-Mare. Nearer Taunton it is Watchet or Westward Ho, while Shaftesbury and Yeovil folk look to Axmouth, Bridport or Lyme Regis.

All these seaside places command the loyalties of inland populations, and a shared loyalty is a bond between strangers, a share in a home from home. It is even more of a bond between friends. Eype in Dorset is a bond between my wife and myself. Long ago, before we ever met or, had we done so, were old enough to have felt a romantic interest in each other, that tiny fishing village a little west of Bridport was the place to which our parents took us on holiday, mine from London, hers from Wincanton. Its physical topography – Balloon Cottages, the Eypemouth Hotel, the New Inn, the Golden Cap, the Chesil Bank and the network of sunken lanes and overgrown footpaths that lead to the shingle where we took our freezing dips into the English Channel – belongs, as a result, to our emotional geography, and in a peculiarly intense form. There are other places, visited later, that belong to our family experience. It is one of the pleasures of England's smallness that it offers the opportunity of intimacy with not one seaside but many, and so we know the Norfolk sea marshes near Blakeney, the enormous cliffs of Hartland Point, the surfing sands at Bude and the crags of Cape Cornwall as well. To our children the tiny village of Bantham, at the mouth of the Devon Avon, visited year after year in the 1970s, has the same meaning as Eype does for their parents, and now our elder daughter is taking her children there as well, reinforcing old acquaintance and generating a new family mythology of 'our seaside', the first, the most enduring, among our grandchildren. Bantham has all the ingredients of an English child's seaside dream: sand, cliffs, rockpools, fishermen's cottages, holiday friendships to be annually renewed, the use of a boat, an estuary leading mysteriously inland and the very slight thrill of danger. To the external 'Don't get out of your depth, darling', Bantham parents can add 'Don't try to ford the river'. Still, for my wife and myself, nowhere will ever surpass Eype.

Other nations have seasides, of course. My sister and I belong to the generation that was despatched across the Channel each summer for the ritual of the holiday exchange, so that between us we have covered much Mr Hulot territory, including La Baule, Deauville, Trouville and the Ile de Ré, each with their small verandahed hotels, wealth of half-timbered holiday cottages, sandy tennis-courts, acres of campings and parkings, and swathes of scented pine plantations fringing the beach that gave aunts and mothers so much concern at what Marie-France and Jean-Pierre might be up to on those long walks they took to digest the two hour lunch that formed the centre-point of every *grandes vacances* afternoon.

Spain has a seaside, now largely ruined by the English; likewise Portugal, not yet desecrated, and Italy; and even Germany has a tiny fringe of sand and islands at the Friesian coast. The United States has some seaside along its thousands of miles of coastline, as does Australia and, though I have never visited that continent, South America. None of these, it seems to me, has a seaside in the English sense, or in geographical extent. It is one of the wonders of England, admittedly part of an island with an extraordinarily long coastline relative to its land area, thanks to its multitude of indentations and wide estuaries, that so small a country should possess so many outlets, so much access to the sea, and confront it in such a spectacular way. The American Atlantic Coast, except in Maine, is dull and low-lying, the Mediterranean countries' coasts are landlocked, the French coast is strangely devoid of harbours, and those of the Dutch, Belgian and German are short, flat and boggy. Only in England does the disjunction between land and ocean combine beauty, variety and utility in the striking form familiar to all of us.

The English relationship with the sea, I have begun by suggesting, is an emotional and social one; but emotion and sociability came late in English life, long after geographical facts had worked to make England what it is and to allow emotion and sociability room for play. England enjoys extraordinary geographical advantages in its relationship both with its near neighbours and with more distant lands. It is those that made it a great European power and eventually, through its European triumphs, the world's leading empire. Let us take the strategic view. Access to the oceans remains, even in the age of air transport and unified continental land transport systems, a major economic benefit. Russia, by comparison with England, is lacking in this advantage. So, too, is Germany, since its North Sea coastline is short and its Baltic outlets are landlocked, a condition applying also to Sweden and Denmark. Norway, better positioned, lacks the resources to be a commercial maritime nation because its topography limits its population. France has many of England's advantages, but its Channel ports are overshadowed by the English coast, while its Atlantic coast has few sheltered harbours. Portugal deprives Spain of much of its access to the Atlantic but is too small and unfavoured to sustain any great maritime effort. Those countries with long coastlines in the Mediterranean all look along the inland sea to the barrier of the Pillars of Hercules, of which Gibraltar, the key to the Atlantic outlet, was fated to fall into, and thus far to remain, in English hands.

Strategically, therefore, England dominates the seaward approaches to and exits from northern Europe. Traffic from the Baltic finds East Anglia, the Thames and Medway ports, and Kent athwart its outward passage; so too, does that from the great rivers, the Rhine and the Meuse, the avenues of movement inside north-western Europe, and from the lowland ports of Holland and Belgium. The whole length of the northern French coast, from Dunkirk to Ushant, is duplicated by the English coast from the Downs to Scilly. Thus it is that no fleet – naval or merchant – can approach or leave North Atlantic Europe without passing under England's maritime shadow.

In England's early history the shadow always fell inwards rather than outwards, Caesar came to Britannia by sea and so did Claudius. One of the great works of the Romans, in the declining years of their occupation, was to build the forts of the Saxon Shore, many of them still visible, to guard the province against the depredations of the fierce Teutonic sea peoples of the North European coast. Later, when land hunger drove the Scandinavians of the Baltic and Norway to a frenzy of raiding, rapine and conquest, it was eastern England that suffered, from York to Sheppey, as well as the future English dependencies in the Orkneys and Shetlands, Hebrides and the offshore island of Ireland. That Norse onslaught culminated, of course, in the second conquest of 1066, launched from the Norseman's coastal enclave in Normandy. This was one of several they had won, the farthest in Sicily and southern Italy, in an early and dramatic demonstration of the potentiality of seafarers commanding the right technology, sufficient will and strategically located bases to carry force across the sea to distant territory.

The real triumph of the Norsemen who conquered England was to transform it into a centralized kingdom that, step by step, would unify the whole British and Irish archipelago into a single polity. As soon as that was done – and we date the achievement, even if concluded at the end dynastically rather than militarily, to the union of the crowns of England and Scotland in 1603 – the fall of the shadow was reversed. The Anglo-Scottish kingdom, which ruled Ireland, potentially controlled all the coasts of Europe from Finisterre in Britanny to the North Cape of Norway. The potentiality was increasingly to be realized during the seventeenth century as the Stuart monarchs built ships with which seapower could be exercised. In the second half of the century the rise of English naval mastery was contested by the Dutch, and very energetically too, in three wars, during one of which the Dutch entered the Thames and burned British ships in the Medway. Holland's marine base, however, was too narrow for the country to sustain a protracted challenge and, after its defeat in the Third Dutch War, its naval effort was increasingly diverted to exploiting and defending the seaborne empire it had already established in the East Indies. The effective truce that ensued was solidified by the offer of the English crown to William III in 1688, and it persisted until the Netherlands fell under French control in the 1790s.

England had East Indian interests also, but those were not its only ones. Thanks to the early decision to use the country's manifold exits to the North Atlantic during the seventeenth century, it succeeded in claiming and colonizing the whole of the eastern North American seaboard between the Hudson and Florida by the early eighteenth century. This served to confine French imperial ventures in the continent to the entry point of the St Lawrence. Thanks to England's naval victories in English seas, it simultaneously succeeded in acquiring the Dutch American foothold along the Hudson. The English American foothold was shallow – a coastal strip closed off from the interior by the Appalachians, behind which the French sketched out an enormous internal claim by their bold and skillful navigation of the network of lakes and rivers that connected with their bases at Quebec and Montreal and led eventually to the Gulf of Mexico at New Orleans. Because of the reluctance of the French to contemplate a life beyond the seas, however, a prospect that by contrast the English, and later the Scots and Irish, took up with enthusiasm, the English colonies were rapidly and heavily populated while New France never was. In 1756, French America had only

50,000 inhabitants, English America more than a million. With the renewal of Anglo-French transatlantic warfare, a contest that had begun as early as 1619, numbers decisively told. By 1763, French America had become British, and Britain dominated a wedge of the North Atlantic that, at its western terminus, extended between the thirtieth and sixtieth parallels.

By then Britain had further exploited its favourable maritime position to extend a chain of bases near and far, all of which impeded its continental rivals' efforts to make effective their own oceanic outreach. An English fleet first appeared in the Mediterranean during the Cromwellian Commonwealth. By 1704, Britain had taken Gibraltar, which can deny ingress to and exit from the Mediterranean. During much of the eighteenth century the country enjoyed the use of the Balearic islands, which watch over Spain's Mediterranean ports. Malta, which controls the neck of the Mediterranean, became British in 1800. For the first half of the nineteenth century, Britain garrisoned the Ionian islands off the west coast of Greece. It acquired Cyprus in 1878 and Alexandria in 1882, from which time for the next 60 years it was as great a Mediterranean power as any state whose coasts are lapped by Mediterranean waters. Indeed, under the Queen Empress Victoria, her son Edward and her grandson George, Britain was *the* Mediterranean power, the Royal Navy's Mediterranean Fleet being the most powerful instrument of naval might in the inland sea and second in importance only to the Channel, later the Grand, Fleet.

Such acquisitions were relatively domestic compared to those Britain was meanwhile making elsewhere. In the sixteenth century, Portugal had attempted to win an empire in the Indian Ocean, and Spain succeeded in creating a major Pacific power centre in the Philippines. Portugal's material weakness, to say nothing of Ottoman strength, and its major involvement in South America, also Spain's chief focus of imperial interest, meant that neither power could find the resources to found solid Indian Ocean outstations. Spain did not try; Portugal succeeded only at Goa. England, later Britain, did better. Perhaps because its American possessions were already by the seventeenth century self-sustaining, drawing population from seaboard townspeople and villagers ready to settle elsewhere, its government, navy and expeditionary army enjoyed the flexibility to seize advantage where it was offered and so to enlarge footholds, originally brought by dynastic bequest, such as Bombay, or trading enterprise, such as Madras and Calcutta, into enclaves for empire building. France had such footholds also, as at Pondicherry, and in the mid-eighteenth century it deployed major fleets to Indian waters. Had the chance of battle so decreed, those fleets might have been victorious, and the European empire in India French rather than British. In the event it did not. A British India was the outcome of the Anglo-French wars in the region, a conquest that gave British power two almost equal centres of military effort on the surface of the globe: one at home, the other 12,000 miles away in the heart of Asia.

The subjection of India, completed by the 1840s, explains almost all other British maritime acquisitions. From it flowed the acquisition of Aden and the Persian Gulf dependencies, Ceylon, Singapore, Malaya and Borneo, Hong Kong and the extraterritorial concessions in China. The thrust to India justified the taking of the Cape, the retention of the West African slaving centres – later so useful as coaling stations – the extension of a protectorate over Zanzibar, the venture into East Africa and, of course, the subordination of Egypt, its canal and its dependency in the Sudan to British administration. The projection of British power from India to such a far-flung network of colonies, bases and trading centres is a marvel in itself. Even more marvellous is that the impulsion derived from the willingness of a small island's population to take to the oceans and to gamble their lives, and the small resources with which they began, in the world's great game of trade and warfare.

Others before them had shown the same willingness: the Scandinavians first, then the Portuguese and the Spanish, while the Dutch and the French were their contemporary competitors in the age when England's first overseas successes were achieved. As I have suggested, however, Portugal and Spain made the mistake of over-investment of effort in their original South American conquests, while France, pulled two ways between oceanic empire and continental commitment, dissipated the preponderant strength that would certainly have made it the world empire Britain became had it chosen to pursue global objectives rather than dynastic prestige. Holland, having survived Habsburg aggression, simply succumbed to its geographical disadvantages relative to England, was defeated and was lucky to be left free to enjoy its East Indian empire thereafter.

What explains the English willingness to go to sea? Proximity, I think, first of all. With access to the oceans nowhere further than 80 miles from home, seafaring was an option of which even the most rooted rustic was aware. Next was the coast itself, which furnished a chain of harbours and anchorages at close intervals its whole length, and supported a numerous fishing and coastal trading population plus a flourishing boat and ship-building industry. Thirdly was the history of England, largely made by maritime invaders – the Anglo-Saxons, Vikings, Danes and Normans who implanted in the English consciousness a vivid awareness of maritime opportunity. In a sense, England became through invasion the principal repository of the tradition of successful north European sea-raiding and conquest. Finally, alone among the north European maritime peoples, the English inhabited a country that enjoyed both the political organization and the productive capacity to form a base for concerted commercial and military activity in oceanic waters. England, in comparison with France, was not rich, but by the sixteenth century it was rich in the sense that it produced more than it consumed – particularly wool and manufactured textiles – possessed accumulated capital – after the dissolution of the monasteries a very great deal – had a trading class and, above all, enjoyed internal peace – a rare benefit at the time – and a centralized and fiscally efficient government. Taxes that in Europe went to support soldiers, and were then wasted in indecisive cross-frontier campaigning, in England could be realized as ocean-going warships, while the wealth that was not taxed appeared as stout trading vessels, manned by tough and venturesome crews ready in an emergency to rally to the crown and see an invader off, as the merchantmen who supported the royal ships in the Armada battles of 1588 so convincingly demonstrated.

One of the most distinctive elements in the relationship of the English with the sea was that the navy was in its origins organic, not an artificial creation. Henry VIII built warships, as did Elizabeth I and Charles I, but the Armada victory, besides Trafalgar – England's most notable sea battle, and one even more crucial to national survival – was a triumph of ordinary seafarers and their workaday vessels over a fleet of dedicated warships. England's continental rivals, France and Spain, continued to build and maintain galley fleets, which, like those of Venice, served no commercial function. When, in the seventeenth century, the British Royal Navy came into being, it was formed of ships essentially mercantile in design and drew its traditions and practices from a homegrown mercantile culture. This then, I suggest, explains the empathy between the navy and the nation that, for three centuries, and still persisting today, so forcibly struck foreigners who did business, diplomatic, commercial or military, with the country. By the eighteenth century, Great Britain, which the English dominated, was a naval nation. By the nineteenth it was navy mad. The reason for that, of course, was the overwhelming, but nevertheless justifiable, pride that the British took in the triumphs of their sailors over all-comers in the French Revolutionary and Napoleonic wars. Britain has had its naval ups and downs. It had a serious down in the 1770s and 1780s when its French and Spanish enemies enjoyed the satisfaction of winning victories in American waters that actually deprived it of the first British Empire over the Thirteen Colonies. It was a humiliation not to be tolerated. English sea captains had always prided themselves on going bald-headed for the enemy, whatever the risks and whatever the costs. When war with France, and then Spain, came round again, the generation of captains and admirals succeeding that which had been beaten in the war of American Independence found a resolve to avenge the down that would not have shamed their Viking ancestors. The gigantic Duncan – victor of Camperdown that extinguished Dutch naval power for good – Howe and Jervis – the victors respectively of the Glorious First of June and Cape St Vincent – and above all Nelson – mercurial genius personified – simply did not countenance caution. Shown an enemy, they closed, fought and ceased the struggle only when victory or death or both gave them a reason for stopping. A rank below these admirals, hundreds of ship and frigate captains followed their example in dozens of single-ship or small fleet actions, very few of which ended in British defeat. It was during those years, from 1793 to 1815, that the Royal Navy set the standards of ruthlessness, implacability and, let it be said also, ship-handling, plus navigational, logistic and strategic efficiency by which all navies have subsequently measured their competence.

The British naval epic of the Napoleonic Wars laid the basis for the Pax Britannica of the nineteenth century, assured by a ship strength that, at its apogee, equalled that of the next seven navies put together. It was underpinned by a worldwide chain of bases that supported the most extensive complex of fleets and squadrons – Home, Mediterranean, African, East Indian, North American and West Indian, South American, China, Australian and New Zealand – the world has ever seen, exceeding in extent even that of the United States Navy during its global dominance in the cold war years. Pax Britannica, which might better have been called the Pax Classis Britannicae, assured the freedom of North Americans to build the world's greatest economy and of South Americans to raise revolution to an art form; it put an end to the oceanic slave trade; it assured freedom of passage for the greatest expansion of maritime commerce and intercontinental emigration in world history; it effectively put an end to naval war throughout the world for nearly a century; and it established the phrase 'word of an Englishman' as the test by which honest business was conducted from Buenes Aires to Borneo.

Yet it may be argued that the greatest impact of the Pax Britannica was felt at home rather than abroad, and there it took a social and cultural rather than military or commercial form. I have said that nineteenth-century Britain was navy mad. Let me expand on that assertion. Who does not, somewhere in a family photograph album, have pictures of a grandfather or grandmother in a sailor suit, around 1900 the universal dress of infants and adolescents of every class from the highest to nearly the lowest in this country? Victoria's infant son, the future Edward VII, was painted by Winterhalter in a sailor costume, of which her great-great-great-great-grandson wore a replica at the wedding of Prince Andrew in Westminster Abbey. Her granddaughterin-law, Princess Mary, wore a sailor costume as a young wife, while her husband, George V, was a serving naval officer. Their son, the future Edward VIII, got such education as he had at Dartmouth. His niece, our Queen, is the daughter, wife and mother of Dartmouth cadets, all of whom fought in battle at sea: Jutland, Matapan and the Falklands respectively. These are weighty ingredients of our national culture, linking the head of our society as well as of our state directly to the most visible instrument of our external relationship with the rest of the world.

The cultural dimension goes further. Think of the influence of the sea on our culture in that word's traditional sense. Which other country's greatest artist – for such I hold Turner to be – devoted so large a part of his output to maritime and naval subjects? Which other national school of watercolour is dominated by marine artists, as ours is by Bonnington, Cotman and Clarkson Stanfield? Which other country's music is so suffused by sea themes, as it is in Elgar's, Vaughan Williams's and Benjamin Britten's, to say nothing of Gilbert and Sullivan's work? Whose children's literature is so heavily dedicated to arousing a sense of mystery and adventure through nautical subject? From Midshipman Easy via Long John Silver – the creation, admittedly, of a Scot – to Captain Hook, Rattie in *The Wind in the Willows*, and John Walker and Nancy Blackett, the leading *Swallows and Amazons*, English children's literature abounds in nautical heroes, villains and alter egos that have followed whole generations through life and been transmitted in vivid and lifelike form to the next. *Swallows and Amazons* was the first proper book I read and when, a few weeks ago, my six-year-old grandson told me he was 'on chapter 2', I felt less pride in his achievement than a pang of envy at the enjoyment and sense of discovery that he must be experiencing, as I did at the same age more than fifty years ago. It is an oddity that England has produced no great maritime novelists, for we have no Herman Melville and we cannot really claim Conrad; but we have invented a vibrant middlebrow literature, whose masters include Tobias Smollet, Capt. Marryat and C.S. Forester, and which has just now found a new exponent in Patrick O'Brian. It is a consolation on that score, moreover, that part of Kipling's extraordinarily eclectic genius was devoted to the life of fishermen, and naval and merchant sailors, in *Captains Courageous* and a large number of his short stories. In his contemporary, John Masefield, England found a leading sea poet, though the association of English poetry with shipwreck, maritime adventure, disaster and triumph ascends through Browning and Coleridge eventually to Shakespeare. *The Tempest* is probably the most powerful vehicle of ideas about the mystery of the sea in English literature.

Think of the power of those ideas in English consciousness: lifeboatmen, lighthouses, wreck, drowning, rescue. A chief element in that British passion for the seaside with which I began derives, I believe, not from any of the reasons for which the seaside holiday was first propagated – the therapeutic properties of seawater and fresh air – but from the exposure it gave to the mystery of the sea and the share it offered in the English triumph over it. John Betjeman has made us all party to the social trivia of seaside life:

> Solihull, Headingley and Golders Green,
> Preston and Swindon, Manchester and Leeds,
> Braintree and Bocking hear the sea! the sea!
> The smack of breakers upon windy rocks,
> Spray blowing backwards from their curling walls

Of green translucent water. England leaves
Her centre for her tide-line. Father's toes
Though now encased in coloured socks and shoes
And pressing the accelerator hard,
Ache for the feel of sand and little shrimps
To tickle in between them. Mother vows
To be more patient with the family:
Just for its sake she will be young again.

But who will grudge
Them this, their wild, spontaneous holiday?
The morning paddle, then the mystery tour
By motor-coach inland this afternoon.
For that old mother what a happy time!
At last past bearing children, she can sit
Reposeful on a crowded bit of beach.
A week of idleness, the salty winds
Play in her greying hair; the summer sun
Puts back her freckles so that Alfred Brown
Remembers courting days in Gospel Oak
And takes her to the Flannel Dance to-night.

Yet Betjeman, as always, sees the eternal under the trivia, the consequential within the commonplace:

And all the time the waves, the waves, the waves
Chase, intersect and flatten on the sand
As they have done for centuries, as they will
For centuries to come, when not a soul
Is left to picnic on the blazing rocks,
When England is not England, . . .

Betjeman's England is not just Cornish cliffs and galoshes in the wet. There is always the hint of the wider, seafaring, war-fighting England that supported the cosy life of villas and seaside golf courses. 'Love in a valley', one of his earliest poems, which begins

'Take me, Lieutenant, to that Surrey homestead!
Red comes the winter and your rakish car'

ends with the poignant

Portable Lieutenant! they carry you to China
And me to lonely shopping in a brilliant arcade;
. . .

The sea means not just the treasured holiday but the fated separation; fated because the sea has called the English to a world empire and its duties: the hard, lonely life of the naval officer and of the merchant seaman ploughing the waves of commerce in the ocean of a lifetime. The same echo is caught in the opening chapter of *Swallows and Amazons*, where the Walker children's hopes of sailing their dinghy on Lake Windermere depend on permission granted by telegram from their naval father, far away in his warship on the China station. When it comes, the telegram brings joy but also a hint of menace: 'Better drowned than duffers. If not duffers won't drown.'

Captain Walker's telegram encapsulates England's sea epic. The English did drown in enormous numbers, not only fighting their country's battles afloat but in carrying her commerce to the ends of the earth. We remember that the Royal Navy was the largest in the world: we forget that the Merchant Navy was also, in its heyday, by far the world's largest mercantile fleet; that seafaring was a way of life for the populations of hundreds of British towns and villages; and that ship-building, with its ancillary trades, was, after coalmining and agriculture, Britain's largest single industry. I must say Britain rather than England for, by the nineteenth century, the life of the sea was as much a Scottish as an English calling, making Glasgow and its shipyards the Empire's second city. The bones of those men and their ships now litter the beds and coasts of the world's seas. They were not, however, duffers. They invented the steamship and built it for the rest of the world. They invented the chronometer and charted the world's seaways. They 'discovered' – a politically incorrect term today – New Zealand, most of Australia and the Pacific islands. Having all too efficiently conducted the oceanic slave trade, they brought it to an end and policed its extinction. They made and kept a great maritime peace in the world's most productive century. Duffers at sea the English certainly were not.

And now? I confess to a profound sadness whenever I recall our maritime past and contemplate our maritime present; the empty yards of Clydeside, the ruined docks of Liverpool, the decaying ports of the West Country. I can now scarcely bear to go to the seaside. What in my childhood brought me in safely diluted strength the essence of a great national enterprise is now merely an anodyne reminder of something that is gone. Can it have gone forever? Is there no way of harnessing once again the unique geographical advantages enjoyed by the inhabitants of these islands? Can there be no reason for doing so? Should we be content to see what was once the greatest merchant navy in existence dwindling into nothingness? Should we accept as inevitable the extinction of a ship-building industry that once enjoyed a virtual global monopoly in the trade? Do we really face a future in which an island at the centre of the world's trade routes is as unmaritime as Switzerland? Should we? Must we? The seas still surround us and the world still lives by shipping. Perhaps, paddling his or her toes in the chilly waters at Eype or Bantham or Cape Cornwall, there is, even now, an infant James Watt or Isambard Kingdom Brunel, watching the horizon, wondering what lies beyond and resolutely not heeding mother's cry of 'Don't get out of your depth, darling.' I do hope so.

INDEX

Italic numbers indicate illustrations. Numbers immediately followed by n indicate notes.